W9-DDT-564

FIXING POWERPOINT ANNOYANCES™

FIXING POWERPOINT ANNOYANCES™

*How to Fix the Most Annoying Things
About Your Favorite Presentation Program*

Echo Swinford

O'REILLY®

Beijing • Cambridge • Farnham • Köln • Paris • Sebastopol • Taipei • Tokyo

Fixing PowerPoint Annoyances™
How to Fix the Most Annoying Things About Your Favorite Presentation Program

by Echo Swinford

Copyright © 2006 O'Reilly Media, Inc. All rights reserved.
Printed in the United States of America.

Illustrations © 2006 Hal Mayforth

Published by O'Reilly Media, Inc., 1005 Gravenstein Highway North, Sebastopol, CA 95472.

O'Reilly books may be purchased for educational, business, or sales promotional use. Online editions are also available for most titles (*safari.oreilly.com*). For more information, contact our corporate/institutional sales department: 800-998-9938 or *corporate@oreilly.com*.

Print History:

February 2006:   First Edition.

Editor: Brett Johnson

Production Editor: Genevieve d'Entremont

Copyeditor: Linley Dolby

Proofreader: Ann Atalla

Indexer: Johnna VanHoose Dinse

Interior Designer: David Futato

Compositor: Phil Dangler

Illustrators: Robert Romano, Jessamyn Read, and Lesley Borash

The O'Reilly logo is a registered trademark of O'Reilly Media, Inc. The *Annoyances* series designations, *Fixing PowerPoint Annoyances*, and related trade dress are trademarks of O'Reilly Media, Inc.

Many of the designations used by manufacturers and sellers to distinguish their products are claimed as trademarks. Where those designations appear in this book, and O'Reilly Media, Inc. was aware of a trademark claim, the designations have been printed in caps or initial caps.

While every precaution has been taken in the preparation of this book, the publisher and author assume no responsibility for errors or omissions, or for damages resulting from the use of the information contained herein.

0-596-10004-3
[C]

Contents

2. DUMB DEFAULTS   19

3. FORMATTING AND EDITING   47

4. IMPORTING   85

6. CHARTS AND GRAPHS   151

7. ANIMATIONS, ACTION SETTINGS, AND HYPERLINKS — 185

8. SOUND AND VIDEO   221

Introduction

I never set out to become a PowerPoint wiz. In fact, I started using PowerPoint by accident.

Way back in 1997, I worked as a temporary employee for a medical meeting planning company. I asked the owner if I could create our presentation slides in-house rather than pay an outside firm to do the work. She agreed with my proposal, which forced me to learn PowerPoint—and learn it fast.

Of course, I soon ran afoul of PowerPoint and its many quirks. For example: Why does the file size increase tenfold after you insert a JPG? How do you plot individual error bars on data points in a column chart? I even remember the panicky feeling I got after I upgraded from PowerPoint 95 to 97 and had to scrounge around for the Write Up tool. Where did it go? How could I make good looking handouts without it?

Over the years, I've had to dodge many such bullets and develop workarounds for PowerPoint's most puzzling dilemmas. (No wonder I thought I could write a PowerPoint book in my sleep.) Hopefully, the tips and tricks you find here will help you master, or at least survive, PowerPoint, and you can learn to enjoy it as much as I do.

Do You Need This Book?

If PowerPoint annoys you, this book is for you. It will appeal to PowerPoint users who regularly run into vexing issues. It should also be helpful to novices as they work their way through the wild and wooly world of PowerPoint presentations.

What's Covered in This Book?

This book is not the ultimate reference to the complete works of the Microsoft PowerPoint development team. And it was a little difficult (okay, a lot difficult) to divide the myriad annoyances into logical chapters. But I tried. Still, the book is set up so you can jump in wherever the water looks good and get out easily whenever you're tired.

Here's a general outline of what you'll find.

Chapter 1, Presenting Your Presentation
> Get a handle on setting up the equipment, troubleshooting projection issues, navigating during a presentation, and using custom shows.

Chapter 2, Dumb Defaults
> Learn how to deal with PowerPoint's dumb default settings: Fast Saves, AutoFit, moving objects, shortened menus, and the lack of default slide layouts and charts.

Chapter 3, Formatting and Editing
> Work with PowerPoint, not against it. Read about creating templates, using multiple masters, leveraging color schemes, working with slide numbers, and using bulleted text and tabs.

Chapter 4, Importing
> Wrap your head around importing a wide variety of materials into PowerPoint, including Word documents, Excel data, charts, pictures, clip art, and PDFs.

Chapter 5, Organization Charts, Diagrams, and Drawing Tools
> Organize organization charts, diddle with diagrams, and feel the power of connectors, edit points, and the alignment tools.

Chapter 6, Charts and Graphs
> Chart a new course through old, tired waters. Learn how to create combination charts, break an axis, add error bars to data points, and update links efficiently.

Chapter 7, Animations, Action Settings, and Hyperlinks
> Make your audience go "Wow" with your cool animations. Learn how to incorporate action settings and hyperlinks to increase the interactivity factor of your presentations.

Chapter 8, Sound and Video
> Stop tearing your hair out trying to get background music and other multimedia playing in your presentation.

Chapter 9, Printing and Distribution
> Deal with getting your presentation into someone else's hands, whether via notes pages, handouts, Flash, web pages, video, or an Autorun CD.

"You Haven't Covered My Pet Annoyance"

We feel your pain! If you'd like to share yours—and any solutions, for that matter—feel free to reach out. Send your emails to *annoyances@oreilly.com*. Also, visit our Annoyances web site *http://www.annoyances.oreilly.com* for more tips and tricks, as well as information on upcoming books.

Conventions Used in This Book

The following typographic conventions are used in this book.

Italic

> Indicates new terms, URLs, filenames, file extensions, directories, and program names.

Constant width bold

> Indicates commands or other text that you should type literally (rather than substituting text appropriate to your computer's configuration or the situation).

Constant width italic

> Indicates commands or other text that you should replace with values suitable to your computer's configuration or the situation.

Menus and navigation

> This book uses arrow symbols to indicate menu instructions. For example, "choose File→Open" means that you should open the File menu and choose the Open item from the menu. But when you need to click a tab, check or uncheck an option box, or click a button in a dialog box, this book tells you that clearly.

Pathnames

> Pathnames show the location of a file or application in the Windows or Mac OS X filesystem. Windows folders are separated by a backward slash—for example, *C:\Temp\Documents*. Mac OS X folders are separated by forward slashes—for example, *~/Library/Preferences*. In Mac OS X, a tilde (~) represents your Home folder.

Safari® Enabled

When you see a Safari® Enabled icon on the cover of your favorite technology book, that means it's available online through the O'Reilly Network Safari Bookshelf.

Safari offers a solution that's better than e-books: it's a virtual library that lets you easily search thousands of top tech books, cut and paste code samples, download chapters, and find quick answers when you need the most accurate, current information. Try it for free at *http://safari.oreilly.com*.

O'Reilly Would Like to Hear from You

Please address comments and questions concerning this book to the publisher:

> O'Reilly Media, Inc.
> 1005 Gravenstein Highway North
> Sebastopol, CA 95472
> (800) 998-9938 (in the United States or Canada)
> (707) 829-0515 (international or local)
> (707) 829-0104 (fax)

We have a web page for this book, where we list errata, examples, and any additional information. You can access this page at:

> *http://annoyances.oreilly.com*

To comment or ask technical questions about this book, send email to:

> *bookquestions@oreilly.com*

For more information about our books, conferences, Resource Centers, and the O'Reilly Network, see our web site at:

> *http://www.oreilly.com*

Acknowledgments

A number of people made the writing of this book possible. I would especially like to thank the Microsoft PowerPoint MVPs for their spirit of cooperation and teamwork, as well as the people in the *microsoft.public. powerpoint* newsgroup for making it a fun and educational place. Thanks also to Ric Bretschneider and April Dalke just for being you. Finally, I would like to thank Robert Luhn and Brett Johnson at O'Reilly.

This book is dedicated to Mom, Dad, Amber, Azure, and Marte Farte.

Presenting Your Presentation

I hate sitting in an audience and having to squint, crane my neck, or turn my head sideways just to make heads or tails of a slide. What's the point of having slides if nobody can read them?

Whether you're an audience member or a presenter, presentations are chock-full of annoying issues. In this chapter, you'll learn how to set up your equipment and navigate your slides to keep your audience focused on your presentation—not on you. You'll also tackle sound issues and other problems you may face when working with hyperlinks, hidden slides, and custom and self-running presentations.

Set Up the Projector

If you've never attached a projector to your laptop, don't worry. Simply plug the projector into an available outlet. If you can, plug your laptop into an outlet as well, to keep the battery from dying during your presentation.

Cable the laptop and the projector together. The projector usually comes with a cable; plug it into the projector and the video-out port on the laptop.

Turn on the projector, and then turn on the laptop. If you're lucky, the laptop will recognize the projector, and your screen will display on both your laptop and through the projector. Otherwise, press Fn+ the appropriate F key to toggle between displays: projector only, monitor only, or both projector and monitor. For example, on a Dell Latitude, press Fn+F8. On a Toshiba, it's often Fn+F5.

SETTING UP YOUR EQUIPMENT

The Slides Look Crooked

THE ANNOYANCE: I got the projector up and running without any trouble, but I notice that my slides are cut off at the bottom of the screen.

THE FIX: You just need to adjust the height and distance of the projector. Either move the projector away from the screen, screw the projector feet out some, or do a combination of both.

If you can't move the projector, or if the feet are as far out as they'll go, prop the projector up on something—a folded piece of paper under each front foot will often do the trick.

The Slides Look All Skinny on the Bottom

THE ANNOYANCE: I got the projector set up, but the slide image looks like a trapezoid on the wall. I mean it's wider at the top than at the bottom. What's happening?

THE FIX: This trapezoidal look is called keystoning, and you can adjust it in the settings of most modern projectors. Simply hit the Menu button on your projector or its remote and look for the keystoning option.

If you don't see a keystoning option on the projector, you'll need to raise the height of the projector by mounting it on some books or other objects.

However, because keystoning is caused by tilting the projector away from a 90° angle to the screen, make sure you raise the entire projector, not just the front of it.

I Can't Hear the Sound

THE ANNOYANCE: I can't hear the audio. There's supposed to be music on this slide.

THE FIX: If you're showing the presentation through a projector, check to see if the projector has speakers and make sure they're turned on. Also, make sure you have the proper audio cable with you to plug the laptop into the projector.

You also need to turn on the sound for your laptop. Most laptops have a Function (Fn) toggle key and an F key with an icon that looks like a speaker. Hold down the Fn key while you repeatedly press the speaker key.

Remember, there's no point in having audio if nobody can hear it. So plan ahead: make sure the audio-visual staff knows your presentation contains audio.

And yes, you need not route the audio through the projector all the time. Often, the laptop output is routed through a sound mixer that in turn sends it to the sound system installed. This works best in dedicated conference venues and auditoriums.

Slides Won't Move Forward

THE ANNOYANCE: When I press the Forward button on the remote during my presentation, the slide won't move. How embarrassing!

THE FIX: Make sure you point the remote toward the remote *receiver*, not at the screen. For whatever reason, the tendency is always to point toward the screen. Most remotes have a limit on how far they can send remote signals, so also make sure you're close enough to the receiver for the remote signal to be picked up.

Of course, always make sure you test and practice with the remote before your presentation. And don't forget to put fresh batteries in the remote before you begin your presentation.

If all else fails, just use the keyboard to advance the slides. The right and up arrow keys, Enter key, spacebar, Page Up key, and the N (for Next) key all move the slides forward; left and down arrow keys, Backspace key, Page Down key, and the P (for Previous) key all move the slides backward.

Silence Is Golden

THE ANNOYANCE: Ugh, this presenter is driving me nuts! He keeps saying "Um" and walking in front of the projector!

THE FIX: Sorry, there's not much that can be done about this type of thing. Poor presentation skills can be overcome through coaching, though, especially if the presenter's willing to learn.

One of the most valuable lessons I learned during a presentation coaching session was not to be afraid of silence. It's okay to look at your slide and gather your thoughts, but don't keep talking when you're doing it! The silent moment will seem long and awkward to you, but it will seem perfectly natural to your audience.

Image Doesn't Show on Projector

THE ANNOYANCE: No matter what I do, I can't get what I see on the laptop to show on the projector.

THE FIX: Use the appropriate keyboard combination to toggle your laptop/ projector display. You can usually control the following three toggle states using Fn in combination with an F key: projector only, monitor only, and both projector and monitor. Look for the symbol on the keyboard F key row and hold down the Fn key while you press the key with the symbol. On a Dell Latitude, for example, press Fn+F8. On a Toshiba, it's often Fn+F5.

Always make it a point to arrive at the venue a little early to test your hardware. If someone else is presenting immediately before you, try to check your laptop the day before, during lunch, or during another break.

VIEWING YOUR PRESENTATION

Presentation Keeps Locking Up

THE ANNOYANCE: Aaaarrrrgggghhhh! My presentation locks up when I try to view it in Slide Show mode. Help!

THE FIX: This problem is often related to the "fade through black" transition, which seems to be very hard on video drivers in PowerPoint 97 and 2000 especially. Switching to another transition will often cure the lockups.

To change your slide transition in PowerPoint 97 or 2000, select Slide Show→Slide Transition, choose another transition from the Effect dropdown menu, and then click the Apply button. If you want this new transition to apply to all slides in your presentation, click the "Apply to All" button. If you don't want a transition, choose No Transition, and each slide will simply appear on the screen with no change or movement between slides (see Figure 1-1).

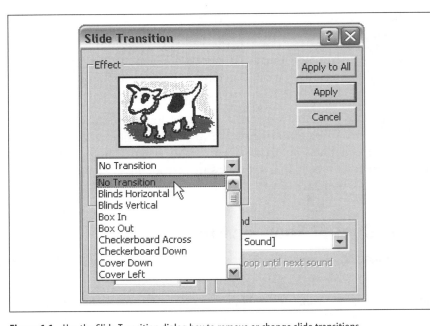

Figure 1-1. Use the Slide Transition dialog box to remove or change slide transitions.

If removing or changing the slide transition doesn't resolve the problem, update your video drivers and change your hardware acceleration.

If you're running Windows 98 or Me, do the following:

1. Choose Start→Settings→Control Panel.

2. In Control Panel, double-click the System icon.

3. Click the Performance tab and click the Graphics button.

4. Drag the Hardware Acceleration slider one notch to the left (see Figure 1-2).

5. Click OK to return to the desktop.

6. Restart the computer if necessary.

7. Test to see if this has resolved the problem. If not, drag the Hardware Acceleration slider one notch farther to the left each time. Your goal is to set the Hardware Acceleration slider to the highest possible setting without locking your presentation.

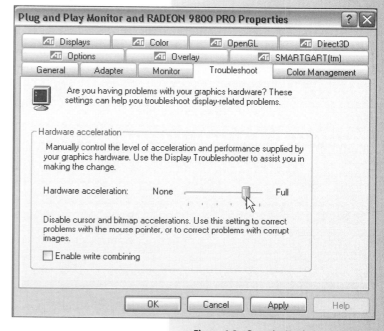

Figure 1-2. Drag the Hardware Acceleration slider to the left to correct display problems.

If you're running Windows 2000 or XP, do the following:

1. Right-click the desktop and choose Properties.

2. Click the Settings tab and then click the Advanced button.

3. Click the Troubleshoot tab.

4. Under Hardware Acceleration, move the slider one notch to the left (see Figure 1-2).

5. Click OK to return to the desktop.

6. Test to see if this has resolved the problem. If not, drag the Hardware Acceleration slider one notch farther to the left each time. Your goal is to set the Hardware Acceleration slider to the highest possible setting without locking your presentation.

You might also want to upgrade your version of DirectX. The latest version of DirectX can be downloaded from *http://www.microsoft.com/directx*.

Video Doesn't Show on Projector

THE ANNOYANCE: No matter what I do, I can't get this video to play on the projector and laptop at the same time; it will only play on the laptop. What am I doing wrong?

THE FIX: You're not doing anything wrong; this is an issue with the combination of hardware and software you're using: the video card, the video driver, the video itself, and PowerPoint.

The most reliable resolution is to toggle the laptop display so that it shows only on the projector. Hold down the Fn button and press the appropriate F key to toggle the laptop display (see "Image Doesn't Show on Projector").

Because the video plays on the primary monitor (the laptop), but not on the secondary monitor (the LCD projector), you can try changing your primary monitor in Windows. This will make the LCD projector the primary monitor, which means you will see the black box on your laptop screen, but your audience will see the video.

To change your monitor, right-click your desktop and select Properties. Click the Settings tab, and then click the Advanced button. Look for a "Monitor" or "Adaptor" tab. You're looking for an option to switch the "Primary" and "Secondary" output. Once you find it, click the Apply button, and then click OK to get back to your presentation. When you finish the presentation, make sure you restore your original monitor settings.

PowerPoint Opens Minimized

THE ANNOYANCE: I can't get my presentation to open properly when I double-click it. I can see the PowerPoint icon on the taskbar, but it won't maximize or restore. How can I view the presentation?

THE FIX: Your slide show is set to display on the secondary monitor, which is no longer attached to your computer. Open PowerPoint from Start→Program Files and select File→Open to open your presentation. Then select Slide Show→Set up Show and choose "Display slide show on primary monitor."

Use White Backgrounds for Acetates

THE ANNOYANCE: I printed colored acetates of my presentation, but when I tried to write in the margins, the audience had trouble reading my notes.

THE FIX: Set up your slides with white backgrounds, and then print the acetates. The colors in the slide text, objects, and charts will print, but you won't have any background colors to contend with when you write on the acetates.

One way to make your slide backgrounds white is to choose Format→ Background, select a white swatch from the drop-down menu, and then click the "Apply to All" button (see Figure 1-3). Make sure you haven't used white for any other objects in your presentation; white objects won't show up against a white background.

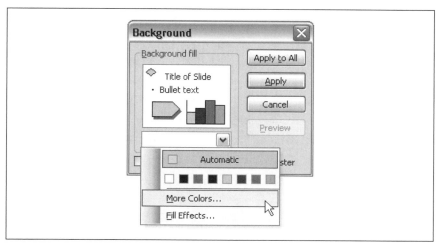

Figure 1-3. Use the Background dialog box to change the color of your slide background.

This is usually what clients really want when they ask for "full-color" acetates. They just don't realize how a printed colored background will affect slides on acetate.

Use Contrasting Text and Backgrounds

THE ANNOYANCE: I had to design a new organizational chart using our company colors and ended up with white text on a yellow background. I can't read a freakin' thing!

THE FIX: Never use white text on yellow fills. Likewise, avoid dark font colors on dark backgrounds and fills. It may look fine on your monitor, but you will likely cause your audience consternation as they squint to read your slides. Instead, think contrast. Use dark backgrounds with light text or vice versa. Be careful with white and very light backgrounds, though—staring at too much glaring expanse of white tends to give people headaches. If you're tired of the oh-so-common blue background with white text, check *http://hubel.sfasu.edu/research/survreslts.html* for some interesting readability information, and perhaps some inspiration for different background-text combinations.

How Big Should My Text Be?

Use the 8H rule, which says "the maximum viewing distance should be no more than eight times the height (H) of the screen. If you then keep your font size at least 1/50th the height of the screen, your text will be legible at the maximum viewing distance."

A slide set for On-screen Show in PowerPoint measures 7.5 inches—about 720 points tall. So the absolute minimum font size would be roughly 14 points (720 divided by 50). If the text seems too small, increase your font size to 1/25th the height of the screen, which translates to roughly 28 points.

Remember that subtle color changes simply get lost on most projectors, and an estimated 1 out of 12 men has some type of color perception problem. So don't rely solely on color to get your point across. For example, if you're working with a line graph, use line thickness and pattern, in addition to color, to help define the different lines.

Finally, most projectors seem to wash out the projected image. Make sure you test your presentation on the projector to alleviate any color visibility issues ahead of time. Also, check both the brightness and contrast settings on the projector. If your slides appear faded, look for a Reset button on the projector and readjust the brightness and contrast as necessary.

If you have control over the slide design, use colors that provide more saturated backgrounds. A saturated blue will appear much less washed out than a dull blue, even if the projector is not up to the mark.

Learn How to Navigate Your Presentation

THE ANNOYANCE: I put a specific slide in this presentation to use as backup information. Now I want to show it, but I can't find it. I know I can close out of Slide Show view and use Slide Sorter view to find slides, but there's gotta be a better way.

THE FIX: Select Tools→Options, click the View tab, and check the "Show menu on right mouse click" box (PowerPoint 2003 and 2002) or the "Popup menu on right mouse click" box (PowerPoint 2000 and 97). You can then right-click your slide, choose Go to Slide, and click the appropriate slide.

Alternatively, use a printout of your presentation and learn the basic navigation techniques. Hit F1 on your keyboard for help in Slide Show view (see Figure 1-4). Some of the basic navigation tools—type the number and hit Enter, right-click for menu, use the B or W key to blank the screen, etc.—will be very helpful to know.

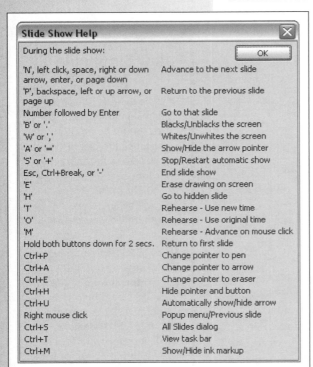

Figure 1-4. Hit the F1 key in Slide Show view to see a list of commands you can use during a presentation.

Navigating to Hidden Slides

THE ANNOYANCE: I have a hidden slide with data included in my presentation. How do I show a hidden slide if I need it to help answer a question?

THE FIX: One way to navigate to a slide—even to a hidden slide—is to type in the slide number and then quickly hit

Enter. Of course, you have to know the number of the slide you want to move to, so it may help to have a numbered printout handy.

If you're using the right-click technique to display a list of slides (see "Learn How to Navigate Your Presentation"), hidden slides will show up with parentheses around the slide number (see Figure 1-5). You can also access this list by pressing Ctrl+S.

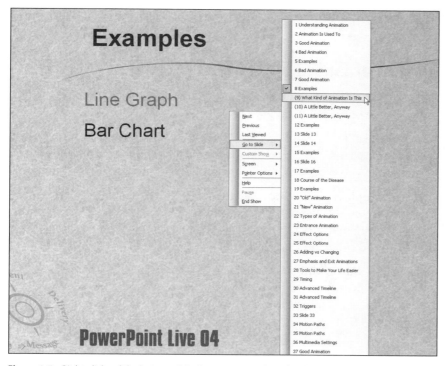

Figure 1-5. Right-click a slide during a slide show to access a list of all slides in the presentation. Hidden slides are indicated with parentheses around the slide number.

Back Up During the Presentation

THE ANNOYANCE: When I right-click during a slide show, I don't get a list of slides in the presentation. Instead, I go backward one slide. What's going on?

THE FIX: Select Tools→Options, click the View tab, and check the "Show menu on right mouse click" box (PowerPoint 2002 and 2003) or the "Popup menu on right mouse click" box (PowerPoint 97 and 2000) to view the list of slides when you right-click during the slide show. If you leave this box unchecked, PowerPoint turns the right-click into a "previous slide" button, as you discovered.

Get Rid of Slide Show Starting Screen

THE ANNOYANCE: Every time I start a presentation in PowerPoint 2002, I get this black screen that says, "Slide Show Starting." How do I get rid of it?

THE FIX: Unfortunately, you can't. This screen is hardwired into PowerPoint 2002 and there's no way around it. Microsoft did remove this irritating intro screen in PowerPoint 2003, so if it really annoys you, an upgrade will resolve it.

Get Rid of End of Slide Show Screen

THE ANNOYANCE: At the end of every presentation, a screen says "End of slide show, click to exit." How do I get rid of it?

THE FIX: Select Tools→Options, click the View tab, and uncheck the "End with black slide" box. If you want the presentation to end with a plain black slide, you'll have to add one yourself at the end of the presentation.

To insert a plain black slide, select Insert→New Slide. Select or go to the new slide, select Format→Background, check the "Omit background graphics from master" box, and choose a black color from the drop-down Background fill menu (see Figure 1-6).

Note that "End with black slide" is a computer-specific setting—it's not part of the presentation. Even if you no longer see "End of slide show" on your computer, you may see it if you show your presentation on a different computer.

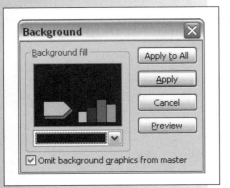

Figure 1-6. Check the "Omit background graphics from master" box to create a plain black slide in your presentation.

Hide the Arrow

THE ANNOYANCE: I just want to hide the arrow when I'm presenting. It's too distracting.

THE FIX: Just press Ctrl+H when you're in Slide Show view. The arrow and the little buttons in the lower-left corner of the screen will disappear. Press the A key to bring the arrow and buttons back.

Pressing A works as a toggle to show and temporarily hide the arrow during a presentation. If you press A to hide the arrow, it will display itself again when you move the mouse. Ctrl+H permanently hides the arrow, even when you move the mouse. You must press A to bring it back.

Draw Straight Lines with the Pen

THE ANNOYANCE: I used to be able to hold down the Shift key while drawing with the Pen tool to draw straight lines during a slide show. I upgraded to PowerPoint 2003, and I can't draw straight lines anymore. What happened?

THE FIX: Unfortunately, Microsoft removed this feature in PowerPoint 2003. They did, however, introduce an option to save annotations created during a slide show, but the straight-line functionality was sacrificed in the process. If you've made any marks during a slide show, you'll be prompted to keep annotations when the presentation finishes.

Access Files from Your Presentation

THE ANNOYANCE: I have to do a presentation on our new corporate branding. I know people will have questions about the brand guide, which is a 50-page PDF. Can I open it without exiting Slide Show view?

THE FIX: If you have to cover something not easily displayed on a slide (such as the 50-page branding guide), open the file, and then start your PowerPoint presentation as usual. The other application and file will run in the background on your system. When you're ready to start using it, press Alt+Tab to switch over to it from your presentation. When you're finished, use Alt+Tab to get back to PowerPoint.

You can also use hyperlinks to navigate to other files from your presentation. Right-click an object on your slide, choose Hyperlink, and then navigate to the appropriate file (see Figure 1-7). The file should open with whatever Windows uses as the default program to open that file.

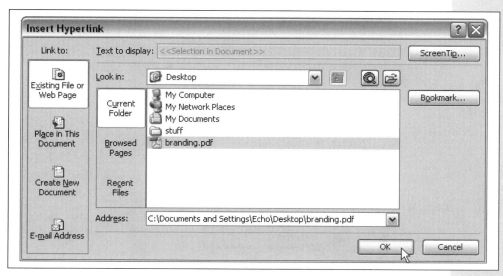

Figure 1-7. You can create hyperlinks on your slides to link to other files.

Avoid the Hyperlinked Files Message

THE ANNOYANCE: I added a hyperlink to a file stored on my hard drive. Now when I click the link in my presentation, I get a stupid warning message. How do I make this annoying thing go away?

THE FIX: A new emphasis on security is the reason for this warning message, which happens in PowerPoint 2003 and PowerPoint Viewer 2003. The warning message says "Hyperlinks can be harmful to your computer and data...Do you want to continue?" (see Figure 1-8). Of course, if you or someone you trust created the file you're linking to, then this warning is simply a nuisance.

Microsoft made it difficult to suppress this warning, even on your own computer with your own presentations. To do so, you need to either hack the registry using the instructions at *http://support.microsoft.com/ ?kbid=829072*, or download a utility that performs these same steps from Microsoft PowerPoint MVP Chirag Dalal (*http://officeone.mvps.org/ download/hyperlink_warning.html*).

Note that these options only prevent the warning message from happening on your computer. You cannot prevent this message on other computers— unless, of course, you use Chirag's utility or perform the registry changes described above on those systems as well.

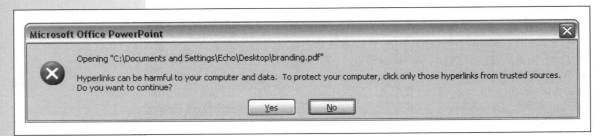

Figure 1-8. You might receive a warning similar to this one when clicking hyperlinks in your presentations run in PowerPoint 2003 or PowerPoint Viewer 2003.

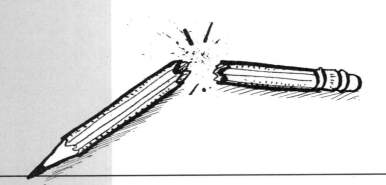

Change Note Size in Presenter View

THE ANNOYANCE: I'm using Presenter view, and I swear, I think I'm blind as a bat! How can I change the size of the notes area in Presenter view?

THE FIX: Presenter view on the PC cannot be changed. (It can be changed on PowerPoint 2004 for the Mac, though.)

If you need this capability, download the PowerShow add-in from Microsoft PowerPoint MVP Chirag Dalal (*http://officeone.mvps.org/powershow/ powershow.html*). This add-in lets you use PowerPoint's views during a presentation, and it keeps the view on the "presenter monitor" synchronized with the view on the "presentation monitor." To set it up, simply install the add-in, select Slide Show→PowerShow, click the Session tab, and check the "Slide design view follows slide show" box (see Figure 1-9).

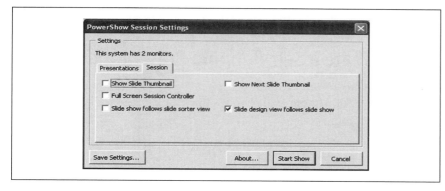

Figure 1-9. PowerShow lets you increase the font size on speaker notes, plus a whole lot more.

Since PowerShow uses PowerPoint's own design views, you can increase the size of your speaker notes by zooming in on them or increasing the font size in PowerPoint. You might also want to download the Shortcut Manager (*http://officeone.mvps.org/ppsctmgr/ppsctmgr.html*), which lets you assign the up and down arrow keys to navigate slides during a PowerShow session.

Practice with Only One Monitor

THE ANNOYANCE: I'd really like to practice with Presenter view, but PowerPoint won't let me use it unless I have a second monitor attached. I don't have a second monitor. Any suggestions?

THE FIX: Select View→Notes Page, and then hold down the Ctrl key while you click the Slide Show button in the lower-left corner of the screen (see Figure 1-10). This opens Slide Show view in 1/4 of the screen, so you can still see your speaker notes if you want. You'll have to advance the notes

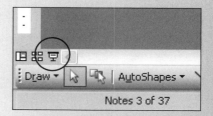

Figure 1-10. Hold down the Ctrl key while you click the slide show icon to open a slide show that takes up only 1/4 of your screen.

pages independently from the small slide show, but it may be enough to let you practice without having to hook up another monitor.

Start Slide Show from the Current Slide

THE ANNOYANCE: I'm working on creating a presentation, and it would sure be nice if there were a keyboard shortcut to start the presentation from the current slide! Otherwise, it takes forever to navigate to the slide I really want to see.

THE FIX: Plain ol' F5 will still begin the slide show on the first slide, but Shift+F5 will, as of PowerPoint 2003, begin the presentation from the current slide.

As a matter of fact, if you happen to have the Custom Animation task pane open in either PowerPoint 2002 or 2003, you can press the Slide Show button at the bottom to start the show on the current slide (see Figure 1-11).

Create a Self-Running Presentation

THE ANNOYANCE: I want to have a presentation running in our booth at an upcoming trade show. How can I create a self-running presentation?

THE FIX: Select Slide Show→Set Up Show and choose the "Browsed at a kiosk" option.

Kiosk mode renders the keyboard useless, so make sure you provide some kind of navigation for the users. You can either set all the slide transitions to automatic, or you can provide buttons with Action Settings so the users can navigate through the presentation at their leisure.

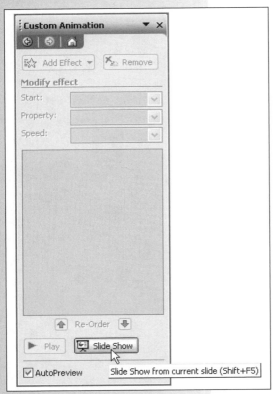

Figure 1-11. Press the Slide Show button at the bottom of the Custom Animation task pane to begin the slide show on the current slide.

You can add action buttons to the slide and title master so they're available on every slide. Select View→Master→Slide Master, and then select AutoShapes→Action Buttons→Forward or Next on the Drawing toolbar and click the slide to create a "next slide" button. Repeat the sequence and select "Back or Previous" to add a "previous slide" button. Don't forget to add the buttons to the Title Master also.

Did I say Kiosk mode makes the keyboard useless? Well, I lied. The Esc key will still work, so you'll want to remove the keyboard from the trade show system after you get the kiosk going. Or you can use Microsoft PowerPoint MVP Shyam Pillai's free No ESCape add-in (*http://skp.mvps.org/noesc.htm*) to disable the Esc key.

Kiosk Mode Is Broken

THE ANNOYANCE: I created a presentation to run at a kiosk, and it should return to the first slide after five minutes of inactivity. However, now it just sits there on the slide and never goes back to the beginning. How'd I manage to break my presentation?

THE FIX: Oh, you didn't break anything, PowerPoint did. Kiosk mode is broken in PowerPoint 2002; it doesn't reset after five minutes of inactivity. It does reset as expected in PowerPoint 97, 2000, and 2003, though.

If you need to use Kiosk mode in PowerPoint 2002, or if you simply want to extend the capabilities of Kiosk mode in PowerPoint 2000 or 2003, download the Kiosk Assistant (*http://officeone.mvps.org/kioskassist/kioskassist.html*) from Microsoft PowerPoint MVP Chirag Dalal. It lets you specify the time interval before the presentation resets, as well as which slide the presentation will reset to.

Loop Your Presentation Continuously

THE ANNOYANCE: I have this computer running a presentation in our lobby, but I want it to start over automatically when it gets to the end.

THE FIX: Select Slide Show→Set Up Show and check the "Loop continuously until 'Esc'" box (see Figure 1-12). This setting is automatically enabled when you choose the "Browsed at a kiosk" option.

Show a Range of Slides

THE ANNOYANCE: My presentation has 20 slides in it, but it stops after showing only half the slides. What's wrong?

THE FIX: There are two common culprits here: hidden slides or a specific slide range. The easiest way to check for hidden slides is to select View→Slide Sorter and look for a gray cross through the slide number.

If hidden slides aren't the problem, select Slide Show→Set Up Show and make sure the All option is selected in the "Show slides" area (see Figure 1-12).

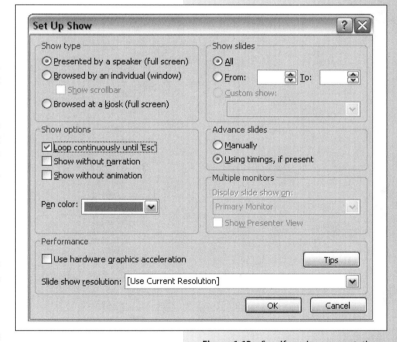

Figure 1-12. Specify various presentation settings in the Set Up Show dialog box. You must have two monitors attached for the Multiple Monitors options to be available.

Add Current Date and Time

THE ANNOYANCE: I have a welcome presentation running continuously on a computer in our lobby. I'd like to add the current date and time, but I can't find a way to do it. I tried using Insert→Date and Time, but it sticks at the time the presentation starts.

THE FIX: You need to download the free AutoDateTime add-in from Microsoft PowerPoint MVP Chirag Dalal (*http://officeone.mvps.org/autodatetime/autodatetime.html*). As with any add-in, before you can install it, you must select Tools→Macro→Security and choose the Medium option. Once installed, select Format→AutoDateTime to determine the format of the date and time (see Figure 1-13). Next, select View→Header and Footer, click the Slide tab, check the "Date and time" box, and choose the "Update automatically" option to display it. If you want to change the location, font, or size of the date and time text, select View→Master→Slide Master, and make the change to the Date Area placeholder.

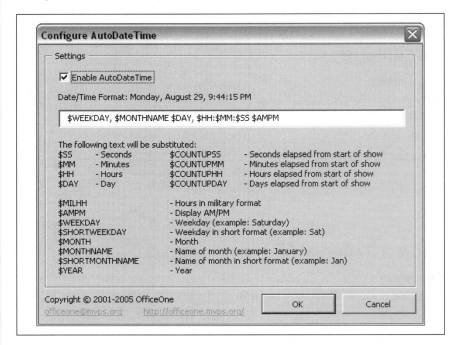

Figure 1-13. Choose Format→AutoDateTime to determine how the date and time will display.

Customize Your Presentation with Custom Shows

You already created your presentation, but now you want to add a three-slide, "side" presentation that goes into more depth on a particular subject, in case the audience asks questions.

One easy solution is to create a custom show within your presentation. Select Slide Show→Custom Shows and click the New button. Give the custom show a name, select the appropriate slides from the list on the left, and click the Add button to add the slides to the custom show (see Figure 1-14).

Figure 1-14. Custom shows let you create "branches" or specific groups of slides in your presentation. Press Shift or Ctrl while clicking on slides in the list to add or remove more than one slide at a time.

After you've created a custom show, use the following steps to enable access to it:

1. Right-click an object and choose Action Settings. (You'll click this object to open the custom show.)

2. Choose the "Hyperlink to" option and select Custom Show from the drop-down list.

3. Select your custom show, check the "Show and return" box, and click OK to close the dialog boxes (see Figure 1-15).

The "Show and return" option returns you to the slide you started on when the custom show finishes. If you don't check this box, the presentation will just end after you finish showing the slides in the custom show.

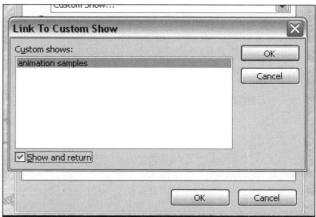

Figure 1-15. When you create the Action Setting link to access a custom show, make sure you check the "Show and return" box so you return to the original slide when you finish the custom show.

Create an Intro Loop

Many users need to have a couple of slides loop at the beginning of a presentation while the audience is seated. They then need to move to the main presentation easily without the audience noticing.

One way to create such an intro loop is to make a custom show that includes just the first few slides you need to loop. (You can even create a custom show containing just one slide.) Create another custom show that includes the slides in the main presentation. See the "Customize Your Presentation with Custom Shows" sidebar.

Next, select Slide Show→Set Up Show and check the "Loop continuously until 'Esc'" box for the custom show with the initial looping slides (see Figure 1-16).

Finally, add a button to each of the slides in the intro loop; you'll click this button to begin the main presentation. Draw an object on an intro slide, right-click it, and choose Action Settings. Choose the "Hyperlink to" option and select Custom Show from the drop-down list. Select the custom show representing the main presentation. Copy the button and paste it on all the intro slides.

Microsoft PowerPoint MVP Taj Simmons has an even more seamless method of looping slides. Check out his tutorial at *http://www.awesomebackgrounds.com/ powerpointlooping.htm.*

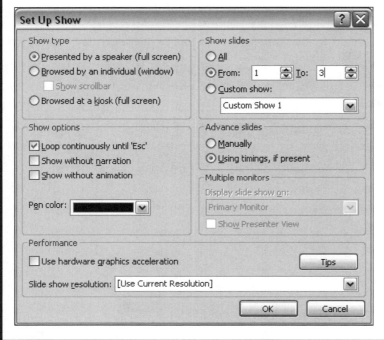

Figure 1-16. Set custom shows to "Loop continuously until 'Esc'" in the Set Up Show dialog box. To loop a custom show, you must specify the slide numbers in the Show Slides area, which is rather counterintuitive.

Dumb Defaults

The development team for every computer application has to decide how the program will act straight out of the box. Sometimes they get the default behavior right, and sometimes they don't.

PowerPoint is no exception. In many places, the PowerPoint development team made very wise decisions regarding the default behavior for the program settings. In other places, well, let's just say those decisions were less than inspired.

In this chapter, we'll discuss some of the default settings in PowerPoint. You'll learn how to keep stuff from moving around when you don't want it to, how to restore some items that seem to be missing, and how to deal with file size issues.

Turn Off AutoFit Body Text to Placeholder

THE ANNOYANCE: Here I am typing along in a placeholder, and my text keeps getting smaller and smaller! How can I make the font size stay put?

THE FIX: You want to turn off "AutoFit body text to placeholder." In PowerPoint 2003 and 2002, select Tools→AutoCorrect Options, click the AutoFormat As You Type tab, and uncheck the "AutoFit body text to placeholder" box (see Figure 2-1). In PowerPoint 2000 and 97, select Tools→Options, click the Edit tab, and uncheck the "Auto-fit text to text placeholder" box.

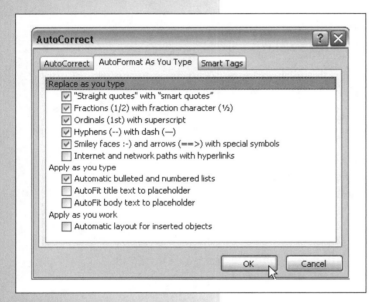

Figure 2-1. Uncheck the "AutoFit body text to placeholder" and "AutoFit title text to placeholder" boxes to prevent your text from shrinking.

The AutoFit feature not only decreases the font size as you type, it also decreases the line spacing in the placeholder at the same time. This can be a problem, especially in PowerPoint 2002 and 2003: on a crowded slide, the line spacing can quickly drop to well below .8 lines, at which point the ascenders and descenders of many letters start getting cut off.

AutoFit works less aggressively in PowerPoint 2000 and 97. In those versions, the font size will only decrease one "level," so you will not see nearly as much adjustment as you will in PowerPoint 2002 and 2003.

If you notice this type of AutoFit adjustment happening when you type slide titles in the Title Placeholder in PowerPoint 2002 or 2003, return to the AutoFormat As You Type tab, and uncheck the "AutoFit *title* text to placeholder" box.

Inserted Pictures Change the Layout

THE ANNOYANCE: Every time I insert a picture into a slide, PowerPoint goes crazy and moves all my stuff around on the slide. Make it STOP!

THE FIX: This behavior first appeared in PowerPoint 2002. To turn it off in 2002, just go to Tools→AutoCorrect Options, click the AutoFormat As You Type tab, and uncheck the "Automatic layout for inserted objects" box. Now when you insert any type of object (image, diagram, table, etc.) onto a slide with text, the existing content will no longer move.

Automatic layout for inserted objects is basically PowerPoint's way of trying to be helpful. If you have a slide with some text on it, and you then insert something else (an image, a diagram, table, etc.), PowerPoint applies the

Title, Text, and Content slide layout for you. Of course, this will often move your existing content to places you don't necessarily want it moved!

This behavior proved confusing enough to users when first introduced in PowerPoint 2002 that Microsoft removed the behavior from the "Automatic layout for inserted objects" option when used with images in PowerPoint 2003. However, the slide layout will still change for inserted diagrams, tables, or charts, and, in those instances, the behavior is usually welcome.

Reverse Flipped Images

THE ANNOYANCE: I opened my file, and my images are flipped! What's going on?

THE FIX: This occasionally happens when you use PowerPoint 2002 or 2003 to open files created in PowerPoint 2000 or 97. To resolve it, download *FlipPict.EXE* from Microsoft (*http://support.microsoft.com/default. aspx?scid=kb;en-us;822228*) or *Unflip.ZIP* from Microsoft MVP Shyam Pillai (*http://skp.mvps.org/unflip.htm*). Or, install Service Pack 3 for Office XP (*http://support.microsoft.com/kb/832671/*).

Why does this happen? PowerPoint 2000 and 97 ignore the FlipVertical and FlipHorizontal properties of images. PowerPoint 2002 and 2003 recognize these properties, so the images show up in their inverted or upside down state. If you drag an image handle past the edge of the image boundary in PowerPoint 2002 and 2003, you will see the image flipped, but in PowerPoint 2000 and 97, you won't—even though the image flip properties have been set.

Prevent Text from Moving Around

THE ANNOYANCE: I worked really hard on this presentation, but when my colleague opened the file on her computer, all the text had moved around. What causes this, and how do I keep it from happening?

THE FIX: You're experiencing a classic font replacement issue. See, if you've used a font that's not available on the recipient's computer, PowerPoint will replace the font with one that is available (usually Arial for sans serif and Times New Roman for serif fonts). When your fonts are replaced, the text will move.

Tell your colleague to open the presentation and select Format→Replace Fonts (see Figure 2-2). If you see a question mark next to any of the fonts in the list, those fonts are not available.

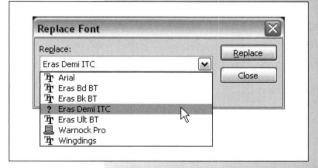

Figure 2-2. A question mark indicates a missing font. The TT symbol indicates a true-type font. The other symbol indicates a PostScript font.

Unfortunately, there's no core set of fonts for Windows computers. The font selection available depends on your operating system, the programs you installed, and what you've done with the fonts in general. The most reliable way around this problem is to stick with Times New Roman and Arial when creating presentations.

If the licensing level of the font you're using allows it, you can embed the font into your presentation. Make sure you test this early in the creation process so that you don't find out you can't embed your font just as you're finishing your presentation! PostScript fonts can't be embedded into PowerPoint presentations. And fonts can't be embedded at all on Mac versions of PowerPoint, nor will Mac versions of PowerPoint recognize fonts embedded in PowerPoint presentations created on a PC.

To embed a font in your presentation, select File→Save As. Click the Tools button and select Embed TrueType Fonts (PowerPoint 2000 and 97) or Save Options (PowerPoint 2002 and 2003) and check the "Embed TrueType fonts" box (see Figure 2-3). In PowerPoint 2002 and 2003, you can also select Tools→Options, click the Save tab, and check the "Embed TrueType fonts" box. Save and close the presentation.

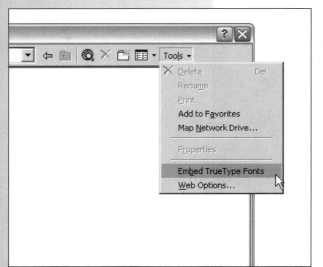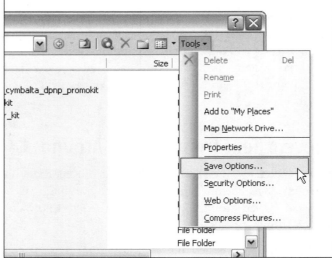

Figure 2-3. To embed a font in PowerPoint 2000 or 97, select File→Save As and click the Tools drop-down menu (left). To embed a font in PowerPoint 2002 or 2003, select File→Save As and choose Save Options from the Tools drop-down menu (right).

To test that the font has been embedded, go to your *C:\Windows\Fonts* folder, select the font, and press Ctrl+C to copy it. Next, navigate to another folder on your hard drive and press Ctrl+V to paste it. After you've created a copy of the font, return to your *Fonts* folder, right-click the font, and select Delete.

Now open your presentation with the embedded font. Does everything look as it should? If so, then the font has been embedded. Return to your *Fonts* folder and choose File→Install New Font to reinstall the font you deleted.

Because of font rendering differences, text tends to wrap differently on Mac and Windows systems. So, text will occasionally move around when a presentation created on Windows is opened on a Mac or vice versa. To work around this issue, leave some extra space in your placeholders and text boxes to compensate for the rendering differences.

Force Complete Menus

THE ANNOYANCE: Whenever I go to choose something on a menu, it's moved or I can't find it at all! How do I make the menus stay the same?

THE FIX: In PowerPoint 2002 and 2003, select Tools→Customize, click the Options tab, and check the "Always show full menus" box. In PowerPoint 2000 and 97, *uncheck* the "Menus show recently used commands first" box. In all versions, changing this setting affects all your Microsoft Office programs.

Make Toolbar Icons Stay in One Place

THE ANNOYANCE: The icons on my toolbars keep moving around, and about half the time, the icon I need is missing. How do I put the freeze on them?

THE FIX: In PowerPoint 2002 and 2003, select Tools→Customize, click the Options tab, and check the "Show Standard and Formatting toolbars on two rows" box. In PowerPoint 2000 and 97, *uncheck* the "Standard and Formatting toolbars share one row" box.

While this will take up a little more space on your screen, keeping the toolbars on two separate rows means there should be enough room for all the icons on both toolbars, so the icons won't appear and disappear as you use them.

If you don't want to give up the extra space it takes to show your toolbars on two rows, you can click at the end of the toolbar to see the rest of the icons that belong on that toolbar (see Figure 2-4).

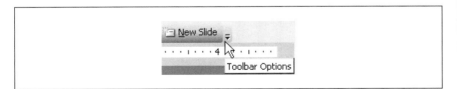

Figure 2-4. Click the end of the toolbar to see the rest of the icons.

Embedded Fonts with PowerPoint 2003

If you or any of the presentation recipients use PowerPoint 2003, you'll want to be wary when embedding fonts.

When embedded, the licensing levels of some fonts will cause the presentation to open as Read Only in PowerPoint 2003. This means you can't edit the file, do a Save or Save As, or even use Format→ Replace Fonts to substitute a different font so that you can edit the presentation.

Also, a bug in PowerPoint 2003 sometimes causes presentations to open as Read Only, even if the embedded fonts are available on your computer! How annoying is that? You created a presentation, embedded the font, and then saved and closed the file. When you proceed to open the file later, it opens as Read Only, which means you can no longer work on it.

Make sure you think long and hard before you embed a font into a presentation that will be opened in PowerPoint 2003. For more information about PowerPoint and font embedding, head to the PowerPoint FAQ (*http://www.rdpslides.com/ pptfaq/FAQ00076.htm*).

CUSTOMIZE POWERPOINT TO SUIT YOUR NEEDS

Restore Missing Images and Charts

THE ANNOYANCE: When I open my file, the images and charts are missing. What's going on?

THE FIX: Are you using PowerPoint 2003? You need to apply the latest Service Pack for Office 2003 by going to Help→Check for Updates.

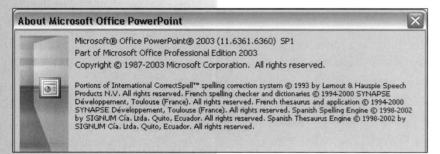

About Microsoft Office PowerPoint

Microsoft® Office PowerPoint® 2003 (11.6361.6360) SP1
Part of Microsoft Office Professional Edition 2003
Copyright © 1987-2003 Microsoft Corporation. All rights reserved.

Portions of International CorrectSpell™ spelling correction system © 1993 by Lernout & Hauspie Speech Products N.V. All rights reserved. French spelling checker and dictionaries © 1994-2000 SYNAPSE Développement, Toulouse (France). All rights reserved. French thesaurus and application © 1994-2000 SYNAPSE Développement, Toulouse (France). All rights reserved. Spanish Spelling Engine © 1998-2002 by SIGNUM Cía. Ltda. Quito, Ecuador. All rights reserved. Spanish Thesaurus Engine © 1998-2002 by SIGNUM Cía. Ltda. Quito, Ecuador. All rights reserved.

Figure 2-5. Make sure you have the latest Service Pack installed by selecting Help→ About.

Service Pack 1 especially is a *critical* patch for PowerPoint 2003. It resolves most of these "missing images" types of issues, as well as a number of others. To see if a Service Pack or update has already been installed, select Help→ About Microsoft Office PowerPoint and look for SP*x*, where *x* is the number of the Service Pack. For example, in Figure 2-5 it says Microsoft Office PowerPoint 2003 (build number) SP1.

Restore Grayed-Out Commands

THE ANNOYANCE: I can't save my PowerPoint file because the save options are all grayed out.

THE FIX: You need to activate Office. Select Help→Activate Product and follow the prompts.

If, for some reason, you are unable to activate using the "Activate by using the Internet" option, choose "Activate by using the telephone" instead. The activation wizard will provide you with the number to dial. For more information on activation, visit the Microsoft web site (*http://office.microsoft.com/en-us/assistance/HA011187761033.aspx*).

Another possibility: If you downloaded a trial version of Microsoft Office, the applications will open in reduced functionality mode after the trial time period has expired. In this case, you must purchase Microsoft Office to make it fully functional.

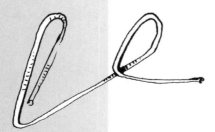

Restore New Animations

THE ANNOYANCE: When I right-click an object and choose Custom Animation, the old custom animation dialog box opens. How can I get the custom animation task pane with the exit and trigger animations and motion paths to open instead?

THE FIX: Select Tools→Options and click the Edit tab. In the "Disable new features" section, *uncheck* the "New animation effects," "Multiple masters," and "Password protection" boxes, and then close the dialog box (see Figure 2-6). Next, close and reopen PowerPoint.

If the three boxes are already unchecked, check them and close the dialog box. Next, close and reopen PowerPoint, return to the Edit tab, and uncheck the three boxes. Close the dialog box, close PowerPoint again, and reopen it. See if you can now get to the Custom Animation task pane.

Bring Back Color Views

THE ANNOYANCE: Oh my god! PowerPoint is all black and white! Where'd the color views go?

THE FIX: You're a victim of a Windows accessibility setting. Select Start→Control Panel→Accessibility Options, click the Display tab, and uncheck the "Use High Contrast" box.

Make Sure You Have a Qualifying Product

THE ANNOYANCE: When I tried to install PowerPoint, I got an error message saying it couldn't find the qualifying product. I have an old version of Office installed on my computer, so what's the problem?

THE FIX: In a nutshell, you purchased an upgrade version of PowerPoint 97, 2000, or 2002. For the most part, you can't install an upgrade version of PowerPoint if you don't have a full version of PowerPoint to upgrade. So you really needed to purchase the full standalone version of PowerPoint, not the upgrade version.

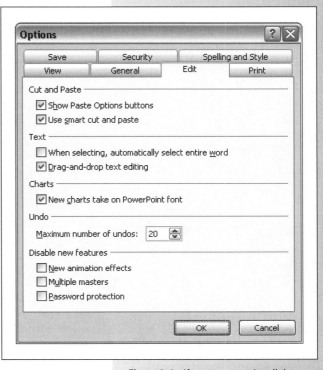

Figure 2-6. If you want to enjoy all the benefits of PowerPoint 2002 and 2003, make sure you uncheck the three items under "Disable new features."

See, your old version of Office might not have PowerPoint. This was pretty typical with Small Business Edition (SBE) versions of Office (i.e., Office XP SBE, Office 2000 SBE, Office 97 SBE). You can try putting your Office installation CD in the CD drive when the PowerPoint installation prompts you to help it find the qualifying product. Sometimes that will work.

Microsoft got smart with PowerPoint 2003, though. Even Office SBE versions now count as qualifying products if you purchase a PowerPoint 2003 Upgrade. That means you can use the PowerPoint 2003 Upgrade version to add PowerPoint to any version of Office XP, 2000, or 97. But beware—many OEMs (Original Equipment Manufacturers, which is a fancy name for a company that manufactures and sells computers) include Office 2003 Basic with the computers they sell. Office 2003 Basic does *not* include PowerPoint, and you *cannot* use the PowerPoint 2003 Upgrade to add PowerPoint 2003. In this case, you need to purchase the full standalone version of PowerPoint 2003. Check the Microsoft web site for the list of qualifying products (*http://www.microsoft.com/office/powerpoint/howtobuy/default.mspx*) if you're thinking about adding PowerPoint to your computer.

Of course, you can always purchase a licensed copy of an older version of PowerPoint to use as your qualifying product—if you can find one. But make sure you check the list of qualifying products before you go this route!

Change the Username in Comments

THE ANNOYANCE: When I installed Office, I typed in a joke name. Now that name shows up in the comment boxes on my slides. How can I change it to my real name, or else my new clients won't be clients for long.

THE FIX: Select Tools→Options, click the General tab, and type your name in the User Information box. Don't forget to update your initials to match! Changing the User Information in one Office application changes it automatically in the other Office applications.

Avoid Saving in Notes Page View

THE ANNOYANCE: How do I get my speaker notes back? I saved my presentation, but when I opened it again, the speaker notes disappeared.

THE FIX: Start looking for a backup or a previous version of your presentation because once those notes disappear, there's unfortunately no way to get them back.

Disappearing notes is most definitely a problem in PowerPoint 97. Saving while in Notes Page view seems to trigger the disappearance. You should also turn off Fast Saves, which may contribute to the problem. Select Tools→ Options, click the Save tab, and *uncheck the* "Allow Fast Saves" box.

To stop the problem from happening again, install Service Release 1 (SR-1)— and possibly Service Release (SR-2)—for Office 97 (*http://office.microsoft. com/en-us/officeupdate/CD010226191033.aspx*). Also, don't save while in Notes Page view.

PowerPoint 2002 and 2003 don't seem to have a problem with disappearing notes. It may not even be a problem in PowerPoint 2000, although most long-time PowerPoint users still refuse to save while in Notes Page view. As the saying goes, once bitten, twice shy....

Add Save as HTML to the Menu

THE ANNOYANCE: I read that I can use Save as HTML to convert my PowerPoint file to a web page, but I don't have that option on my menu.

THE FIX: Save as HTML isn't part of the default installation for PowerPoint 97. If you performed a Typical Installation, the Save as HTML option is either grayed out or simply does not appear.

To install this feature, insert your Office (PowerPoint) 97 installation CD into the CD drive and choose Custom Installation when prompted. Find Web Authoring Tools and put a checkmark next to it.

If you have Adobe Acrobat 4.0 (and maybe 5.0, too), the Acrobat add-ins for PowerPoint could be conflicting with the Save as HTML feature. To resolve this, you'll need to disable the *PDFMaker.PPA* and *PDFMakerA.PPA* files. Close PowerPoint, find the two PPA files on your hard drive (e.g., *C:\Program Files\Acrobat\Macros\Office97*), and rename them *PDFMaker.PPX* and *PDFMakerA.PPX*. Restart PowerPoint and see if File→Save as HTML is now available.

Renaming these two PPA files disables the add-ins that let you make one-click PDF files from PowerPoint. However, you can still select File→Print and select Acrobat Distiller from your list of printers to create PDFs in PowerPoint.

Outline View Icon Gone

THE ANNOYANCE: In PowerPoint 2000, I could click the little icon at the bottom left of the screen to open Outline view. How come I can't seem to find that in PowerPoint 2002?

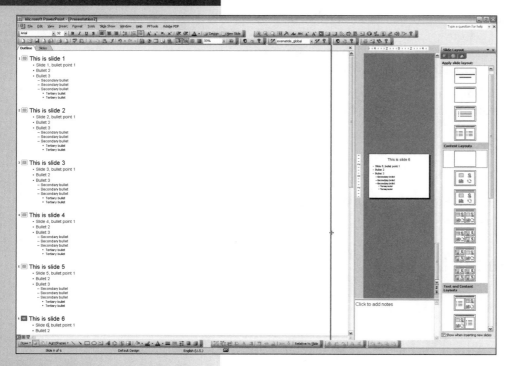

Figure 2-7. Drag the edge of the Outline pane to resize it.

THE FIX: If you need a full-screen Outline view, hold down the Ctrl+Shift keys and click the slide sorter icon at the lower left of the screen. Microsoft removed the Outline View icon in PowerPoint 2002 and 2003, maybe because you can resize the Outline pane on the left to nearly full screen (see Figure 2-7).

To add the Outline View icon to your toolbar, select Tools→Customize, click the Commands tab, select the View category, and drag the Outline command to one of your toolbars (see Figure 2-8).

Figure 2-8. Click and drag a command to any toolbar so it's always within easy reach.

WHAT'S GOING ON WITH THESE FILE SIZES?

Turn Off Fast Saves Feature

THE ANNOYANCE: Okay, this makes no sense. I deleted a slide, saved my presentation, and the file size actually got bigger! What in the world is going on?

THE FIX: Select Tools→Options, click the Save tab, and *uncheck* the "Allow Fast Saves" box (see Figure 2-9). Don't ever recheck it. After you turn off Fast Saves, you might want to select File→Save As and save your file with a new name.

Fast Saves works by *appending* changes to your file rather than rewriting the file when you save. This was helpful in speeding up the time it took to save a file back in the days of slower processors, but it's no longer necessary. And it's notorious for increasing file size. Fast Saves may also contribute to corrupt PowerPoint files, so it's really best to turn it off and leave it off.

Choose the Correct "Save as type" Option

THE ANNOYANCE: Yikes! What'd I do? I saved my presentation as a PowerPoint 97 file and it's enormous. And no, I don't have the Fast Saves feature turned on.

THE FIX: There is no such thing as a "PowerPoint 97" file.

PowerPoint 97, 2000, 2002, and 2003 all share the same file format. However, when you click the "Save as type" drop-down menu in the Save As dialog box, you will see several different options. In this case, your file size increased because you chose the option with the "& 95" in its name (see Figure 2-10).

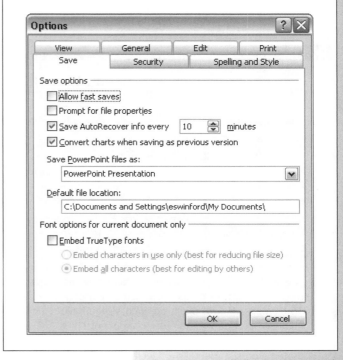

Figure 2-9. Turn off Allow Fast Saves—and leave it off!

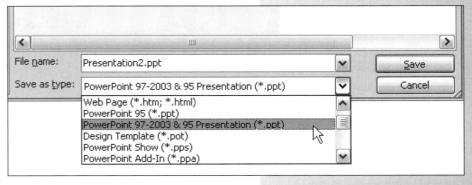

Figure 2-10. Avoid anything with "& 95" in the "Save as type" drop-down menu, unless you want very large file sizes.

It's the "& 95" part that'll getcha. PowerPoint 95 didn't maintain the internal compression of images. When you save a file with one of those "& 95" options, any images in the file become uncompressed, which causes the file size to blow up.

In the future, always choose "Presentation (*.ppt)" from the "Save as type" drop-down menu to save your work as a regular PowerPoint file.

Cut Your Files Down to Size

"Huge" is a relative term, but a *lot* of things can cause your PowerPoint files to grow. The following is a list of the more common causes:

- The Fast Saves option can increase file size because it *appends* changes to your file rather than rewriting the file when you save (see "Turn Off Fast Saves Feature," earlier in this chapter).

- If you save your presentation as PowerPoint 95 file type, your file size will increase (see "Choose the Correct 'Save as type' Option," earlier in this chapter).

- Overscanned images can also bloat file sizes. However, you should remember that PowerPoint is at the mercy of your monitor or projector, which can display only 96 (sometimes 120) pixels per inch. If you have higher resolution images, you're simply wasting pixels and causing the system to work much harder during a presentation. To understand more about this issue, visit *http://www.awesomebackgrounds.com/ powerpointgraphics.htm*. If you need to optimize the images in your presentation, you can use the Compress Pictures tool on the PowerPoint Picture toolbar (View→Toolbars→Picture). Or, you can purchase the RnR Presentation Optimizer (*http://www.rdpslides. com/pptools/FAQ00013.htm*) for $99.95. You can also download a free trial version of NXPowerLite (*http://www.nxpowerlite.com/*), but it will cost you $46 if you wish to purchase it.

- Object Linking and Embedding (OLE). When you paste or drag and drop images and other objects onto a slide, PowerPoint sometimes creates embedded OLE objects. Embedded OLE objects let you edit the object from within PowerPoint, but they can really bloat your PowerPoint file. Excel charts pasted in PowerPoint can be especially problematic—you may not know it, but the whole Excel workbook comes along with those charts.

- Extraneous stuff on your slides, such as audio files, charts, and images, add to your file size. When you're looking for oversized images, OLE objects, etc., make sure you check the slide, handout, and notes masters as well.

- Most embedded fonts don't give you a huge file size hit, but double-byte and Unicode fonts can be huge! You may want to check the file size of the font before you embed it.

- Review Features (File→Send to→Mail Recipient (for Review)) are available in PowerPoint 2002 and 2003. They work by appending the recipients' changes to the original file, so the file size will increase even if the change consists of deleting slides. You'd think that choosing File→Send to→Mail Recipient (as Attachment) would keep this from happening; however, Outlook has been known to turn on the Review feature all by itself! To turn this feature off for good, open Outlook and select Tools→ Options→Preferences→E-mail Options→Advanced E-mail Options and uncheck the "Add properties to attachments to enable Reply with Changes" box.

Ungroup Your Excel Charts After Pasting

THE ANNOYANCE: I pasted a chart from an Excel spreadsheet into my PowerPoint file, and the entire spreadsheet came along with it. I just sent confidential salary information to our whole company.

THE FIX: When you copy data or charts from Excel and paste them on a PowerPoint slide, you're actually pasting the *entire* Excel workbook into your presentation. Not only can this greatly affect your file size, it can also lead to embarrassing situations!

The easiest way around this is to ungroup your Excel chart when you're finished working with it. To do this, select the chart and, on the Drawing menu, choose Draw→Ungroup (see Figure 2-11).

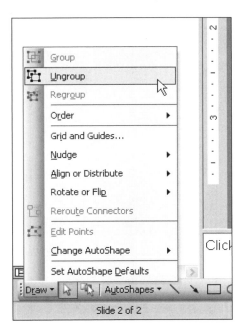

Figure 2-11. Ungroup Excel charts to prevent including unwanted data in your presentation.

SLIDES, TEMPLATES, AND OTHER RELATED DEFAULTS

Specify a Default Template

THE ANNOYANCE: How can I make our corporate template my default template?

THE FIX: Simply rename the corporate template *Blank.pot* (PowerPoint 2002 or 2003) or *Blank Presentation.pot* (PowerPoint 2000 or 97). The location of your templates depends on which version of Office and Windows you're using. Open the corporate template, select File→Save As and type **blank** in the "File name" box. Choose "Design Template (*.pot)" from the "Save as type" drop-down menu (see Figure 2-12). The "Save in" box will automatically change to the location where templates you create are stored.

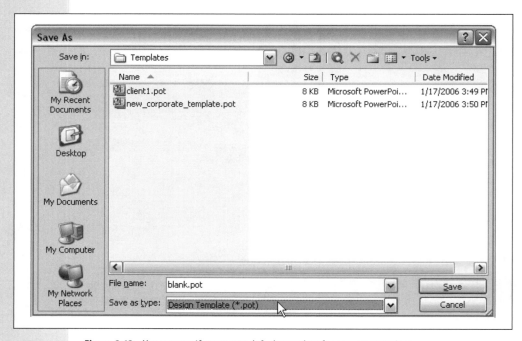

Figure 2-12. You can specify your own default template for new presentations.

In PowerPoint 2003, you have another option. In the Slide Design task pane, click the drop-down arrow to the right of your corporate template and choose "Use for All New Presentations" (see Figure 2-13).

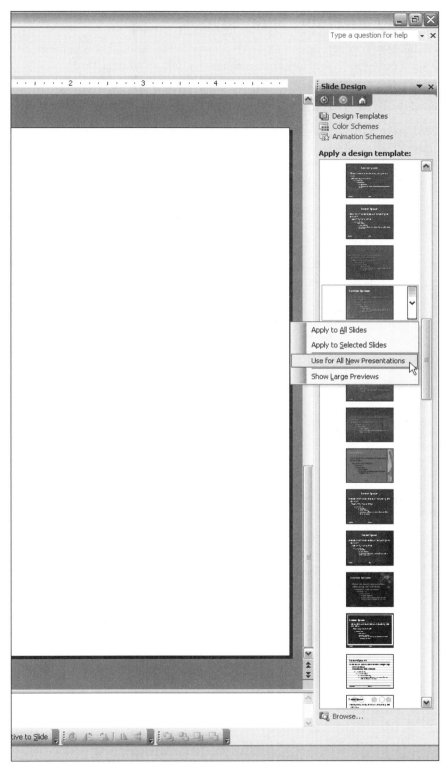

Figure 2-13. PowerPoint 2003 makes it easy to specify a default template for new presentations.

Specify a Default Slide Layout

THE ANNOYANCE: When I press Ctrl+M to insert a new slide, I don't necessarily want a bulleted slide. How can I change the default slide layout?

THE FIX: Download the Set Default Slide Layout add-in from Microsoft PowerPoint MVP Chirag Dalal (*http://officeone.mvps.org/sdsl/sdsl.html*).

Before you install this or any other add-in, you must open PowerPoint, select Tools→Macro→Security, and choose Medium security level (see Figure 2-14). Close PowerPoint and then double-click the Set Default Slide Layout add-in to install it.

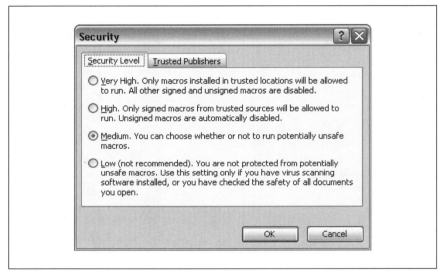

Figure 2-14. You must temporarily change your macro settings to medium or low before you can install PowerPoint add-ins. After installing an add-in, you can change the macro security setting back to high if you wish.

Once installed, open PowerPoint and choose Tools→Set Default Slide Layout. In the Set Default Slide Layout dialog box, select your desired default layout and check the "Use this layout for all new slides too" box (see Figure 2-15).

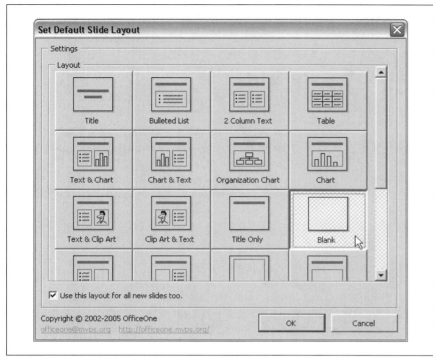

Figure 2-15. You can use the free Set Default Slide Layout add-in to force new slides to use a default layout different than PowerPoint's usual "Title and Text" layout.

Create a Default Chart Style

THE ANNOYANCE: I'm making a template for a bunch of corporate users, but there's no way to specify a default chart. I can't expect these people to format each chart by hand.

THE FIX: Unfortunately, you can't really set a default chart style.

One option is to create a few sample charts on some slides in your template. Teach users to open the template file (instead of *applying* it to a file), copy the slide with the chart, and change the data in the graphs as appropriate.

You can also create user-defined graphs, but be aware that these are machine-specific—not template-specific—settings. To create a user-defined graph, do the following:

1. Format a chart the way you want it.

2. Right-click and choose Chart Type.

3. Click the Custom Types tab and choose the User-defined option (see Figure 2-16).

4. Click the Add button.

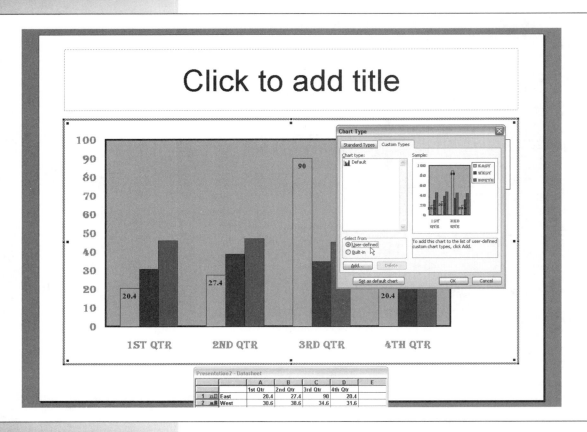

Figure 2-16. To create a custom chart style, select Custom Types in the Chart Type dialog box. Be aware that custom chart styles do not travel with a PowerPoint template— they're only available on the computer where you create them.

5. Enter a name (required) and description (optional) for your chart and click OK.

6. Click the button to Set as Default Chart and choose Yes when asked, "Are you sure?"

PowerPoint saves these settings in a file named *Grusrgal.gra*. This file is usually located in *C:\Documents and Settings\[YourUserName]\Application Data\Microsoft\Graph*. If you want to share your custom graphs with the world, you can copy and send this file to other users; however, start with a small group to make sure it works properly. You should also warn people that if they overwrite their own *Grusrgal.gra* file with yours, they will lose any customizations they made to their own chart styles.

Add a Placeholder to the Slide Layout

THE ANNOYANCE: I need to add a subtitle placeholder and another text placeholder to the slide layout. How do I do this?

THE FIX: Unfortunately, you can't. Time to send another thank you letter to the folks in Redmond.

Find a Template on the Task Pane

THE ANNOYANCE: I've been staring at this stupid task pane for 10 minutes. How in the world is the list of templates organized? Can I specify the way I want them sorted?

THE FIX: In PowerPoint 2002, the task pane lists templates alphabetically. In PowerPoint 2003, it sorts them by background color. You can't change these settings.

If you have PowerPoint 2003 alongside another version of PowerPoint on your computer, you will see the first half of the templates—the PowerPoint 2003 templates—sorted by color, followed by the second half of the templates—from the other version of PowerPoint—listed alphabetically.

File→New Doesn't Do Anything

THE ANNOYANCE: I hit File→New to start a new presentation, but PowerPoint doesn't do anything.

THE FIX: In PowerPoint 2002 and 2003, File→New actually opens the New Presentation task pane, where you can choose to start a new blank presentation, one based on a design template or the AutoContent Wizard, or open an existing presentation or template (see Figure 2-17). If you already have the New Presentation task pane open, you will notice a quick flash at the top of the task pane prompting you to choose an option. You can also press Ctrl+N in all versions of PowerPoint to open a new, blank presentation.

> **NOTE**
>
> *In PowerPoint 2002 and 2003, many commands (such as Format→Slide Layout and Insert→Picture→Clip Art) simply open task panes. You then have to look in the task pane to find your desired tool or command.*

Turn Off Snap to Grid

THE ANNOYANCE: When I use the arrow keys to nudge objects on a slide, they seem to move by huge increments. How can I better control this feature?

THE FIX: By default, PowerPoint aligns objects to a one-pica (.083") invisible grid. It automatically kicks in when you move objects with your mouse or the arrow keys on your keyboard. To toggle this off in PowerPoint 97 and 2000, click the Draw button on the Drawing toolbar and choose Snap→To Grid. If you can't see your Drawing toolbar, select View→Toolbars→Drawing.

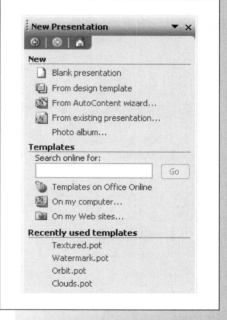

Figure 2-17. You can choose from a variety of options in the New Presentation task pane.

Figure 2-18. Use Draw→Grid and Guides, or View→Grid and Guides, to control PowerPoint's grid settings.

Once you turn off the grid, your arrows will nudge objects .01" at a time if you're viewing the slide at 100% zoom. If you zoom in more, your arrows nudge objects in even smaller increments—for example, .005" per nudge when you're viewing at 200% zoom.

In PowerPoint 2002 and 2003, you can not only turn off the grid, but also define your own grid spacing. Select Draw→Grid and Guides, or View→Grid and Guides, and uncheck the "Snap objects to grid" box or change the Grid settings (see Figure 2-18).

Alternatively, you can override Snap to Grid by holding the Alt button while you nudge the object with the arrow keys.

In what may be a related feature, PowerPoint often tries to snap objects to the edge of your slide. Holding down the Alt key may help then, too, but sometimes zooming in is the best solution when you need very fine control. If you have a mouse with a wheel, you can hold down the Ctrl button while rolling the mouse wheel to zoom in and out on your slide. Otherwise, use the zoom box on the Standard toolbar or View→Zoom on the menu.

Make PowerPoint Rulers Show Centimeters

THE ANNOYANCE: PowerPoint is so U.S.-centric. I can't believe there's no way to change the ruler to show centimeters.

THE FIX: To change PowerPoint's measurement system, open the Windows Control Panel and choose Regional and Language Options. Click the Customize button on the Regional Options tab and select Metric from the "Measurement system" drop-down menu (see Figure 2-19). Be aware that changing this setting may affect the way other applications behave.

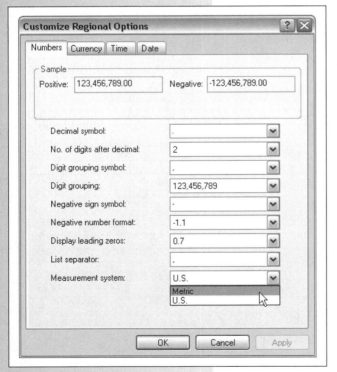

Figure 2-19. Change PowerPoint's measurement system in your Windows Control Panel.

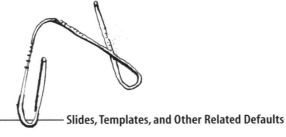

Slides, Templates, and Other Related Defaults

ACTIVATION, VERSIONS, AND CORRUPTION

Transfer Your Settings to a New Computer

THE ANNOYANCE: I'm getting a new computer next week, and I want to keep all my customizations. Is it possible to save them, or am I destined to hunt down individual toolbar files and such?

THE FIX: In Office XP and 2003, you can use the Save My Settings Wizard to save your customizations. Go to Start→All Programs→Microsoft Office→ Microsoft Office Tools→ Save My Settings Wizard. Unfortunately, the Save My Settings Wizard is no longer available for Office 2000.

If you just need your PowerPoint toolbar, you can try saving the *.pcb* file and moving it to the appropriate location on the new computer. (This file is where PowerPoint stores all your customizations.) To locate your *.pcb* file, right-click the Start button and select Search. Type ***.PCB** in the "file name" box, and remember to check both the "Search system folders" box and the "Search hidden files and folders" box. If you have multiple versions of PowerPoint installed, you may have multiple *.pcb* files, too.

Office Tells Me to Reactivate

THE ANNOYANCE: I reformatted my hard drive and reinstalled Office a couple of weeks ago, and I keep getting a screen that says I have to activate. Why? I already activated when I installed Office the first time.

THE FIX: Yeah, certain changes to your computer, and sometimes a reinstall, will prompt Office to request activation. If you let it go long enough, your Office applications will revert to reduced-functionality mode. You should be able to start the Office applications 50 times before you have to activate.

Just follow the prompts to activate, or go to Help→Activate Product. If you're unable to activate by Internet, choose the option to activate by telephone. The activation wizard will give you the appropriate telephone number to dial.

Microsoft has this to say about your privacy and Office activation: "During activation, the product ID and a non-unique hardware identification are sent to Microsoft. The product ID is generated from the product key used to install the software and a generic code representing the version and language of Office being activated. The non-unique hardware identification represents the configuration of your PC at the time of activation. The hardware identification does not include any personally identifiable information about you, any information about other software or data that may reside on your PC, or any information about the specific make or model of your PC.

Microsoft Redefines the Centimeter

Microsoft, in its infinite wisdom, redefined the centimeter in PowerPoint 95, 97, and 2000. In those versions, 1 inch equals 2.4 centimeters instead of 2.54 centimeters (which is the conversion in the rest of the world).

If you're using one of these versions and need an accurate measurement on your printout, you can do a few different things.

1. If your printer driver allows it, set your print scale to 106%.

2. Right-click the object, choose Format→AutoShape, and input the correct size on the Size tab.

3. Use inches instead of centimeters for your rulers (see "Make PowerPoint Rulers Show Centimeters") and uncheck the "Scale to fit paper" box in the Print dialog. For a conversion table showing inches, actual centimeters, and PowerPoint centimeters, visit *http://support. microsoft.com/?id=189826*.

Although it seems ridiculous and arrogant, Microsoft actually did this for a reason: they wanted PowerPoint's invisible one-pica grid to work consistently with either inches or centimeters. By making 2.4 centimeters equal 1 inch, it makes 12 grid units equal 1 inch and 5 grid units equal 1 centimeter. In PowerPoint 2002 and 2003, Microsoft centimeters equal "real" centimeters.

The hardware identification identifies only the PC and is used solely for the purpose of activation. Office can detect and accept changes to your PC configuration. Minor upgrades will not require re-activation. If you completely overhaul your PC, you may be required to activate your product again."

Edit PPS Files

THE ANNOYANCE: Someone sent me a PPS file and I want to edit it. Someone else told me that you can't edit a PPS file. Who's telling the truth?

THE FIX: The only difference between a regular PowerPoint file (PPT) and a PowerPoint Show file (PPS) is the last letter, which tells Windows how to open the file. PPS files open in Slide Show view when double-clicked, and PPT files open in Normal (edit) view when double-clicked. PPS files can be edited. Simply open PowerPoint, go to File→Open, navigate to the PPS file, and click Open. Voila!

Help Files Only Available Online

THE ANNOYANCE: Office 2003 really tires me. I hate having to be online to use the Help files.

THE FIX: Actually, you don't have to be online to use the Help files. A scaled-down version of Help ships with Office and is available on your hard drive. The benefit of using online Help is that it's continually updated based on customer feedback.

If you find that your Internet connection is too slow or otherwise interfering with your work, you can limit your searches in Help to just those files on your hard drive. In PowerPoint 2003, select Help→Customer Feedback Options, choose the "Online Content" category, and uncheck the "Show content and links from Microsoft Office Online" box (see Figure 2-20).

Understand the Background Printing Setting

THE ANNOYANCE: I get an *mso9.dll* error when I try to print. What do I do?

THE FIX: Select Tools→Options, click the Print tab, and uncheck the Background printing box.

Contrary to popular belief, the Background printing setting does not help you print slide backgrounds. Rather, this setting prints your presentation as a background process so you can continue working in PowerPoint while you're printing. You might find it helpful if you're using a printer that relies on your computer's memory when it prints.

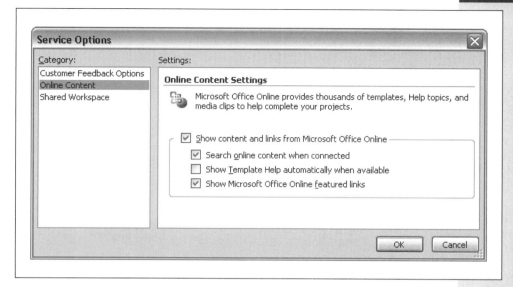

Figure 2-20. The Online Content settings determine whether you search online content or not when using the Help files.

Dealing with Different Versions of PowerPoint

THE ANNOYANCE: I use PowerPoint 2002 at home, but my office uses PowerPoint 2000. Will this cause me problems?

THE FIX: It shouldn't. The easiest solution is to disable the new features in PowerPoint 2002. Select Tools→Options, click the Edit tab, and check the "New animation effects," "Multiple masters," and "Password protection" boxes. That way you won't be tempted to use these new features that PowerPoint 2000 doesn't support. (Turning off "New animation effects" also turns off the new transitions, which include comb, fade smoothly, newsflash, push, various shapes, wedge, and wheel.)

These features can be turned off in PowerPoint 2003 as well. If you're only moving between PowerPoint 2002 and 2003, you don't need to worry about turning these features off, as the new animation, multiple masters, and password protection features are the same in these two versions.

If you already created a presentation using some of the new animations and transitions, and need to show the file to someone using PowerPoint 97 or 2000, you can download PowerPoint Viewer 2003 to show the presentation (*http://www.microsoft.com/downloads/details.aspx?FamilyId=428D5727-43AB-4F24-90B7-A94784AF71A4&displaylang=en*).

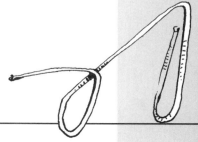

Password-Protect Your Presentations

THE ANNOYANCE: I don't want anyone to change my presentation. How can I protect it?

THE FIX: PowerPoint 2002 and 2003 offer password protection. To set or modify a password, select Tools→Options and click the Security tab. You can also select File→Save As, click the Tools button, and choose Security Options.

You can require a password to open the presentation, modify the presentation, or both. If you just want to prevent people from making changes to your file, enter a password in the "Password to modify" box (see Figure 2-21).

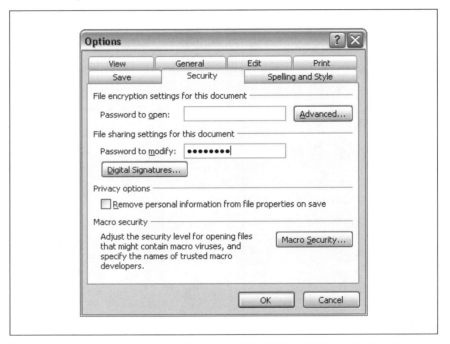

Figure 2-21. You can apply passwords to files in PowerPoint 2002 and 2003 using the Security tab.

If you protect a file with a password, the file can be opened only in PowerPoint 2002, 2003, or PowerPoint Viewer 2003. If you attempt to open a password-protected file in PowerPoint 97 or 2000, you will see the following error message: "PowerPoint can't open the type of file represented by <*filename*>."

The PowerPoint Viewers

Microsoft has two PowerPoint Viewers, which you can download for free. Both allow people to view PowerPoint files without having to purchase and install the full PowerPoint application.

Both viewers have limitations, but generally, PowerPoint Viewer 2003 supports the new features introduced in PowerPoint 2002 and 2003, including passwords, multiple masters, and some animations and transitions. PowerPoint Viewer 97 is mostly useful for showing presentations created in PowerPoint 97 or 2000.

You can include the viewer(s) when you send a PowerPoint file to someone, or, better yet, just include a link to the appropriate download page on the Microsoft web site. PowerPoint Viewer 2003 is available at *http://www.microsoft.com/downloads/details.aspx?FamilyID=428d5727-43ab-4f24-90b7-a94784af71a4&DisplayLang=en*, and PowerPoint Viewer 97 is available at *http://www.microsoft.com/downloads/details.aspx?FamilyID=7C404E8E-5513-46C4-AA4F-058A84A37DF1&displaylang=EN*.

Other options for protecting a presentation include creating a self-extracting file using WinZip (*http://www.winzip.com/*), distributing a PDF of the file, and creating a series of images of the slides. Or, consider using Secure Pack (*http://skp.mvps.org/securepack/index.htm*) to protect your files. You can download a free, 20-day trial version, but the retail version will cost you $100. For more information on each of these software packages, visit the PowerPoint FAQ (*http://www.rdpslides.com/pptfaq/FAQ00038.htm*).

My Presentation Is Corrupt

THE ANNOYANCE: A client emailed me her presentation, but I get an error message that says the presentation is corrupt. She worked on this thing for two weeks! Any way to recover the file?

THE FIX: Before you determine that the file is indeed corrupt, find out if a password was added to it in PowerPoint 2002 or 2003. If the file does have a password and you're trying to open it in a previous version of PowerPoint, you will receive the following error: "PowerPoint can't open the type of file represented by *<filename>*." Ask the person who created the file to resave it without the password, or use PowerPoint Viewer 2003 if you simply want to view the presentation.

If you're using PowerPoint 2003 and have problems opening files created in previous versions of PowerPoint, click Help→Check for Updates and install the latest Service Pack (SP) or Service Release (SR) for Office 2003.

If you received the file as an email attachment, it may have become corrupted as it traveled through cyberspace. Ask the sender to zip the file using Microsoft Windows XP's built-in zip function or a program such as WinZip, and then resend.

You can also select Insert→Slides From File, browse to the corrupt file, and click the Insert All button (see Figure 2-22). If Insert All fails to work, select and insert individual slides.

Figure 2-22. If you have a corrupt presentation, you may be able to recover at least part of it using Insert→Slides From File.

If that doesn't work, try Impress, the presentations application found in the StarOffice (*http://www.staroffice.com/*) and OpenOffice (*http://www. openoffice.org/*) productivity suites. Because Impress does not include all of PowerPoint's functionality, or support certain elements in its import utilities, it may open files PowerPoint identifies as corrupt, allowing you to recover at least part of the presentation file.

Still stuck? The following steps show you how to open the file in Word.

1. Open Word and select File→Open.

2. In the Open dialog box, choose "Recover Text from Any File" from the "Files of type" drop-down menu.

3. Navigate to your corrupt file, select it, and then click the Open button.

Prevent PowerPoint File Corruption

The following tips will help you prevent corruption of your PowerPoint files:

- Never work from removable media. "Removable media" means anything other than your hard drive. Floppy disks, CD-ROMs, Zip or Jaz disks, USB flash drives, network servers—any and all of the above count as removable media. If you value your work, use those media types only for transporting your files. If you have a file stored on some kind of removable media, use Windows Explorer to copy the file to your hard drive and then open it. When you finish working on the file, save the file to your hard drive, and then copy it to your removable media.

- Turn off fast saves. Select Tools→Options, click the Save tab, and uncheck the "Allow fast saves" box.

- Save, Save, Save. Select Tools→Options, click the Save tab, and check the "Save AutoRecover info every *xx* minutes" box. This creates temporary copies of your PowerPoint file every *x* number minutes. If PowerPoint crashes, it may be able to retrieve some of your file. Note that this option does not perform a regular save every *x* number of minutes. It's up to you to save your work regularly. Press Ctrl+S or select File→Save every now and then. And, of course, make sure you save to your hard drive, not to removable media.

- Make backups. This should be a no-brainer, but for some reason, it's not. In addition to "formal" backups

to a CD-ROM, backup tape, or second hard drive, you might consider creating your own "backup" copies of PowerPoint files as you work on them. For instance, before you make a major change to a file, select File→ Save As and save the file with a new name (for example, *MyFile1.ppt*, *MyFile2.ppt*, and *MyFile3.ppt*). You can also use Sequential Save, a free add-in from Microsoft PowerPoint MVP Shyam Pillai, which makes this task much easier (*http://skp.mvps.org/seqsave.htm*).

- Practice good hard drive maintenance. Good hard drive maintenance can help your computer run more smoothly and cut down on file corruption as well. Standard practices include searching for and deleting *.tmp* files, emptying the Temporary Internet Files folder, and running ScanDisk and Disk Defragmenter regularly.

- Zip files before sending through email. Sending PowerPoint files as email attachments sometimes corrupts them, although this doesn't seem to happen nearly as often as it used to. As a precaution, you can use the built-in zip capability in Windows XP or a program such as WinZip to zip the files before you send them. Although zipping is often associated with compressing the file size, if you're using PowerPoint 97 or later, you probably won't see much file size benefit. You will, however, ensure that your PowerPoint file arrives at its destination intact.

If you are able to recover the text in Word, you can move the text back into PowerPoint. First, spend some time with the styles in Word so that the text ends up where you want it in PowerPoint. All text formatted as Heading 1 will become slide Title text in PowerPoint. Heading 2 styles will become primary bulleted text. Heading 3 styles will become secondary bulleted text, and so on. When you finish formatting the text, select File→Send To→ Microsoft Office PowerPoint. Word starts PowerPoint if it's not already running, creates a new presentation, and enters the text on the slides.

After you finish, return to the Open dialog box in Word and choose All Word Documents from the "Files of type" drop-down menu. Otherwise, you may see strange things happen when you subsequently open Word documents.

If you use CorelDraw or Presentations (part of the WordPerfect Office Suite), you can try to import the PowerPoint slides as a last-ditch effort to recover a corrupted file. You could also try PowerPoint Recovery (*http://officerecovery.com/powerpoint/*), which lets you recover corrupted presentations, although I have not had any luck using this tool. You can download a free demo, but the full version will cost you $149.

Unhide Windows File Extensions

Windows XP hides file extensions (*.doc*, *.ppt*, *.xls*, etc.). Talk about a dumb default! If you type the file extension along with the filename in the Save As dialog box, or change the filename in Windows by right-clicking and choosing Rename, Windows will append the file extension to the filename—but you won't see it. So you can end up with files named *presentation.pps.ppt* and *myfile.ppt.ppt*. Of course, if you intended to create a *.pps* file by simply renaming the file in Windows, the file won't behave like a *.pps* if Windows automatically adds *.ppt* to the end.

To keep Windows from being so very helpful, open My Documents, select Tools→Folder Options, click the View tab, and uncheck the "Hide extensions for known file types" box.

Formatting and Editing

3

Those of us who create presentations for a living have our own pet peeves about PowerPoint's editing and formatting tools. We also know how important it is to start a presentation right, using well-developed templates, masters, and default settings to speed production along.

This chapter begins by showing you how to overcome issues with design templates and slide masters to help you lay a good foundation for your presentations. It also explains how to create your own templates, work with multiple masters and slide layouts, take advantage of various tools to align objects, and tackle formatting issues such as changing case and setting hanging indents.

TEMPLATES AND MASTERS

Locate Your Templates

THE ANNOYANCE: I made a design template, but it doesn't show up in the template list when I select File→New. Why can't PowerPoint find my templates?

THE FIX: To see where PowerPoint stores these templates, select File→Save As and choose Design Template (*.pot) from the "Save as type" drop-down menu. Next, click the "Save in" pull-down arrow to see the full path to where the templates live (see Figure 3-1). Save or copy your *.pot* file to that folder.

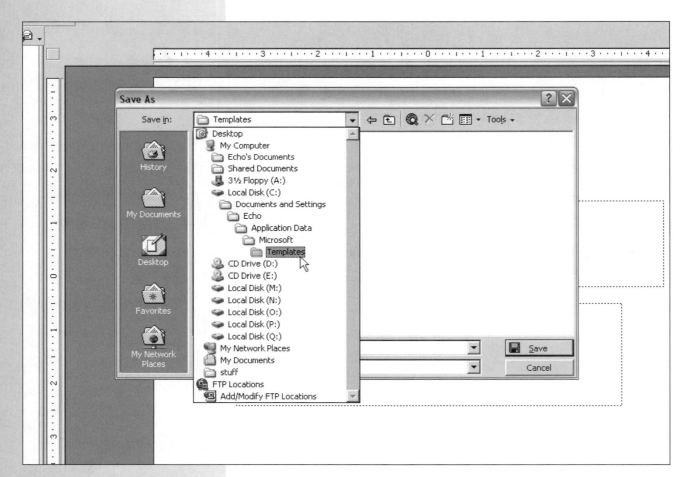

Figure 3-1. To see where PowerPoint stores your templates, choose Design Template (*.pot) from the "Save as type" drop-down menu, and then check the path to the folder in the "Save in" menu.

When you install PowerPoint 2002 or 2003, the program stores its templates in a folder on your hard drive; for example, *C:\Program Files\Microsoft Office\Templates\Presentation Designs*. You can usually see these templates by clicking the "From design template" link in the New Presentation task pane (see Figure 3-2). To see your own design templates, you may need to click the "Browse" link at the very bottom of the Slide Design task pane.

Force Templates to Show in the Task Pane

THE ANNOYANCE: I put my templates in the right place, but they still don't show up in the Slide Design task pane.

THE FIX: Even if you put your templates in the right place, sometimes you must use them on a presentation once or twice before they show up in the task pane.

Open a new, blank presentation (File→New→Blank Presentation), click the "Browse" link at the very bottom of the Slide Design task pane, and apply the template you want to display. Save the blank presentation on your desktop using a generic name like *test1.ppt*. After you do this, the template usually shows up on the list in the Slide Design task pane.

Find More Templates

THE ANNOYANCE: I'm sick of these templates. Where can I find some new ones?

THE FIX: You can find PowerPoint templates in about a million different places. The following site offers a good list to get you started: *http://www.rdpslides.com/pptfaq/FAQ00080.htm*. In addition, Microsoft PowerPoint MVP Geetesh Bajaj offers a number of free templates (*http://www.indezine.com/powerpoint/templates/freetemplates.html*).

Microsoft also has lots of templates available: go to *http://office.microsoft.com*, select "Templates" from the Search drop-down menu, and type **PowerPoint** in the keyword area. If you have a more specific idea of what you need—a medical template, for example—type **PowerPoint Medical** in the keyword area.

In addition, you can select File→New→Templates on Office Online or click the "Templates on Office Online" link in the New Presentation task pane (see Figure 3-3). This takes you directly to the Microsoft Office Templates home page, where you can type your search terms (e.g., PowerPoint Medical) into the keyword area. It saves you from having to remember *http://office.microsoft.com*, anyway!

Figure 3-2. In PowerPoint 2002 and 2003, select File→New to open the New Presentation task pane. From here you can open existing presentations or create new ones.

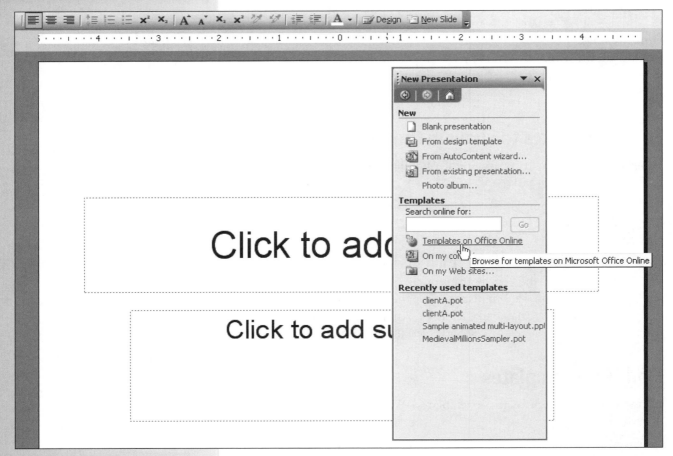

Figure 3-3. Click the "Templates on Office Online" link to go directly to the Microsoft Office Templates home page.

Microsoft has also made most of the legacy templates—templates released with previous versions of PowerPoint—available for anyone to download. You can find them at the following sites:

- *http://www.microsoft.com/downloads/details.aspx?FamilyID=3a8b90ac-2bcb-4fec-a8b4-bfbd509baefb&DisplayLang=en*

- *http://www.microsoft.com/downloads/details.aspx?FamilyID=e903488f-0f1d-4cae-aa2f-6de7afc8db59&DisplayLang=en*

- *http://www.microsoft.com/downloads/details.aspx?FamilyID=47cedf97-b910-4a17-96c8-18c155492a9a&DisplayLang=en*

Finally, use your favorite search engine to find templates. For example, I typed "PowerPoint Templates" into the Google search box and turned up more than 1.2 million hits.

Create a Template

THE ANNOYANCE: I made a template, but when I apply it to a new presentation, nothing happens and I still have a blank slide. This template thing just doesn't work.

THE FIX: You probably didn't make your changes to the slide master, so the template you created is really just a blank master with one formatted slide in the presentation.

To create your own template, you must make your changes to, or do your creating on, the slide master itself. To get to the slide master, choose View→Master→Slide Master. Now make your changes. For example, you can change the background color; the font color; and the color of objects, including bullets, lines, and fills. You can also change the font size, adjust the text indents, or move things around. When you're done, save the template by selecting File→Save As and choosing Design Template (*.pot) from the "Save as Type" drop-down menu (see Figure 3-4).

> **NOTE**
>
> *You can apply an actual PowerPoint file as a template. In PowerPoint 97 and 2000, select Format→Apply Design Template, and choose "All PowerPoint Files" from the "Files of type" drop-down menu. In PowerPoint 2002 and 2003, click the Browse link on the Slide Design task pane and select "All PowerPoint Files" from the "Files of type" drop-down menu. In all versions, locate your file and click the Apply button.*

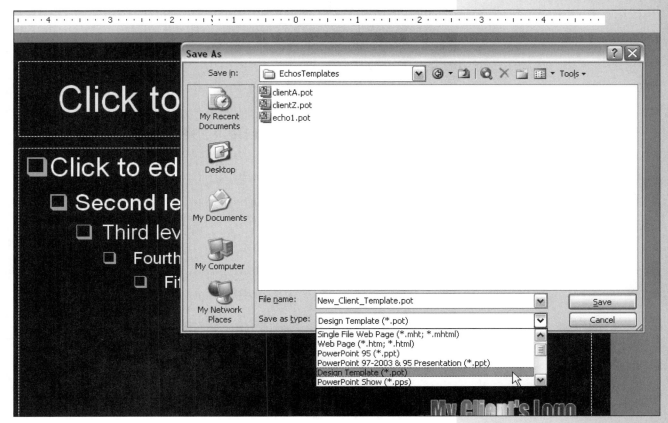

Figure 3-4. Choose Design Template (*.pot) from the "Save as type" drop-down menu.

You can also download the free Template Creation Wizard from Microsoft (*http://www.microsoft.com/downloads/details.aspx?familyid=D1BD0173-ED7C-4EF0-B7F3-290424D5012E&displaylang=en*). After you install it, you should see a Wizards toolbar the next time you open PowerPoint. If you don't see it, select View→Toolbars→Wizards to open the toolbar. Click the Template Wizard button, and the Wizard will automatically create a template using background images you select for the slide and title masters. The final screen of the Template Wizard gives you the option to create a presentation based on the template, save and close the template, or keep it open for further modification (such as font sizes, color schemes, etc.).

For more information, see "Creating PowerPoint Templates" by Microsoft PowerPoint MVP Geetesh Bajaj (*http://www.indezine.com/products/ powerpoint/ppcreatemp.html*) and "Creating a Template" by Microsoft PowerPoint MVP Sonia Coleman (*http://www.soniacoleman.com/Tutorials/ PowerPoint/create_template/index.html*).

Add a Title Master

THE ANNOYANCE: I'm creating a PowerPoint design template and I want the title slide to look different than the other slides. How do I add a title master?

THE FIX: Select View→Master→Slide Master. Once in Master view, select Insert→New Title Master. No, it's not terribly intuitive, is it?

Slide Thumbnail View Disappears

THE ANNOYANCE: I'm in Slide Master view, but I don't have a slide thumbnail pane on the left. And I can't get it back!

THE FIX: Yeah, unfortunately, if you closed the slide thumbnail pane in Normal view, it doesn't come back automatically when you select View→ Master→Slide Master. And once you're in Slide Master view, there's no way to turn the slide thumbnail pane on!

To get the slide thumbnails pane back, select View→Normal to exit Master view. Then select View→Normal (Restore Panes) to turn the left and right panes back on. Once the panes are visible, you can go back to Master view (View→ Master→Slide Master).

Create Multiple Masters

THE ANNOYANCE: I know you can have multiple masters in PowerPoint 2002 and 2003, but I can't figure out how to make them. Help!

THE FIX: First select View→Normal so that all of your task panes are visible (see "Slide Thumbnail View Disappears"). Then select View→Master→Slide Master to see all the available master slides in the left slide thumbnail pane (see Figure 3-5).

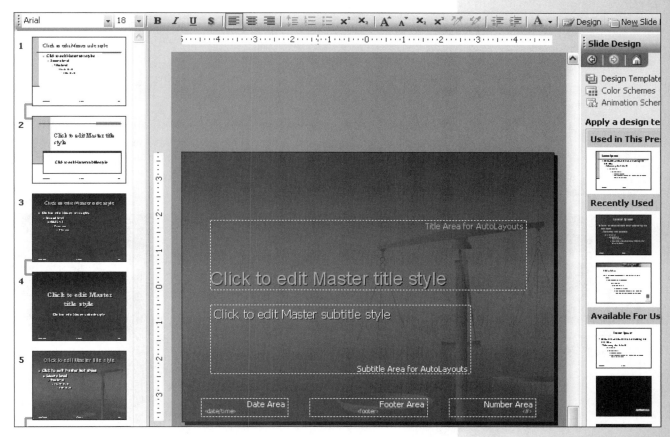

To add a new blank master with a plain white background, select Insert→ New Slide Master or Insert→New Title Master, whichever one you want. It will appear immediately after the slide you have selected in the slide thumbnails pane. If it appears in the wrong place, you can always drag it to the correct position in the slide thumbnail pane. You must add a slide master before you can add a title master because while you can have a standalone slide master, you can't have a standalone title master. Once you've created the slide and title masters, select and format them just as you would any other master.

Figure 3-5. Make sure you can see the slide thumbnail pane on the left of your screen, and then select View→Master→Slide Master to see the masters used in the presentation and create more as desired.

If you have a master in your thumbnail list that is similar to the master you want to create, you can click that thumbnail and select Insert→Duplicate Master. Once the duplicate has been created, select the duplicate slide or title master in the thumbnail pane and format it just as you would any other master.

Distinguish One Master from Another

THE ANNOYANCE: Okay, I have a bunch of section break slides with really long titles, so I duplicated my slide Master and made the font smaller in the title area. The problem is, I can't tell the masters apart in the Slide Design task pane. I keep applying the wrong one.

THE FIX: Just name the new master. The name will show up when you hover over the master in the Slide Design task pane.

To name a master, choose View→Normal so you can see the slide thumbnail pane on the left of your screen, and then choose View→Master→ Slide Master. Right-click the master in the slide thumbnail pane and select "Rename Master" (see Figure 3-6). Type a new, descriptive name for your master and click OK.

Figure 3-6. While you're in Slide Master view (View→Master→Slide Master), right-click a master in the slide thumbnail pane to access a number of options.

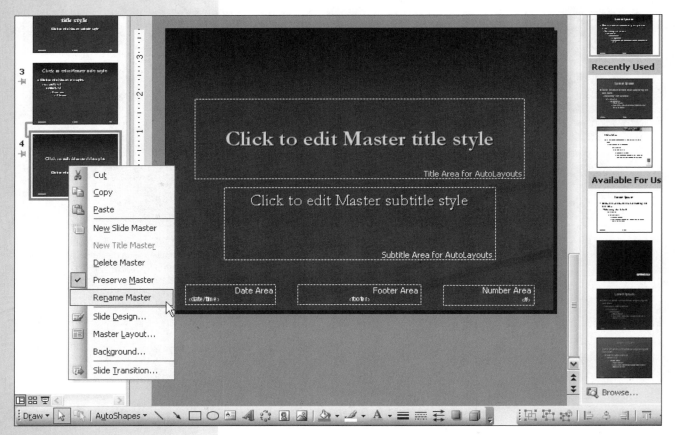

Apply a Template to Only a Few Slides

THE ANNOYANCE: I clicked a design template in the task pane on the right, and the template applied to *all* my slides. I only wanted to use it on a couple of slides.

THE FIX: Oh, yeah, this is annoying. First hit Ctrl+Z or Edit→Undo to unapply the template from all your slides.

Next, choose View→Normal so you can see the slide thumbnail pane on the left and the Design Template task pane on the right. (You may have to choose View→Normal twice to restore all the panes.) In the slide thumbnail pane on the left, select the slides you want to change. (If you want to choose noncontiguous slides, press the Ctrl key as you click.)

Once you've selected the slide thumbnails, click the design template thumbnail in the Slide Design task pane. Because you've selected the slides to change, the design template will apply only to those slides, not to every slide in your presentation.

This is only an issue in PowerPoint 2002 and 2003 because earlier versions don't support multiple masters.

Masters Disappear from the Presentation

THE ANNOYANCE: I deleted some slides from my presentation, and their slide Master disappeared. I'm screwed!

THE FIX: To prevent this from happening, preserve the slide Masters in your presentations. Otherwise, PowerPoint will automatically delete them if no slides in the presentation use that master.

To preserve a master, select View→Normal so you can see the slide thumbnail pane, and then select View→Master→Slide Master. Right-click the master in the slide thumbnail pane and select "Preserve Master" (see Figure 3-6).

Deleting Slide Masters

THE ANNOYANCE: When I delete a slide Master, the attached title Master gets tossed as well. Can I delete the stupid slide Master without PowerPoint mucking with my title Master?

THE FIX: Although slide masters can stand alone in PowerPoint, title masters must always be paired with a slide master. In the master slide thumbnail pane, you can see the line connecting the title master to its slide master (see Figure 3-7). Delete the slide master, and the title master is also deleted. But you can delete a title master, and the slide master will still be available.

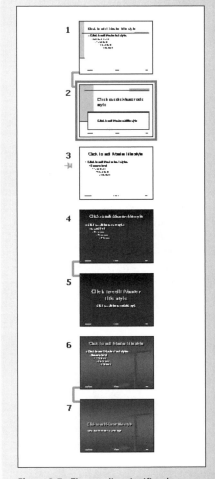

Figure 3-7. The gray line signifies the connection between the slide master and title master—think of them as a pair.

It's really nothing to worry about. Let PowerPoint attach slide masters to your title masters and then just don't use those slide masters. You can even put a big "don't use" WordArt object across them if you want something to help you remember.

Font Size Changes on Title Master

THE ANNOYANCE: When I change the font attributes in the title placeholder on my slide master, the font on my title master also changes. What's the deal?

THE FIX: The slide and title masters are tied together, and some things on the title master change based on changes to the slide master. Usually, if you haven't made changes to the text placeholders on the title master, but you make changes to the text placeholders on the slide master, the title master will update to reflect the changes made to the slide master. If you format the title master first—even if you just change the font color to a different color and then back again to its default color—it shouldn't change when you make modifications to font on the slide master.

"Pickling the Master"

A user in the Microsoft PowerPoint newsgroup posted a question about master slides. She mentioned that she'd make the master look the way she wanted, pickle it, and close out of Master view. It took me a little while to figure out what she meant by "pickling the master," but once I did, it was so obvious! To pickle is to preserve, so pickling the master is the same as preserving the master. Perfect!

Add Placeholders to the Masters

THE ANNOYANCE: I need to have a title placeholder, a subtitle placeholder, and three text placeholders on every slide. How can I add placeholders to the masters?

THE FIX: Unfortunately, you can't add placeholders, either on slides or on masters.

It's not an ideal workaround, but you might consider creating some slides with text boxes and dummy text in the appropriate spots, and then copying those "model slides" and replacing the dummy text as necessary. One drawback of this workaround, however, is that the text you type in the manual text boxes (as opposed to the text placeholders) will not show up in the presentation outline.

You might also want to look into RnR ShapeStyles (*http://www.rdpslides.com/pptools/shapestyles/index.html*), a $99.95 add-in developed by Microsoft PowerPoint MVPs Steve Rindsberg and Brian Reilly. This add-in lets you specify "styles" based on existing objects and apply those styles to other objects with one mouse click.

Add a Color Scheme to a Template

THE ANNOYANCE: I tried to add a color scheme to my design template, but nothing happened—my new color scheme doesn't show up on the list. What's the deal?

THE FIX: It's not a very widely known fact, but there's a limit of 16 color schemes per design template. When you apply a new color scheme to a slide, PowerPoint automatically adds the scheme to the list of standard color schemes (see Figure 3-8). You may not have noticed the "Add As Standard Scheme" button on the Edit Color Scheme dialog box (see Figure 3-9), but it is actually grayed out once you reach your color scheme limit.

After that, even if you apply a color scheme to a slide, it's not added to the list of color schemes available with the design template. If you want the scheme to be available on the list, you'll have to delete some of the existing color schemes. To do so, use the Delete Scheme button on the Standard tab of the Edit Color Schemes dialog box.

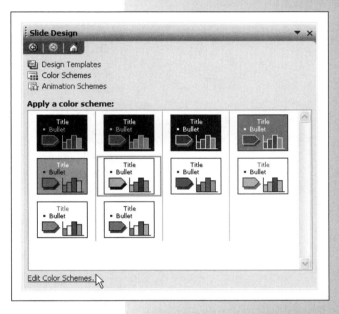

Figure 3-8. Click the Color Schemes link on the Slide Design task pane to see the various color schemes available for a given template. Edit or add to the color schemes by clicking the Edit Color Schemes link at the very bottom of the task pane.

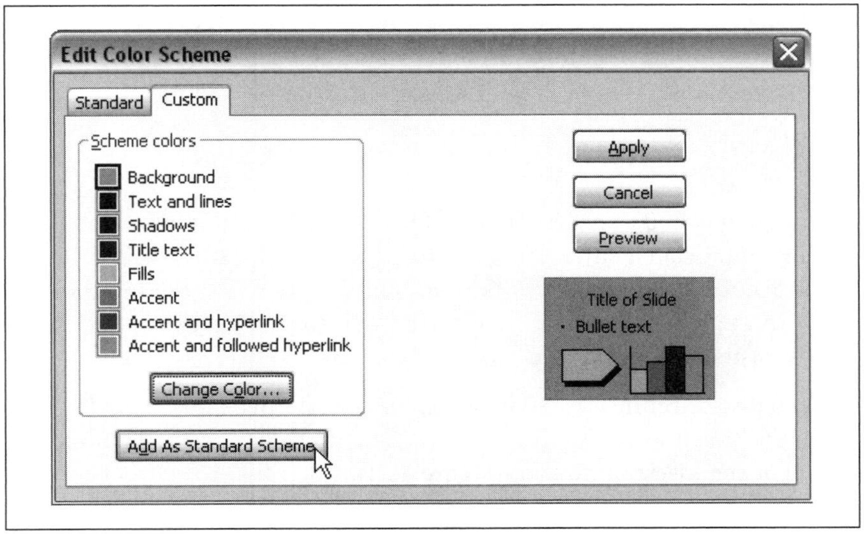

Figure 3-9. To edit color scheme colors, select a color swatch and click the Change Color button. Choose the new color, and back in the dialog box, either apply the new color scheme to the selected slide or slide master, or opt to save the color scheme by choosing Add As Standard Scheme.

The available color schemes you see in the Slide Design task pane depend on which slides you have selected in the slide thumbnail pane on the left of your screen and what templates have been applied to them. Choosing one of these color schemes will apply the new color scheme to the selected slides, but it won't change the actual design template of the selected slides. That means all font sizes, placeholder positions, images, etc., will remain on the slides, although the colors may change.

Add Color Schemes Without Applying Color Schemes

THE ANNOYANCE: Can I add a color scheme to a template without actually applying it to my slides?

THE FIX: Yes. Just create a new slide master and apply the color scheme to the master.

To do so, select View→Normal to turn on the slide thumbnail pane on the left, and then select View→Master→Slide Master to switch to Master view. Select the slide master in the slide thumbnail pane and choose Insert→ Duplicate Slide Master. In the Slide Design task pane on the right of your screen, click the Color Schemes link. With the duplicate slide master selected in the slide thumbnail pane on the left, click a different color scheme in the Slide Design task pane on the right.

Apply Multiple Masters in a Presentation

THE ANNOYANCE: I copied a bunch of slides from one presentation into another, but the formatting all changed. I don't want the formatting to change! I'm screwed!

THE FIX: How you deal with this depends on which version of PowerPoint you're using.

In PowerPoint 2002 and 2003, look for the Smart Paste Options tag that appears immediately after you paste (see Figure 3-10). Click it and choose "Keep Source Formatting." If the Smart Paste Options tag doesn't show up when you paste, select Tools→Options, click the Edit tab, and check the "Show Paste Options buttons" box.

You can also select Insert→Slides From Files. In the Slide Finder dialog box, check the "Keep source formatting" box, and then click either the Insert All button or the Insert button (see Figure 3-11).

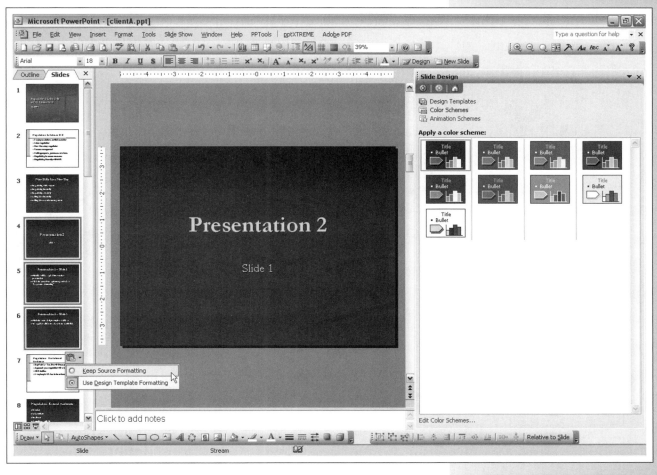

Figure 3-10. Use the Smart Paste Options tag to maintain the formatting of slides you paste into a presentation based on a different template.

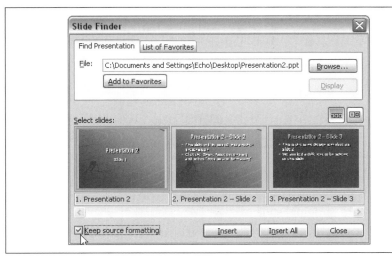

Figure 3-11. The Slide Finder dialog box has an option to "Keep source formatting" in PowerPoint 2002 and 2003.

If you decide you want to use a different slide master on a slide already in a presentation, simply select the slide in the slide thumbnail pane on the left and choose a different master in the "Apply a design template" area of the Slide Design task pane on the right.

PowerPoint 2000 and 97 do not have a multiple masters feature, so there is no option to "Keep source formatting" when you insert or paste slides into an existing presentation. And by default, slides will take on the template attributes of the presentation they're being pasted into.

One workaround is to paste an embedded slide object into the target presentation. This sounds really complicated, but it's really not. Just follow these steps:

1. Open the target presentation (the file you're copying to) and the source presentation (the file you're copying from) and select Window→Arrange All so you can see both presentations side by side.

2. Insert a new slide into the target presentation and give it a blank slide layout. Select Insert→New Slide and choose the Blank AutoLayout (see Figure 3-12).

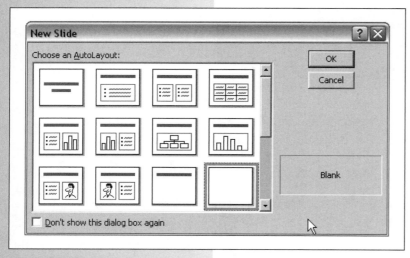

Figure 3-12. To insert a new slide in PowerPoint 2000 or 97, choose Insert→New Slide and select an appropriate layout in the New Slide dialog box. For this particular purpose, use the blank slide layout.

3. Put the source presentation into Slide Sorter view (View→Slide Sorter).

4. Select one of the source presentation slides in Slide Sorter view, and press Ctrl+C to copy it.

5. Click the slide in the target presentation to activate that window, select View→Normal to make sure the target presentation is in Normal view, and press Ctrl+V to paste the source slide onto the slide in the target presentation.

6. This creates an embedded PowerPoint slide object in the target presentation. Drag the embedded slide object by the corners until it covers the entire target presentation slide.

7. Double-click the embedded PowerPoint slide object if you need to edit it. This will change only the copy inside the target presentation; it will not affect the original slide.

You can actually use this same technique in PowerPoint 2002 and 2003, but instead of a "regular" paste, you must select Edit→Paste Special and choose "Microsoft PowerPoint Slide Object" from the list.

If you apply multiple masters in PowerPoint 2002 or 2003, they might not show up if you view the presentation in PowerPoint 97. They probably will show up in PowerPoint 2000. Also see the sidebar, "What Happens to Multiple Masters in Earlier Versions?". For additional information and workarounds, see *http://www.echosvoice.com/multipletemplates.htm*.

Determine Which Master Will Apply

THE ANNOYANCE: When I paste slides in PowerPoint 2003, I never know which template the pasted slides will take on by default. It seems so random.

THE FIX: It might seem random, but when you paste slides into another presentation in PowerPoint 2002 or 2003, your slides at first take on the template of the slide just before them. Of course, if you then opt to use the Smart Paste Options tag to "Keep source formatting," it's a moot point.

Can't See Text When You Type

THE ANNOYANCE: Aaaarrrrgggghhh! When I type in a placeholder, I can't see the text. This is making me crazy!

THE FIX: You need to change your slide color scheme so the background color contrasts with the text color. In PowerPoint 97 and 2000, select Format→ Slide Color Scheme, click the Custom tab, choose the Background or Text and lines color, and click the Change Color button. In the Color dialog box, choose a new color and click OK.

If you place a picture as a background on the slide master and adjust the font color to work with the picture, make sure you remember to change the background color to contrast with the new text color. Otherwise, you end up with an unworkable color combination, such as white text on a white background.

Fortunately, Microsoft fixed this annoyance in PowerPoint 2002 and 2003. In those versions, the program automatically adjusts to a contrasting background while you're typing.

What Happens to Multiple Masters in Earlier Versions?

If you use multiple masters in a presentation you're building in PowerPoint 2003, what happens when your client opens the presentation in PowerPoint 2000? Will the multiple masters work?

Well, "work" is a relative term. Microsoft built some multiple masters features into PowerPoint years before they were actually implemented. This means that most of the time, the multiple masters will show up just fine when you open the presentations in earlier versions of PowerPoint. However, you (or, in this case, your client) won't be able to actually get to the additional masters or edit them.

Be sure to test any multiple masters in the previous version to be on the safe side. If you don't have PowerPoint 2000 or 97 handy, download and install the free PowerPoint 97 Viewer to see if your multiple masters will look the way they should (*http://www.microsoft. com/downloads/details. aspx?FamilyID=7c404e8e- 5513-46c4-aa4f-058a84a37d f1&DisplayLang=en*).

The Automatic Contrast Is Ugly

THE ANNOYANCE: I can always see what I'm typing in PowerPoint 2002, but sometimes those contrast colors look really nasty. Can I change them?

THE FIX: No, PowerPoint creates these temporary colors automatically so you can see text against the slide background as you're typing. They're just for contrast, and you only have to put up with them for as long as you're typing.

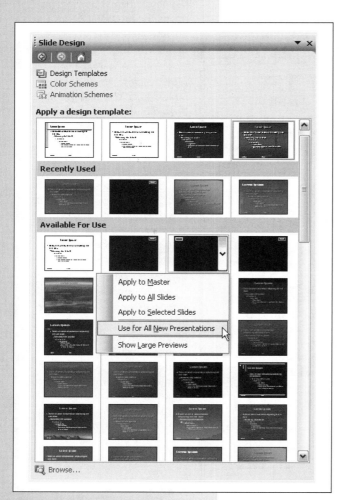

Figure 3-13. PowerPoint 2003 makes it a breeze to specify a new default template.

Set a New Default Template

THE ANNOYANCE: I'd like for all new presentations to open up with my corporate template already applied. Is there an easy way to make this happen?

THE FIX: In PowerPoint 2003, simply choose "Use for All New Presentations" from the drop-down menu when you hover your mouse over your corporate template in the Slide Design task pane (see Figure 3-13).

In PowerPoint 97, 2000, and 2002, you need to modify or overwrite PowerPoint's existing blank template. Open your corporate template, select File→Save As, and choose Design Template (*.pot) from the "Save as type" drop-down menu. In the "File name" box, type `Blank Presentation.pot` (PowerPoint 97 and 2000) or `Blank.pot` (PowerPoint 2002), navigate to the folder that contains the existing blank template file, and click the Save button.

If you mess up, simply close PowerPoint and delete *Blank.pot* or *Blank Presentation.pot*. PowerPoint will automatically recreate its old blank template the next time you open PowerPoint.

Set a New Default Master Slide

THE ANNOYANCE: I use the slide layout with two bulleted text placeholders more often than I use the slide layout with one bulleted text placeholder. It's extremely tedious to have to change the slide layout every time I insert a new slide. Can I just make the one I want the default slide layout?

THE FIX: Download Microsoft PowerPoint MVP Shyam Pillai's free Set Default Layout add-in to your desktop (*http://skp.mvps.org/setlayout.htm*). Open the zip file and extract the *layout.ppa* file to a folder on your hard drive (for example, *C:\layout_addin*).

Figure 3-13. PowerPoint 2003 makes it a breeze to specify a new default template.

In PowerPoint, select Tools→Macro→Security and choose the Medium option, if necessary. If Macro Security is set to High or Very High, you will not be able to install any add-ins. You can always switch the setting back after you install the add-in. (I promise this add-in is safe.)

Next, select Tools→Add-Ins→Add New. Navigate to the folder you created (in this case, *C:\layout_addin*) and choose the *layout.ppa* file. You will see a security warning that says, "C:\layout_addin\layout.ppa includes macros. Macros may contain viruses. It is usually safe to disable macros, but if the macros are legitimate, you might lose some functionality." Click the Enable Macros button and then click the Close button to exit the add-in dialog box.

After installing the Set Default Layout add-in, you should see a new tool on your Standard toolbar (see Figure 3-14). Simply click the drop-down box and choose your default layout.

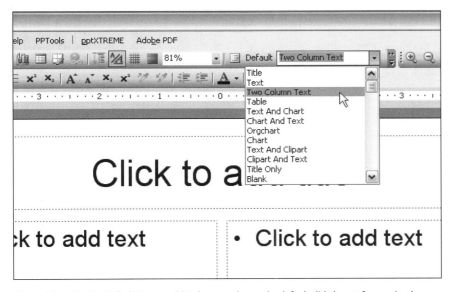

Figure 3-14. The Set Default Layout add-in lets you choose the default slide layout from a simple drop-down list.

How Does PowerPoint Arrange Templates?

In PowerPoint 2003, the Slide Design task pane sorts templates by color and saturation. Graphic artists at Microsoft developed the palette with the goal of making the template list seem less random. In early versions of PowerPoint, the templates are sorted alphabetically.

And if you have templates from more than one version of PowerPoint on your system, you'll see the 2003 templates sorted by color, and you'll see the older templates sorted alphabetically at the end. Older versions of PowerPoint simply sort the templates alphabetically.

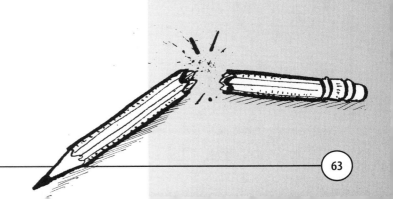

Understanding Color Schemes

Most users know very little about color schemes, one of the most powerful features in PowerPoint. Why? One reason is that color schemes are fairly complicated. Another, and perhaps more likely, reason is that Microsoft hid color schemes deep within the PowerPoint interface and provided inadequate documentation.

Every design template from Microsoft comes with a variety of color schemes. After you apply a design template to your presentation, select Format→Slide Color Scheme (PowerPoint 97 and 2000) or Format→Slide Design→Color Schemes (PowerPoint 2002 and 2003) to see the available color schemes.

Simply click one of the color schemes in the task pane to apply it to your slides. The default behavior is to apply the color scheme to all slides using the specific design template in the presentation, but you can hover over the color scheme and click the arrow to see more options. In PowerPoint 2002 and 2003, you must click the link to "Edit Color Schemes" at the very bottom of the Slide Design task pane if you want to create more or adjust existing schemes (see Figure 3-15). In PowerPoint 2000 and 97, simply click the Custom tab in the Color Scheme dialog box.

To change a color, simply select a swatch, click the Change Color button, choose a new color, and click the Apply button. The changes will be applied to your slides, and the new color scheme based on these changes will appear in the list of available color schemes.

The swatches in the Edit Color Schemes box are labeled according to their default behaviors. For example, the first swatch is labeled "Background," and the second swatch is labeled "Text and lines." You can see which color applies to what objects by default if you look closely at the miniature slide graphic on the right of the dialog box (see Figure 3-15).

However, you can use the colors to change more than the default object. For example, if you changed the Shadows color (swatch three) and the Accent color (swatch six) in Figure 3-15, you will also affect the slide background (see Figure 3-16). Why? The background for the slide master uses a gradient based on the colors typically assigned to the Background (swatch one) and Shadows (swatch three).

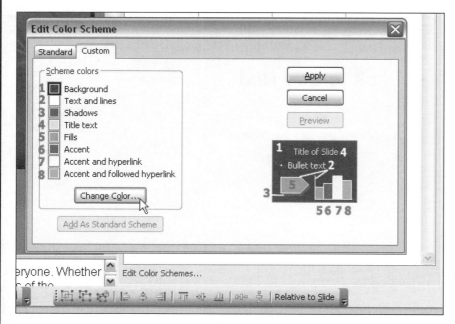

Figure 3-15. Click the Edit Color Schemes link at the bottom of the Slide Design task pane to display the Edit Color Scheme dialog box in PowerPoint 2002 and 2003. This is the same as the Color Scheme box in PowerPoint 97 and 2000.

Understanding Color Schemes (*continued*)

Click a text box and then click the Font Color icon on the Drawing toolbar. Do those eight color swatches look familiar? They should—they're the eight colors from your color scheme (see Figure 3-17).

Now most people don't know the next part of the story. Objects that use these colors follow the slide color scheme. If you change the slide color scheme—which almost always happens if you apply a new design template—the objects will change colors to follow the new color scheme. This is an extremely efficient way to work for most presentations, as it allows you to make global changes by modifying just one color swatch. Or, if you combine presentations, the slides will automatically update to the new template and color scheme, saving you a lot of tedious, manual editing.

What if you don't want an object to update colors based on a new color scheme? For example, maybe your product should *always* be green, your competitor's product should *always* be yellow, and your vendors' products should *always* be blue. In this case, click the Fill Color icon on the Drawing toolbar and choose More Fill Colors. In the Colors dialog box, choose green, yellow, or blue and click OK.

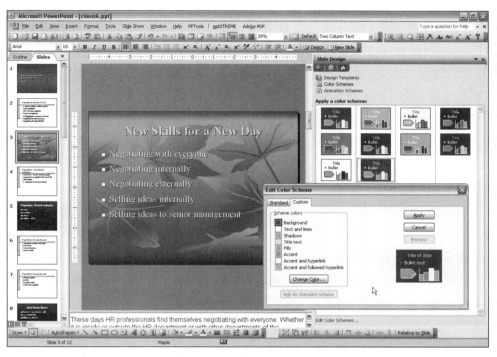

Figure 3-16. By default, the eight color swatches come directly from the slide color scheme.

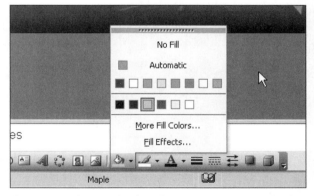

Figure 3-17. Selecting colors from the More Fill (or Line or Text) Colors forces the color to always stay the same when a new template or color scheme is applied to the slide. Selecting from the eight color swatches at the top of this pop-up box forces the object to follow the slide color scheme.

Set Default Graphs and Org Charts

THE ANNOYANCE: I'm setting up a corporate template. I've tried everything to set up a default graph and organization chart, but I'm starting to believe it can't be done.

THE FIX: Unfortunately, you can't really set up a default organization chart. However, organization charts in PowerPoint 2002 and 2003 will pick up whatever default text attributes you've set for manual text boxes (see "Set Default Text Box and AutoShape Settings," later in this chapter).

The same goes for graphs—you can't set up a default graph that travels with a template. (Although you can set up user-defined graphs, but these are machine-specific settings and don't stay with a template.)

Your best bet is to create one slide with a sample graph and another with a sample organization chart, and teach your users how to copy the slides and adjust the data as necessary for new graphs and organization charts.

Determine Default Colors for Charts

THE ANNOYANCE: Where in the world do the colors in graphs and org charts come from? I can change the colors, but when I create a new chart, it uses the same ol' boring colors.

THE FIX: Colors for graphs and diagrams are tied to your slide color scheme. Org Chart fills are assigned to the Fills color (swatch five) in your slide color scheme (see "Understanding Color Schemes"). Graph colors pull from swatches five through eight of your slide color scheme, and then swatches three and four. The last two "Microsoft blues" are default Microsoft-specified colors (see Figure 3-18).

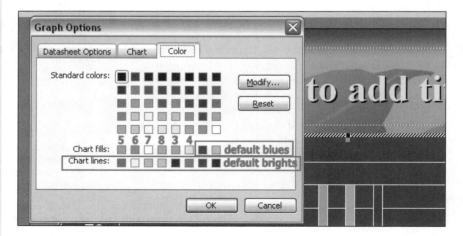

Figure 3-18. Graph colors are tied directly to your slide color scheme. The last two colors on the top row always default to these two blues, and the bottom eight colors (labeled Chart lines, for some reason) always default to the "Microsoft brights."

If necessary, you can add a slide master with a different color scheme and teach users to apply that slide master to their graph and org chart slides.

Add Filename to Every Slide

THE ANNOYANCE: How do I put the filename and path into the footer of a slide? In Word, it takes two seconds.

THE FIX: I don't know why this is so easy in Word. In PowerPoint, you have to create a macro.

Select Tools→Macro→Macros, type in a temporary name for the macro (something like *FileName*), and click the Create button to open a Visual Basic window. Delete the text in the window. Copy the code from Microsoft (*http://support.microsoft.com/default.aspx?scid=kb;en-us;222797*) and paste it into the Visual Basic window. Click the X in the upper-right corner to close the Visual Basic window and return to the presentation. The macro takes its actual name from the first line of the code you pasted in, Sub UpdatePath().

To run the macro, select Tools→Macro→Macros, select UpdatePath, and click the Run button (see Figure 3-19). The name of the file and the path to it will appear in the footer area of your slide (see Figure 3-20). If you want to format this text differently, choose View→Master→Slide Master, select the Footer Area placeholder, and make modifications just as you would to any other placeholder.

Figure 3-19. Select Tools→Macro→Macros to run a macro.

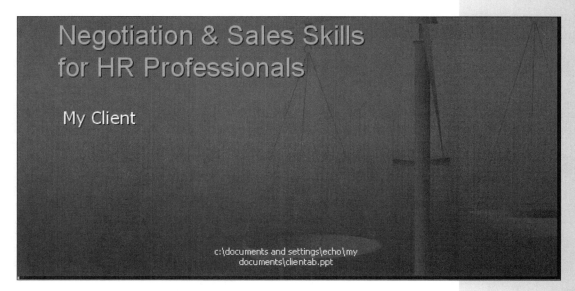

Figure 3-20. This macro adds the name of your file and its path to the footer area on your slide.

If this macro doesn't work, you may have deleted the footer placeholder from your slide master (see "Masters and Headers and Footers," later in this chapter, for more information).

Number Slides XX of YY

THE ANNOYANCE: How do I number my slides XX of YY? I went to File→Page Setup, but I can't find any options for this.

THE FIX: Until recently, the only way to number slides XX of YY (e.g., Slide 5 of 18) was to type in the total number of slides in the slide number area of the slide master (see Figure 3-21). This is still a useful workaround.

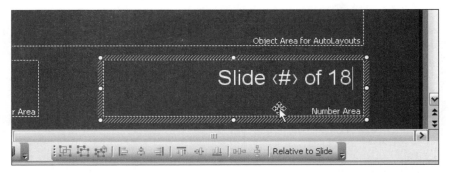

Figure 3-21. You can type in the total number of slides on the slide master to create "Slide XX of YY" numbering.

You can also download a free add-in from Microsoft PowerPoint MVP Bill Dilworth (*http://billdilworth.mvps.org/PageXXofYY.htm*). Unzip the file to a folder on your hard drive and extract the *SaveSelection.ppa* and *SaveSelection.txt* files.

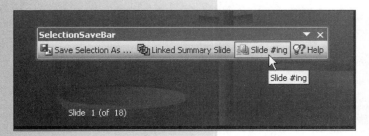

Figure 3-22. Click the Slide #ing button to add Slide XX of YY to the footer area of your slides.

As always, when installing macros, set your macro security to Medium (Tools→Macro→Security), and then select Tools→Add-Ins→Add New, navigate to the *SaveSelection.ppa* file, and click OK. Click the Enable Macros button, if prompted.

To use the add-in, simply click the Slide #ing button on the toolbar (see Figure 3-22). The text "Slide XX (of YY)" will appear in the footer area of your slide. If clicking the button on the toolbar doesn't add this text to your slide, you may have deleted the footer placeholder from your slide master (see "Masters and Headers and Footers" for more information).

This handy add-in also gives you one-click options to save selected slides as a new presentation file and create summary slides with text hyperlinks back to the original slides.

Masters and Headers and Footers

You can add header and footer information to slides, handouts, and notes pages in quite a few different places. In fact, the sheer number of possibilities can make it difficult to pinpoint problems in header and footer text. The following information will help you solve common knotty problems.

A slide must have the appropriate placeholders on the master in order for header and footer information to show up. Select View→Master→Slide Master to switch to Slide Master view, and choose Format→Master Layout to reapply missing placeholders to the masters (see Figure 3-23).

Figure 3-23. Add missing placeholders, such as slide number and footer, to the slide master.

Remember to add placeholders to both your slide master and your title master. If you skip this step, it can cause you a lot of frustration.

If you want, you can type text directly into these placeholders on the masters. Again, you need to type your text in the placeholders on both the slide and title masters if you want the text to show up even on title slides. And if your presentation uses more than one master, you must type the text into the placeholders on each master on which you want the text to appear.

Even if you don't type text directly in these placeholders, you can still format the font attributes and fill and line colors. You can also move the placeholders on the slide. For example, you might want your slide numbers located in the upper-left corner of the slide. In this case, change the alignment of the placeholder text to the left, and drag it to the upper-left corner of the slide and title masters.

Of course, you can't really type in text to represent a slide number on a slide master and expect PowerPoint to know you want to add the actual slide number on each slide. That's why, if you look closely at the date/time, footer, and slide number placeholders, you'll see <> bracketing the text. The information included inside those brackets (in this case, the slide number) is linked to your selections in the Header and Footer dialog box and will update accordingly. If you need to include information that will update, add it in the Header and Footer dialog box. Any text you type into the placeholders on the master slides will show up on the slides *exactly* as you typed it.

To open the Header and Footer dialog box, select View→ Header and Footer (see Figure 3-24). The Slide tab is for text added to the slides themselves. You can enter a fixed date, or opt to let the date update automatically each time you open the file. You can also choose to show slide numbers and add text to the footer placeholder. If you elect not to show these on slides using the Title Slide layout, check the "Don't show on title slide" box. Finally, click the "Apply to All" button to see the header and footer information applied throughout the presentation.

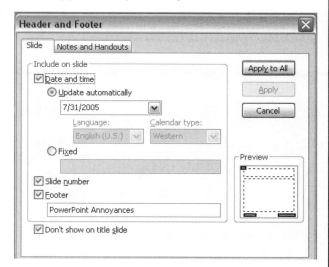

Figure 3-24. Here you can add slide numbers, dates and times, and other text to your slides, handouts, and notes pages.

—continued—

Masters and Headers and Footers (*continued*)

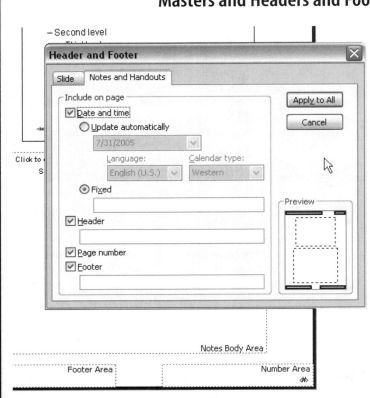

It's not unusual for people to add information in both the placeholders on the masters themselves as well as in the Header and Footer dialog box. This behavior seems especially prevalent on the handouts and notes masters. For example, many of my clients type the presenter's name on the notes master itself for internal tracking, but they add the date and time and the page numbers, and sometimes even the presenter's name again, in the Header and Footer dialog box (see Figure 3-25).

The moral of the story? Make sure you check for text in the individual slide, handout, and notes masters as well as the Header and Footer dialog box.

Figure 3-25. Be careful about adding text directly on the slide, handout, or notes master and again on the Header and Footer dialog box.

Numbers Still Show on Title Slide

THE ANNOYANCE: I'm unable to remove page numbering from the title slide, even though I checked the "Don't Show on Title Slide" box on the Slide tab of the Header and Footer dialog box. Should it really be this hard to add or remove numbering?

THE FIX: Are you sure that the slide in question is in fact a title slide? Try inserting a new title slide and see if it ignores your numbering.

You know, you're right, it should be easier. Part of the problem is that you can set slide numbering in so many places. For instructions on how to troubleshoot this problem, see "Masters and Headers and Footers."

Add Slide Numbers

THE ANNOYANCE: I'm having hard time adding a slide number in my presentation. I tried to add it to the slide master and then as a footer without success. Any suggestions?

THE FIX: Click View→Header and Footer, click the Slide tab, and check the Slide number box.

If the slide number still does not show up, choose View→Master→Slide Master, and then choose Format→Master Layout and check the "Slide number" box in the Master Layout dialog. Also, make sure you have a slide number placeholder on the title master.

FORMATTING

Move Slide Layouts

THE ANNOYANCE: I use the chart slide layout a lot. I'd like to move it up in the task pane so I can reach it more easily.

THE FIX: Unfortunately, they can't be moved. You can use a "content" layout, though. Simply apply a content layout to your slide and click the graph icon on the slide to add a chart (see Figure 3-26).

Figure 3-26. Content layouts let you click the appropriate icon on the slide to add an object such as a graph, a diagram, or clip art.

What Exactly Can You Change on a Master Slide?

Well, let's see. You can change design templates, color schemes, font colors and sizes, bullets for each level of text, text indents (View→Rulers), and background colors, as well as the placement and size of placeholders. You can add elements like pictures, drawings, logos, and text boxes if you want text to appear on every slide. You can even add slide transitions and placeholder animations to the slide masters, but if you do, you'll lose some control over those options in normal editing mode.

On the flip side, you can neither specify the text case (sentence case, title case, all caps, etc.) in place-holder text, nor add placeholders. You also can't change the text that says "Click to add text" or "Click to add title."

Reapply a Slide Layout

THE ANNOYANCE: Sometimes when I reapply the slide layout, it doesn't "take." What do I have to do to get my slide to reset?

THE FIX: Depending on the changes you made to the slide, sometimes you have to apply the slide layout twice. Select Format→Slide Layout, hover over the layout in the Slide Layout task pane until you see the drop-down arrow, and choose Apply to Selected Slides. Hover again, but this time choose Reapply Layout.

If the slide layout in question has already been applied to the slide, select Format→Slide Layout, hover over the layout, and choose Reapply Slide Layout twice.

Set Default Font

THE ANNOYANCE: My slide master works fine: the placeholder text uses our corporate font. What do I have to do to get the other text boxes to use this font?

THE FIX: You must create a text box, format the font to your specifications, choose Format→Font, and check the "Default for new objects" box (see Figure 3-27).

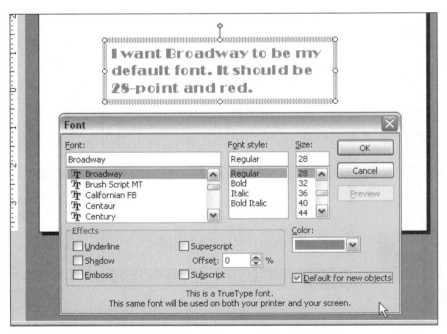

Figure 3-27. Set the default font for manual text boxes in the Font dialog box.

Set Default Text Box and AutoShape Settings

THE ANNOYANCE: Whenever I add a text box to a slide, it has a stupid bullet point in it. How do I turn it off permanently?

THE FIX: Setting text box defaults isn't intuitive at all. Format a text box the way you want it to look, and then right-click and choose "Set AutoShape Defaults" (see Figure 3-28). Why Microsoft didn't add a "Set Text Box Defaults" option, I don't know. I suppose you can think of text boxes as rectangle AutoShapes, basically a subset of the AutoShape family.

The Set AutoShape Defaults command will not pick up any fill color and line color or size you add to the text box. It will, however, pick up font color and size; line spacing attributes; text box attributes (select Format→Text Box and click the Text Box tab); alignment; bullet character, color, and size; and indent specifications (select View→Ruler).

Note that adding a fill color and line colors or sizes to a text box before selecting Set AutoShape Defaults will affect your actual AutoShapes defaults. To see this in action, apply a fill color and a line to a text box, and set the default text box as described above. Then draw an oval on the slide. The color and line attributes you set on the default text box have become the default settings for AutoShapes (see Figure 3-29).

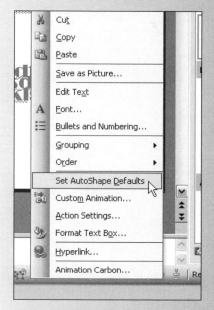

Figure 3-28. Right-click and choose Set AutoShape Defaults to set the default text box style.

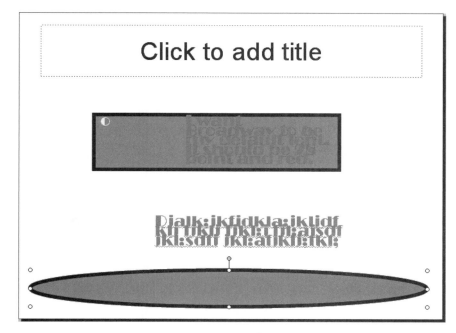

Figure 3-29. The oval drawn on the bottom of this slide picked up the purple fill and black, 6-pt line settings from the top text box, which was used to specify the text box defaults. The middle text box, created just after setting text box defaults, shows that default text box settings don't include fill and line colors.

If you don't apply fill and line colors to the text box before you set it as the default, the next time you draw a line or AutoShape, it may not be visible on your slide! To rectify the situation, simply format the AutoShape with appropriate line and fill colors, right-click it, and choose Set AutoShape Defaults once again. This applies the line and fill attributes to AutoShapes, but it will not affect the existing text box default settings.

If you type in an AutoShape, both your AutoShape defaults and your text box defaults will apply, so if you need filled text boxes, use AutoShapes instead. Simply add one to the slide, make sure it's selected, and start typing.

Whew! Got all that? Let's recap: To apply default settings to text boxes and AutoShapes, first format a text box and format an AutoShape. Right-click the text box and choose Set AutoShape Defaults. Then right-click the AutoShape and choose Set AutoShape Defaults.

When You Draw a Line or a Rectangle, Nothing Shows Up

THE ANNOYANCE: When I draw a line or a rectangle, nothing shows up on my slide. Something's really screwy.

THE FIX: This could be an issue with your AutoShape default settings. Format a rectangle the way you want the default to look, right-click it, and select Set AutoShape Defaults. See "Set Default Text Box and AutoShape Settings" for more information.

This could also be an issue with your video drivers. Turning down hardware acceleration may take care of it (see "Presentation Keeps Locking Up" in Chapter 1).

Not All Slides Appear After You Paste

THE ANNOYANCE: I select slides in existing presentations, copy them, and paste them into new presentations. Once in a while, only one slide copies over. Why?

THE FIX: If you copy *from* Slide Sorter view or from the slide thumbnail pane *to* Slide Sorter view or the slide thumbnail pane, this shouldn't happen. But if you copy from one of these areas and paste onto the one slide in the main editing area of Normal view, you'll get just one slide when you paste.

If you use Insert→Slides From Files instead of copy-paste, you won't have to worry what view you're copying from or pasting to.

Changing Font Locks PowerPoint

THE ANNOYANCE: PowerPoint keeps locking up every time I try to change a font or type in some text.

THE FIX: PowerPoint really, really, really likes local printer drivers. If you install a printer and set it as the default printer, PowerPoint will be much happier. You don't have to actually have a printer hooked up to your computer, and you never have to print to this printer, you just need to have the drivers for one installed. A basic printer driver like the HP LaserJet III is a good bet.

If you do have a printer installed, the drivers are probably on a network somewhere, and you're seeing this happen when you're not connected to the network.

To install printer drivers, choose Start→Control Panel→Printers and Faxes, and then select File→Add Printer. When prompted, specify you're installing a local printer, and do not use "Automatically detect and install my plug-and-play printer," if offered. Choose HP in the manufacturers area, and scroll down in the printers area until you find HP LaserJet III. Click Next until you complete the wizard. Say "No" when asked if you want to print a test page.

Group Objects

THE ANNOYANCE: I selected a bunch of stuff, but I can't group it—the Group command is grayed out on the Draw menu.

THE FIX: You probably selected a text or title placeholder along with the other objects, and these placeholders can't be grouped. If everything's still selected, press the Shift key and click the placeholder to deselect it. You should be able to group the remaining objects.

If you must group the placeholder for some reason, copy it, and then delete the original placeholder or drag it off the edge of the slide if you need to keep it (so you can see its text in the outline area, for example). You'll be able to group the copy of the placeholder with other objects.

Chart placeholders can be grouped with other objects in PowerPoint 2000, 2002, and 2003.

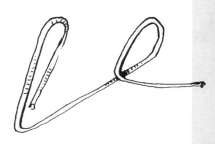

Align Objects

THE ANNOYANCE: The align tools are all grayed out. What's the problem?

THE FIX: You must have more than one object selected for the align tools to work.

Alternatively, you can select Draw→Align or Distribute→Relative to Slide, and the various alignment options will be available, even if you have only one item selected.

Make Grid Visible

THE ANNOYANCE: I want to be able to see the grid when I use Snap to Grid. How do I do that?

THE FIX: You can't see or set the grid in PowerPoint 97 or 2000. You can select Draw→Grid and Guides to set the grid options in PowerPoint 2002 and 2003 (see Figure 3-30). In these versions, you can bypass the Grid and Guides dialog by pressing Shift+F9 to toggle the grid on and off and Alt+F9 to toggle the guides.

Change the Grid Setting in PowerPoint 97 and 2000

THE ANNOYANCE: I need a smaller grid to help align stuff on my slide in PowerPoint 2000, but I can't figure out how to change the grid setting.

THE FIX: There's no way to change the grid setting in PowerPoint 2000 or 97; Microsoft introduced this functionality in PowerPoint 2002.

Some users find it helpful to create additional guides, which can act as sort of a grid. Press Ctrl+G to show the guides. Press the Ctrl button while you click a guide and drag your mouse to create another guide (see Figure 3-31). You can have a total of eight horizontal guides and eight vertical guides on the slide. To get rid of a guide, drag it off the edge of the slide.

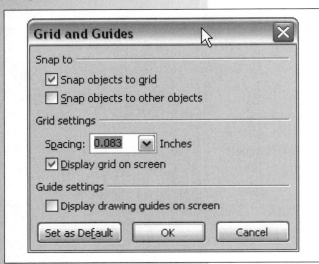

Figure 3-30. The Grid and Guides dialog box lets you control the grid visibility and other settings.

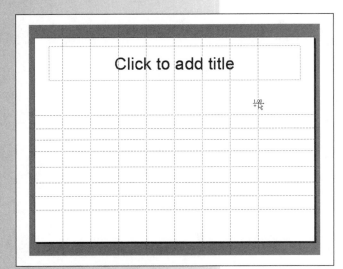

Figure 3-31. Press Ctrl while you click and drag on the guides to create more guides.

Another workaround is to use the Line tool on the Drawing toolbar to draw lines. Next, select the lines, choose Draw→Align or Distribute, and use the Relative to Slide, Distribute Horizontally, and Distribute Vertically commands to place them in a grid. Paste the grid onto your slide master and delete it when you're finished creating the presentation.

Arrow Keys Jump by Leaps and Bounds

THE ANNOYANCE: I'm using the arrow keys on my keyboard to nudge some objects on the slide, but they're jumping in huge bounds. How can I get more control over these arrows?

THE FIX: Turn off Snap to Grid, and you'll have more control over your arrow key nudges. To do so, choose Draw→Grid and Guides (PowerPoint 2002 and 2003) or Draw→Snap→To Grid (PowerPoint 2000 and 97), and uncheck the Snap to Grid box. If you prefer to leave Snap to Grid on, you can press the Ctrl key while nudging with the arrows to override the snap.

Text Ends Up in Placeholder

THE ANNOYANCE: I pasted some text onto a slide, and as I was dragging it around, it ended up being sucked up by the placeholder. What happened?

THE FIX: If you drag a text box and then let go of it when you're on top of the word "Click" in the placeholder (where it says, "Click to add text"), it drops the text into the placeholder in PowerPoint 97 and 2000.

This feature can be a prime annoyance or a great blessing. It's incredibly useful for quick slide reformatting, but it's a royal pain if you don't want it to happen. There's no way to turn it off in PowerPoint 97 and 2000, but Microsoft changed this behavior in PowerPoint 2002 and 2003.

If you took advantage of this behavior when formatting slides, it gives you a good excuse to keep PowerPoint 2000 around.

Change Text Case

THE ANNOYANCE: I have a client who sends me slides with the titles typed in all capital letters. It's soooo tedious to retype them. Is there an easier way?

THE FIX: Select the text and press Shift+F3 to toggle the case. If you've selected text in a title placeholder, this key combination toggles between lowercase, title case, and uppercase. If you've selected text in a text placeholder, this key combination toggles between lowercase, sentence case, and uppercase.

You can also select Format→Change Case and choose from a list of options (see Figure 3-32).

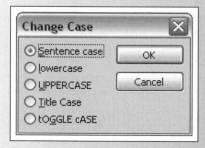

Figure 3-32. The Change Case dialog box gives you all the text case options in one place. This tool is handy for changing text typed in all caps to something easier to read.

Change Text Case Adds Strange Capitalization

THE ANNOYANCE: When I press Shift+F3 to toggle text in a title placeholder, even small words (of, and, the) end up starting with capital letters. What was Microsoft thinking?

THE FIX: Microsoft clearly *wasn't* thinking, because this problem didn't exist in PowerPoint 97 and 2000. This annoyance is a great excuse for keeping a copy of PowerPoint 2000 around.

The only workaround, and it isn't much of one, is to select only individual words before pressing Shift+F3 to toggle the case. Or change the case of a single word and then press F4, which works as a repeat key. It's a little faster to work your way through a presentation using F4 than Shift+F3.

Go from Word to PowerPoint

THE ANNOYANCE: I have a client who sends me slides as a long Word document. Copying and pasting from Word to PowerPoint takes too much time. Is there an easier way?

THE FIX: Select File→Send to→Microsoft PowerPoint. PowerPoint automatically starts if it's not already running, creates a new presentation, and enters the text on the slides.

If you spend some time adding styles in Word before sending the file to PowerPoint, it will make your life a bit easier. All text with Word Heading 1 style will come into PowerPoint as a slide title. Text with Heading 2 style will end up as a primary bullet, Heading 3 entries turn into secondary bullets, and so on. Anything set to the Normal text style will not show up in PowerPoint.

Graphics will still have to be copied and pasted. As an alternative, save the Word file as a web page (File→Save as Web Page), which creates a folder full of graphic images and other files supporting the "web page." Select Insert→ Picture→From File to get the graphic images into PowerPoint.

You can even do this with Notepad, but use tabs instead of styles. No tab equals slide title text. One tab equals primary bulleted text. Two tabs equal secondary bulleted text, and so on. Select File→Save As to save the file. In PowerPoint select File→Open, choose All Outlines (*.txt, etc.) from the "Files of type" drop-down menu, and navigate to the file you created in Notepad (see Figure 3-33).

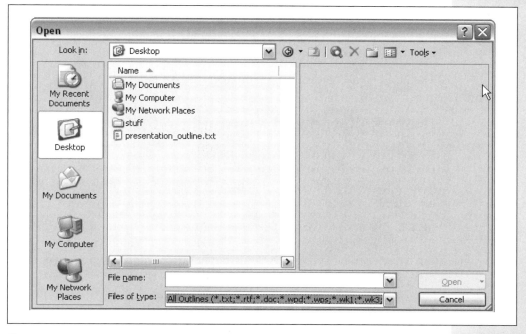

Figure 3-33. To open a text file, select File→Open and choose All Outlines from the "Files of type" drop-down menu.

Set Hanging Indents on Bulleted Text

THE ANNOYANCE: My bulleted text doesn't do a proper hanging indent, so the text doesn't align. I end up putting in about a million manual line breaks, and that messes up the line spacing between the bullets. And it's a nightmare if I have to change the font size later. How can I keep my text aligned without all the hassle?

THE FIX: Select View→Ruler to turn on the horizontal ruler. Drag the indent carats to place the bullets and hanging indents where you want them. Do this on your master slide (View→Master→Slide Master) if you want the indent settings to apply automatically to all text slides.

Each indent marker has three parts: the top caret, the middle caret, and the bottom caret. The caret on the top aligns the leftmost edge of the bullet itself (see Figure 3-34). If you want to place this caret directly over one of the other carets, press the Ctrl key while you drag the caret. This gives you more control over the placement of the carets.

Figure 3-34. Press the Ctrl key while dragging the indent markers on the ruler to gain more control over their placement.

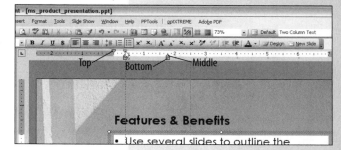

The middle caret sets the placement of the text itself and determines where the hanging indent will occur. If the hanging indent overlaps the bullet on the left, the top and middle indent carets are probably too close. Move the middle caret a bit to the right to correct the hanging indent.

The bottom caret moves the set of indent markers together.

Using Bulleted and Non-Bulleted Text Together

THE ANNOYANCE: My first point is two lines of text. It doesn't have a bullet. The rest of the text has bullets. I don't want the first point to have a hanging indent. Is there a way to do this besides creating a separate text box with no bullet?

THE FIX: You have to be kind of sneaky to make this one work. Select the first level of text and select Format→Bullets and Numbering and choose the None option. This removes the bullet but leaves a hanging indent (see Figure 3-35).

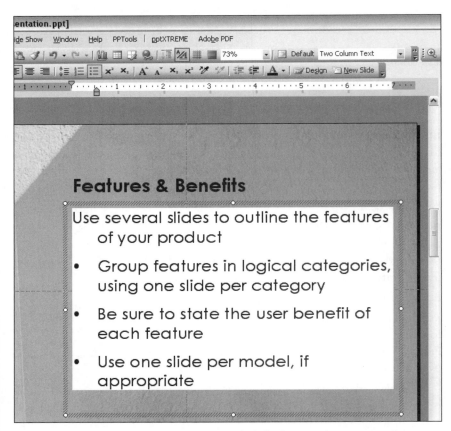

Figure 3-35. This is what happens when you remove the bullet from text that spans more than one line.

Move both indent carets all the way to the left to fix the hanging indent on the first level of text. This will cause the lower level of bullet points to temporarily look bad (see Figure 3-36).

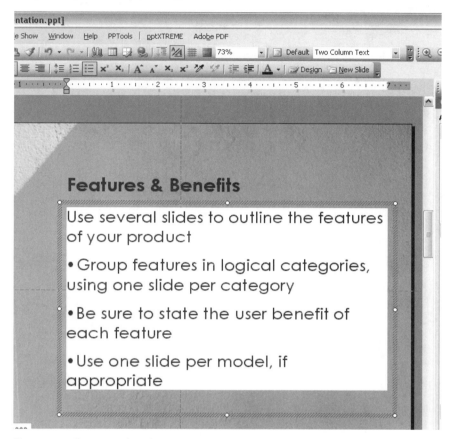

Figure 3-36. If you move the indent caret to the left to fix the first bullet point, the other bullet points look bad.

Select the lower level bullet points and click the Increase Indent icon to demote them. Select Format→Bullets and Numbering and choose an appropriate bullet character to match the primary bullets in the rest of the presentation. Finally, press the Ctrl key while you drag the top-level bullet all the way to the left on the ruler so it will overlap with the other indent carets. Place the middle caret an appropriate distance from the top caret (see Figure 3-37).

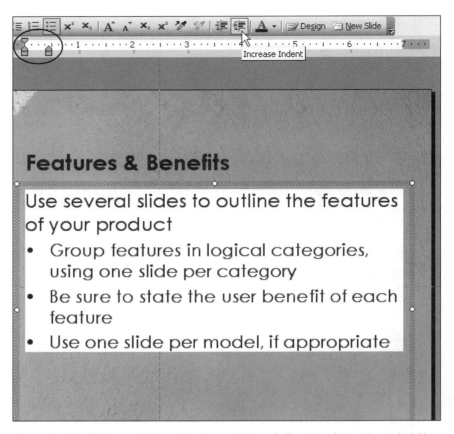

Figure 3-37. Use the Increase Indent tool to demote the lower bullet points, format them to look like the original primary bullet points, and drag the indent markers to the left to realign the secondary bullets.

Create Small Caps

THE ANNOYANCE: Where do I set text attributes like small caps and strike-through? I've looked everywhere!

THE FIX: Unfortunately, PowerPoint doesn't have as many text options as Word. For things like small caps and strikethrough, you'll have to create that text in Word, copy it, and choose Edit→Paste Special→Microsoft Office Word Document Object to paste the text into PowerPoint.

The RnR PPTools Starter Set, a free add-in, has a small caps tool (*http://www.rdpslides.com/pptools/starterset/index.html*). Simply download and install the PPTools Starter Set add-in, select the text, and click the Small Caps icon (see Figure 3-38).

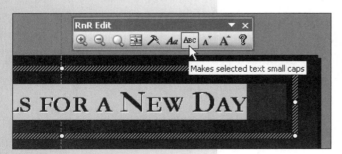

Figure 3-38. The RnR PPTools Starter Set, a free add-in, has a small caps tool.

Line Spacing Cuts Off Text

THE ANNOYANCE: I really like the AutoFit Body Text to Placeholder option because it shrinks my text automatically as I type it. If I get too long-winded, though, it cuts off the bottoms of some letters. Is there any way to keep that from happening?

THE FIX: Unfortunately, AutoFit Body Text to Placeholder works with a combination of decreasing the font size and shrinking the line spacing assigned to the text box. The problem is that once the line spacing goes below about .7 lines, it tends to cut off the ascenders and descenders on the letters. The only workaround is to stop typing earlier or turn off AutoFit Body Text to Placeholder and manually resize the text when you finish typing.

In PowerPoint 2002 and 2003, select Tools→AutoCorrect Options, click the AutoFormat As You Type tab, and uncheck the "AutoFit Body Text to Placeholder" box. In PowerPoint 97 and 2000, select Tools→Options, click the Edit tab, and uncheck the "Auto-fit text to text placeholder" box.

Set Font Size Increments

THE ANNOYANCE: Sometimes I need to resize the font on a bulleted slide, but the font size jumps too much. It's a pain to go back and manually change each level of text by just a point or two. Is there a way I can set the amount the font increases or decreases when I use the Increase and Decrease Font Size tools?

THE FIX: There's no way to change this in PowerPoint, but the free RnR PPTools Starter Set add-in (*http://www.rdpslides.com/pptools/starterset/index.html*) has a set of one-point font increment tools that will solve this problem for you.

PowerPoint's font increase and decrease increments are tied to the sizes in the font size drop-down menu. So the size increment will be one, two, or four points, depending on the size of the text you're working with. The Shrink and Enlarge tools on the RnR PPTools Starter Set always change the font size in one-point increments, making it very easy to experiment with text sizes in multilevel bulleted text boxes.

Set Tabs on a Slide

THE ANNOYANCE: I've been all over the Format and Insert menus, and I still can't figure out how to set a tab in my text box. Doesn't PowerPoint do tabs?

THE FIX: Sure, PowerPoint does tabs. Choose View→Ruler to turn on the ruler, select the text to which you want to apply the tab setting, and click on the ruler to add the tab (see Figure 3-39). Click in the box on the left to move through the tabs you can use in PowerPoint: left-aligned, center-aligned, right-aligned, and decimal-aligned. If you place the tab in the wrong spot on the ruler, simply drag it to the right spot or drag it off the ruler altogether to delete it.

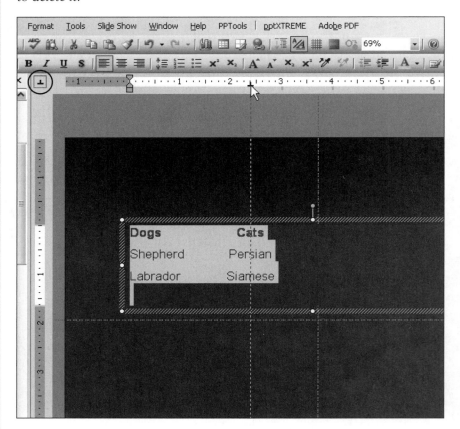

Figure 3-39. Select View→Ruler to make the ruler visible, choose the type of tab you want, and then click on the ruler to add a tab.

PowerPoint tabs aren't as powerful as those in Word. If you need dot leaders or features of that nature, create your tabbed text in Word, copy it, and choose Edit→Paste Special→Microsoft Office Word Document Object to paste it onto your slide.

Importing

4

Although you can create new content in PowerPoint, it seems like we're just importing existing material most of the time. Maybe you're importing sales charts from market research reports, Word documents from product support catalogs, product manual PDFs, pictures of a new facility from the construction manager, or animated GIFs of a new process from the corporate web site—sometimes all in the same presentation.

Importing these disparate materials can be very straightforward or very painful, depending how you go about it. In this chapter, we'll cover the difference between OLE-linked and OLE-embedded objects, the best way to insert graphics, various ways to import information from Excel, inserting PDF and Word content, and the various paste options PowerPoint offers.

GRAPHICS

Don't Drag and Drop or Paste Graphics

THE ANNOYANCE: I dragged and dropped a picture into my PowerPoint file, and now my file is humongous. What happened?

THE FIX: When you paste or drag and drop an image onto a PowerPoint slide, it sometimes creates what is known as an embedded OLE object. It's much better to save the image to your hard drive and then use Insert→Picture→ From File to insert your images onto your slides.

OLE stands for Object Linking and Embedding, which is kind of a dumb name because you can't link *and* embed at the same time. When you paste an image directly from Adobe Photoshop onto your PowerPoint slide, you're pasting not only the image itself, but also a bunch of application overhead that lets you double-click the image on the slide to open up a Photoshop window and edit the photo *from within* PowerPoint. Although that can be handy, it comes at the price of increased file size.

To see this for yourself, insert a JPG into a new, blank presentation file using Insert→Picture→From File. Double-click the picture on the slide. You should see the Format Object dialog box (see Figure 4-1). Save the presentation to your desktop.

Now open a new, blank presentation file, as well as the *.jpg* file in Photoshop or another image-editing program. Select the photo and copy it. Then move over to PowerPoint and paste it onto a slide. Close the image-editing application, and then double-click the photo in PowerPoint. If your photo uses OLE embedding, the photograph will open in the default image-editing application you've assigned to *.jpg* files. Make a small change to the photo—maybe scribble on it with a pencil or brush tool—and then close it. It will update in your presentation file. Save this presentation to your desktop also.

Now go to your desktop, right-click the first presentation, and choose Properties. What does it say under Size? Look at the second presentation's properties. Its size is probably substantially larger than the first presentation (see Table 4-1). That, my friend, is OLE in action.

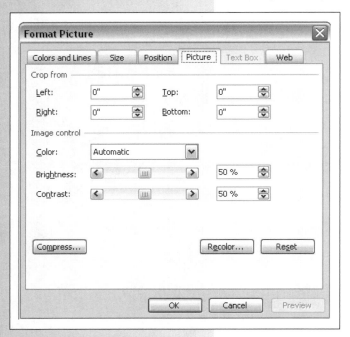

Figure 4-1. If you double-click a photo in your presentation and see this dialog box, it means that your image does not use OLE embedding. OLE embedding can increase your file size tremendously.

Table 4-1. If you paste a graphic onto your slide from another application (in this case, Photoshop), you greatly increase the file size of your presentation

	Original JPG	PowerPoint using Insert→Picture→From File	PowerPoint using Copy/Paste from Photoshop
File Size	97 KB	133 KB	2.48 MB

Interestingly enough, PowerPoint is very smart once the image has been inserted onto a slide. If you copy and paste the image from one slide to another *within the presentation*, PowerPoint recognizes that you're using the same photo, inserts an internal reference to the original photo, and doesn't increase the file size.

My Presentation Tries to Connect to the Internet

THE ANNOYANCE: When I open my presentation, PowerPoint tries to connect to the Internet. Is Microsoft trying to phone home or something?

THE FIX: Your presentation probably contains an image copied from the Internet and pasted directly onto a slide.

The problem is that the web site where you copied the image from really only contained a *link* to the image. The actual image was located on a different web site. If you paste a linked image onto your slide, you create an HTML object in your presentation, which sometimes causes PowerPoint to try to connect to the Internet. It won't happen with every pasted image, and it won't always happen even with the same presentation on different machines, so it may be difficult to pinpoint.

You can try making a copy of your presentation and deleting images one at a time, saving after each deletion until you can isolate the problem image.

If you must use graphics from a web site, right-click the graphic and choose Save Target As or Save Picture As to save it to your hard drive. Then use Insert→Picture→From File to insert the image into your presentation.

And make sure you have permission to use the images. Just because it's on the Internet doesn't mean that copyrights don't apply. See the "Mother, May I?" sidebar in Chapter 8 for links to sites with copyright assistance.

Inserted Pictures Are Really Big

THE ANNOYANCE: All right already. I started using Insert→Picture→From File to get images into my slides, but they're too big when they come into PowerPoint. They hang off the edge of the slide.

THE FIX: There are a whole bunch of different reasons for this. One reason is some file types—GIFs, for example—don't carry information about the file size or the dots per inch in the image. As a result, PowerPoint doesn't have anything to use to determine the actual size of the picture when you import it. Another is you've scanned your image at a size way too large to fit onto the slide, or otherwise not optimized it for use in PowerPoint.

In all honesty, you probably don't need to worry too much if your images appear slightly larger than desired. Just make sure you properly size your images before you insert them into your presentation (see the sidebar, "Image Size in a Nutshell"). If you have a lot of pictures to size, download the free RnR PPTools Starter Set add-in (*http://www.rdpslides.com/pptools/starterset/index.html*) and use the Place Exactly tool (the hammer icon) to quickly position images on your slides (see Figure 4-2).

Figure 4-2. The Pick Up Size/Position tool and Place Exactly tool let you quickly position and place objects on your slides.

To use the Place Exactly tool, you first need to set the parameters. Hold down the Ctrl button and click the Pick Up Size/Position tool (to the left of the Hammer icon). In the resulting dialog box, you can choose where to align pictures relative to the position of your first object. Don't forget to select the Resize button if you want the tool to automatically size your pictures and make them the same size. Click OK to close the dialog box. Note that the Place Exactly tool will not strip pixels from your pictures and change their file sizes.

After you set the parameters, format one picture to your desired size and location. Select the picture and click the Pick Up Size/Position tool so the size and position of this picture become the basis for hammering other pictures into place. A dialog box explains the location of the object on the slide. Click OK to close the dialog box.

Next, select any picture you want to hammer into place on any slide, and click the Place Exactly tool to resize and position it. The settings will hold until you select another object and click the Pick Up Size/Position tool to establish a new baseline size and position.

Can't Make Part of a Picture Transparent

THE ANNOYANCE: I tried unsuccessfully to use the Transparency Wand to make the background of my picture transparent. What's the problem? Is the wand broken?

Image Size in a Nutshell

Knowing how big to make your images for use in a PowerPoint presentation is kind of a tricky subject.

With PowerPoint you really just want to think in pixels. After all, you're at the mercy of your monitor or LCD projector, which can only display a limited number of pixels.

If you need your image to look good when it fills the slide, and therefore, the screen, size it to 1024x768 or thereabouts in an image-editing application. To fill half of the screen or slide, an image sized ~500x~400 pixels should give you a good display. For a quarter of the screen or slide, shoot for ~250x~200 pixels.

"Why should I resize my pictures?" you ask. "Who cares if they're bigger than they need to be?" Overscanned pictures eat up a lot of resources and can quickly make your PowerPoint file difficult to manage. As your file grows larger, it takes longer to open, edit, save, and run. Keeping your images optimized will go a long way toward ensuring you have a successful presentation.

So what do you do when you want to include images from your five-megapixel digital camera in your presentation? Well, you have several options:

- You can resize the images manually in a photo-editing application before you insert them into your presentation. See Microsoft PowerPoint MVP TAJ Simmons's fantastic graphics tutorial for the nitty gritty (*http://www.awesomebackgrounds.com/ powerpointgraphics.htm*).

- You can use PowerPoint's own Compress Pictures feature, located on the Picture toolbar (see Figure 4-3). Opt to compress all the pictures or only selected pictures, etc.

- You can purchase the $99.95 Presentation Optimizer add-in from RDP (*http://www.rdpslides.com/ pptools/FAQ00026.htm*). The add-in lets you choose your compression level, and optimize images and OLE-embedded objects. It also lets you specify the conversion file type (for example, *.jpg*, *.gif*, or *.png*).

- For $46, you can purchase Neuxpower Solutions's NXPowerLite (*http://www.nxpowerlite.com*). This standalone utility lets you choose your compression level, set *.jpg* compression levels, and flatten embedded objects.

Figure 4-3. The Compress Pictures feature on the Picture toolbar lets you optimize images for screen or print.

THE FIX: You'll generally have better results editing your images in an image-editing program and then using Insert→Picture→From File to get them into PowerPoint.

However, in a pinch, you can use the Transparency Wand on your images (see Figure 4-4). This works better with some images than others because it sets exactly *one* color transparent. Some images may look as if they have only one color in the background, when they really have a *blend* of colors in the background. That white background on your *.png* might actually be composed of different colored pixels. Your eye can't discern the different colors, but the Transparency Wand can.

Figure 4-4. The Transparency Wand lets you make one color transparent in an image. You can see how it affected one specific shade of blue in this image.

There is a bug with the Transparency Wand in PowerPoint 2002. If you try to apply transparency to white pixels in an image, and nothing happens, you probably need to apply Service Pack 2 (SP2) for Office XP. Microsoft has information on downloading and installing SP2 (*http://support.microsoft. com/?kbid=325671*).

Too Much of the Picture Is Transparent

THE ANNOYANCE: I used the Transparency Wand, and more than my background ended up transparent.

THE FIX: The Transparency Wand makes *all* pixels of a specific color transparent throughout the entire image. You'll need to edit your image in an image-editing application if you need more control over the transparent areas.

Transparent Parts Turn Black

THE ANNOYANCE: I created some *.png* files with transparent backgrounds, but when I insert them into PowerPoint, the transparent parts appear black. How can I make them transparent again?

THE FIX: See if using the Transparency Wand on the black parts will fix it. If not, you'll need to go back and resave the original images.

Fortunately, you can prevent this annoyance from happening in the first place. If you're creating your images in Photoshop, make sure you turn off color management. Select Edit→Color Settings, and in the Color Management Policies area choose Off from each of the drop-down menus when saving files. In some versions of Photoshop, you may need to choose "Discard embedded profiles" in the same area.

Image-Editing Applications

When working with PowerPoint, you should always have a good image-editing application available. The following lists some of the best. If possible, give the trial version of the product a thorough workout before you buy.

- Irfanview (*http://www.irfanview.com/*) is one of the most versatile and comprehensive image viewers. It also has some editing options, and it's available for free.

- PaintShop Pro (*http://www.corel.com/servlet/Satellite?pagename=Corel3/Products/Display&pfid=1047024307383&pid=1047023911984*), recently purchased by Corel, costs $129 and offers the usual editing and manipulation tools, as well as borders and edges for your photos.

- Photoshop Elements (*http://www.adobe.com/products/photoshopelwin/main.html*) is a scaled-down version of Photoshop with a scaled-down price of less than $100. Still, it has *plenty* of features and should appeal to most photo enthusiasts.

- Photoshop (*http://www.adobe.com/products/photoshop/main.html*), the granddaddy of all image-editing applications, will cost you $649. Unless you plan to become a professional image editor, you can probably do without it.

- Included in Microsoft Office 2003 and later versions, Picture Manager offers very basic image editing. You can find out more about it at *http://office.microsoft.com/en-us/assistance/HP010017211033.aspx*.

- Although Microsoft discontinued its Photo Editor application, you can still install it if you have your Office 2000 or 2002 installation CDs. To learn more about it, visit *http://office.microsoft.com/en-us/assistance/HP011454871033.aspx*.

- Another digital editing application from Microsoft? I'm afraid so. Digital Image (*http://www.microsoft.com/products/imaging/ProductDetails.aspx?pid=002*) costs $49.95 and has some decent photo editing options, including a red-eye fix and a noise reducer.

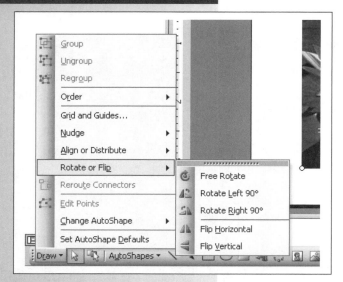

Figure 4-5. You can use the rotation tools on the Drawing toolbar to rotate images in PowerPoint 2002 and 2003.

Rotate Images

THE ANNOYANCE: I want to rotate an image I inserted, but the rotation options appear grayed out in PowerPoint 2000. What's the deal?

THE FIX: You can't rotate images in PowerPoint 97 and 2000. You can, however, rotate the image in an image-editing program, save it, and then insert it into PowerPoint (Insert→Picture→From File).

Or upgrade. You can rotate pictures in PowerPoint 2002 and 2003 (see Figure 4-5 and Figure 4-6).

Figure 4-6. Or you can use the green rotation handle to rotate a picture in PowerPoint 2002 and 2003.

Batch Import Images

THE ANNOYANCE: I have a whole bunch of photos from my vacation. Do I have to insert them all into PowerPoint individually, or is there an easier way?

THE FIX: You can batch import photographs into PowerPoint in quite a few ways. Here's a rundown:

- PowerPoint 2002 and 2003 include the Photo Album utility. Select Insert→Picture→New Photo Album to eliminate tedious labor by importing all your photos at once (see Figure 4-7). The Photo Album feature lets you choose to insert files from your hard drive or directly from your camera. You can also insert one, two, or four pictures on each slide, apply a shape to the photos, add empty text boxes for captions, rotate individual pictures, and do basic brightness and contrast adjustments.

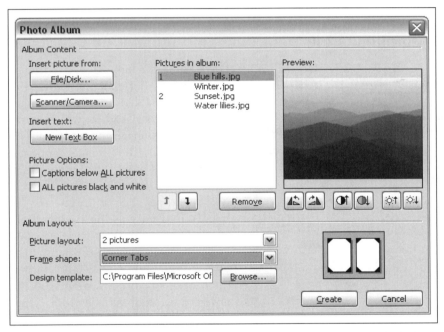

Figure 4-7. The Photo Album interface in PowerPoint 2002 and 2003 helps you import multiple photos at once.

If you're using PowerPoint 2000, you can download the free Photo Album add-in from Microsoft (*http://www.microsoft.com/downloads/ details.aspx?FamilyID=55D24B47-C828-4141-A8DE-9A459C63DB1A &displaylang=en*). Next, select File→New and choose the Photo Album Wizard on the General tab (see Figure 4-8). After that, the interface looks similar to the one in PowerPoint 2002 and 2003.

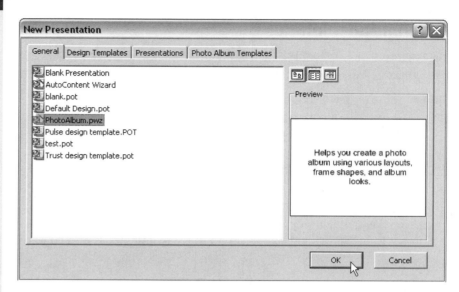

Figure 4-8. To use Photo Album in PowerPoint 2000, you must go to File→New and choose the Photo Album Wizard from the General tab.

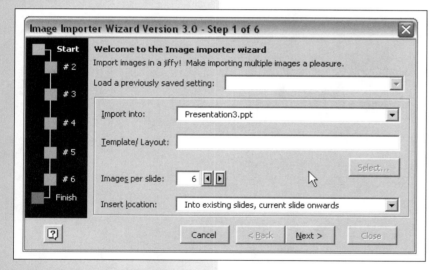

Figure 4-9. The Image Importer Wizard add-in has become an essential tool for many advanced users in all versions of PowerPoint.

PowerPoint 97 has no batch import capabilities. Fortunately, Microsoft MVP Shyam Pillai created the Image Importer Wizard add-in, which works with all versions of PowerPoint (see Figure 4-9). The Image Importer Wizard offers more functionality than PowerPoint's native Photo Album utility, including the ability to import images into an existing presentation, resize images on the fly, search and import specific image formats from folders and subfolders, and format the captions before insertion. You can download a trial version from *http:// skp.mvps.org/iiw.htm*, but once the trial expires, it will cost you $35.

- Pixerter is a relative newcomer to the PowerPoint batch import arsenal. You can download a trial version from *http://members.fortunecity.com/ dreed/pixerter/*. The full version costs $15 and lets you insert up to five images per slide with an option to import from an image list.

- If you need batch importers for the Mac, check Microsoft Macintosh Office MVP Jim Gordon's add-ins, which cost $15 for PowerPoint 2004 (*http://www.agentjim.com/MVP/PowerPoint/ppt2004.htm*) and $10 for PowerPoint X and PowerPoint 2001 (*http://www.agentjim.com/MVP/ PowerPoint/ppt.html*).

Crop Images Before Insertion

THE ANNOYANCE: I inserted a bunch of images using Photo Album, but now I can't crop them. Help!

THE FIX: You can't crop images inserted using Photo Album in PowerPoint 2002 and 2003, as they're actually inserted as fills to AutoShapes.

If you need to crop after insertion, you can save the file as an image, and then reinsert it: right-click the image on the slide (which is really an AutoShape) and choose Cut. Then select Edit→Paste Special and choose an appropriate image type, such as *.png* or *.jpg*. You should now be able to crop the image.

Alternatively, crop the image before you insert it into your slide with Photo Album, or purchase Image Importer Wizard (see Figure 4-9), a third-party add-in for PowerPoint.

Add Pictures to a Photo Album

THE ANNOYANCE: I made a Photo Album using Insert→Picture→New Photo Album in PowerPoint, and now I need to add some more pictures.

THE FIX: Forgot to include that picture of your Uncle Eddie? No problem. Open the Photo Album you want to change and select Format→Photo Album. In the Photo Album dialog box, click either File/Disk or Scanner/Camera button, locate the picture, and then click the Update button.

Flippin' Graphics Flip

THE ANNOYANCE: I opened an old presentation in PowerPoint 2002, and about half the graphics appeared upside down. The presentation looked fine when I last saved it. What happened?

THE FIX: First, close the file and do *not* save it. Just close it for now. Then head to Microsoft PowerPoint MVP Shyam Pillai's web site and download the free Un-flip add-in (*http://skp.mvps.org/unflip.htm*). Save it to a folder on your C drive, something like *C:\unflip*.

Double-click the *unflip.zip* file and extract *Un-Flip.ppa* and *readme.txt* to the folder *C:\unflip*. In PowerPoint, select Tools→Macro→Security and choose the Medium setting, if necessary. If your Macro Security is set to High or Very High, you will not be able to install any add-ins. You can restore this setting once you've installed the add-in.

Select Tools→Add-Ins→Add New. Navigate to *C:\unflip* and choose *Un-Flip.ppa*. You will see a security warning that says, "C:\unflip\Un-Flip.ppa includes macros. Macros may contain viruses. It is usually safe to disable macros, but if the macros are legitimate, you might lose some functionality." Click the Enable Macros button and then click Close to exit the add-in dialog box.

Select Tools→Enable Corrective Flip. You will see a checkmark beside it on the menu when enabled. Open the PowerPoint file with the flipped images and save the file. Un-flip will unflip the images automatically.

In case you're wondering, objects in PowerPoint have both FlipVertical and FlipHorizontal properties. PowerPoint 97 and 2000 ignore these properties, but PowerPoint 2002 and 2003 do not. Therefore, it was possible to inadvertently flip an object in earlier versions of PowerPoint without even knowing it. This issue can also happen with PowerPoint charts and linked or embedded OLE objects, such as Excel charts, Organization Charts, or Word Art.

Photo Album Pros and Cons

The Photo Album utility in PowerPoint 2002 and 2003 works, however, it imports images as AutoShape fills.

What seems like a minor annoyance can turn into a real problem when you try to crop an image on a slide and realize you can't. If you're going to use Photo Album to batch import your images into PowerPoint, make sure you crop them in an image-editing program first.

You might also want to adjust the brightness and contrast of your images while you're in the image editor. Although you can change these settings in Photo Album, the interface offers few controls and a limited viewing area.

On the upside, importing images as AutoShape

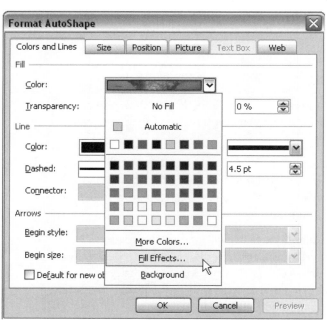

Figure 4-10. To replace an AutoShape fill, choose Fill Effects from the Color drop-down menu.

fills makes it easy to swap out an image or two without losing animations. Let's say you've animated some of the imported images (or AutoShapes) in Photo Album, and then want to change the image. Normally, you'd have to delete the image, reinsert it, and then reapply the animation from scratch. However, Photo Album images are actually AutoShape fills, which means you can double-click the image and click the Colors and Lines tab. In the Fill area, choose Fill Effects from the Color drop-down menu (see Figure 4-10). On the Picture tab, navigate to the picture you want to use. This switches your images but leaves the animation settings intact on the AutoShape itself.

EXCEL

Excel Data Cut Off

THE ANNOYANCE: I pasted cells from an Excel spreadsheet into my presentation, but a bunch of rows got cut off. How can I get the whole thing onto my slide?

THE FIX: The easiest way to fix this is to upgrade to PowerPoint 2002 or 2003, which fix the limitation PowerPoint and Excel seem to have when exchanging information on the clipboard.

There is a limit to the size of the PowerPoint 97 and 2000 clipboard—about 33x33 cm. Anything outside that area may be cut off. If you can, reformat your data to make it fit within this 33×33 cm area (for example, decrease the font size or the width of your columns). On a default spreadsheet, this would be about 72 rows long by 17 columns wide.

Depending on your operating system, you may also be able to copy more data if you change your display setting from, say, 800×600 to 1024×768 or 1280×1024. Right-click your desktop, choose Properties, click the Settings tab, and move the slider in the Screen resolution area (see Figure 4-11).

The only other solution is to paste pieces of your spreadsheet onto your slide and then realign the data once you get everything in PowerPoint.

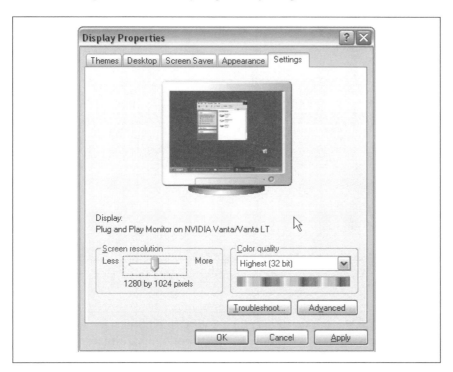

Figure 4-11. Changing your display resolution may let you paste more data from Excel onto your slide.

Colored Text Turns Black

THE ANNOYANCE: I imported my spreadsheet okay, but the colored text turned black. It's really bizarre.

THE FIX: Make sure your default printer is a color printer. Yeah, it's weird, but that really is the fix!

To set your default printer, click Start→Control Panel→Printers and Faxes. Right-click the color printer in the list and choose "Set as Default Printer" (see Figure 4-12).

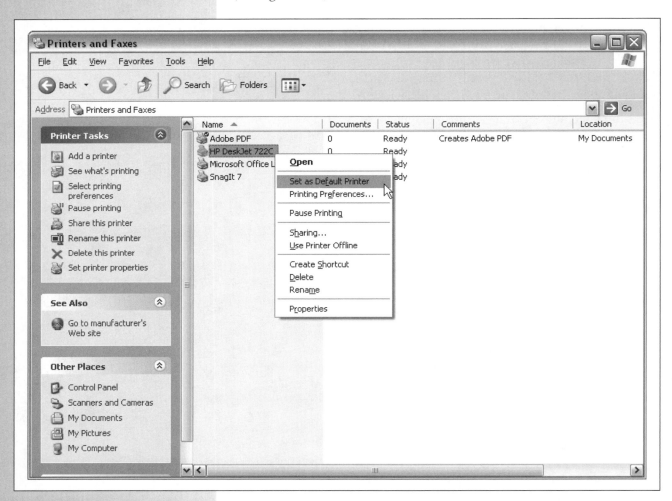

Figure 4-12. Make your default printer a color printer to force your Excel text to remain colored when you paste it into PowerPoint.

You don't actually need a color printer connected to your computer. You can still install the printer drivers for a color printer and set it as the default while you work on the presentation. To install color printer drivers, click Start→Control Panel→Printers and Faxes. In the Printers and Faxes dialog box, select File→Add Printer. Follow the prompts to install a local printer to LPT1, and choose something like HP DeskJet 722C from the list.

Get Rid of Gridlines

THE ANNOYANCE: I pasted in a bunch of Excel data, but I can't get the gridlines to go away. Help!

THE FIX: You have to remove the gridlines in Excel before you paste the data into PowerPoint. Open the file in Excel, choose Tools→Options, click the View tab, and uncheck the Gridlines box in the Window options area (see Figure 4-13).

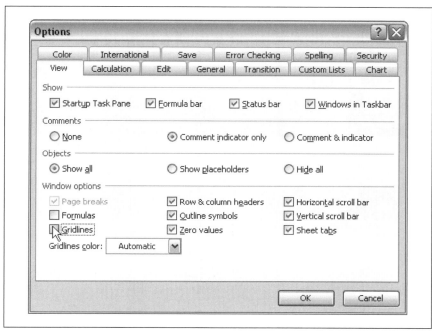

Figure 4-13. To make gridlines disappear, uncheck the Gridlines box before you paste your data into PowerPoint.

Extract Data from an Embedded Excel Chart

THE ANNOYANCE: Some doofus embedded an Excel chart into the presentation, but we really only want it linked so the market research people can update the data without messing up our PowerPoint file. Is there a way to get this information out of PowerPoint, or do we have to start over and create a new workbook in Excel for the research folks?

THE FIX: Just right-click the chart and choose Chart Object→Open. Then select File→Save Copy As. This saves a copy of the chart and data in an Excel workbook you can let your market research people work on. Delete the original chart in the PowerPoint file and create a link to the chart in the new Excel workbook: copy the chart in Excel, select Edit→Paste Special in PowerPoint, and choose the "Paste link" option to link the chart to the presentation. As long as you don't break the link to the Excel file by moving it to a different folder, the data will update each time you open the PowerPoint file. To change this behavior, select Edit→Links and choose the desired options.

Paste the Whole Workbook with the Chart

THE ANNOYANCE: I've copied Excel charts into PowerPoint for years, but I just realized that it pastes the entire workbook. Has PowerPoint always behaved this way?

THE FIX: By default, when you paste Excel charts into PowerPoint, it embeds the entire workbook. This can cause problems—large file sizes, data being inadvertently included in presentations, etc.

In PowerPoint 97 and 2000, if you do not want the entire workbook included in your presentation, you must select Edit→Paste Special and choose an image type from the list (see Figure 4-14). This pastes a simple image of the Excel chart, which is no longer connected to the data used to create it.

In PowerPoint 2002 and 2003, you can select Edit→Paste Special to choose an image, or you can simply click the Paste Options icon to paste a picture of the chart (see Figure 4-15). The Paste Options button appears when you paste an object onto a slide, and the available options depend on what type of object you've pasted. For example, pasting data cells from an Excel spreadsheet pastes a "PowerPoint-style table" by default. The Paste Options button lets you paste as an Excel Table (entire workbook), a Picture of Table (smaller file size), or Keep Text Only.

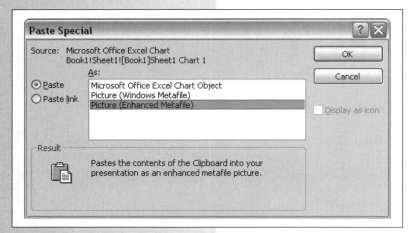

Figure 4-14. The Paste Special dialog box lets you specify what format you want to paste.

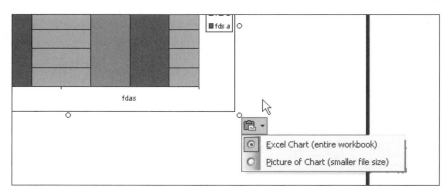

Figure 4-15. The Paste Options icon shows up immediately after you paste something on a slide. The options you see change with the type of object that you paste.

Font Size Goes Wacky When I Resize

THE ANNOYANCE: When I try to resize the data I pasted by dragging the edges and corners on the slide, the font size goes crazy and gets distorted. How can I make this stop?

THE FIX: Select Edit→Paste Special, choose the "Paste link" option, and then choose "Microsoft Office Excel Workbook Object" to link to the spreadsheet as opposed to embedding it in the slide. You can break the link later if necessary.

Create Separate Chartsheets

THE ANNOYANCE: I have a bunch of charts in a workbook, which I linked to my presentation. When I update the links, the different charts in the PowerPoint file all change to the same chart, so it looks like I just linked to the same chart over and over. This is not good.

THE FIX: Put the charts on separate chartsheets in Excel, and then link them to the PowerPoint slides. To change a graph from a chart object to a separate chartsheet, right-click the chart in Excel, choose Location, and select "Place chart as new sheet." Then reinsert them into your presentation. If the charts continue to change when updating, save the separate chartsheets as separate Excel workbooks.

OLE Linking Versus Embedding

The main difference between OLE linking and OLE embedding is where the data is actually stored.

If you copy a cell range in an Excel spreadsheet and paste it onto a PowerPoint slide, you have created an OLE embedded object. In this case, the entire spreadsheet is embedded within the PowerPoint file. OLE embedded objects increase your PowerPoint file size because they include not only all the data from the source file, but also the overhead that allows you to open the source application and edit the file from within PowerPoint. You can delete the Excel file and it will not affect the data on your PowerPoint slide.

If you copy the same cell range in Excel, select Edit→Paste Special, and then choose Paste Link, PowerPoint creates a shortcut to the Excel file. Thus, when you update the data in Excel, it will also update on your PowerPoint slide.

This is known as OLE linking. The upside is that the size of your PowerPoint file will be much smaller than if you simply pasted the spreadsheet onto your slide, creating an OLE embedded object. The downside is that you must keep the Excel file readily available for PowerPoint. You must also make any changes to the data in the actual Excel file.

To get the best of both worlds, create OLE linked objects using Edit→Paste Special→Paste Link while you're working on the file, and then ungroup the object before finalizing the presentation and/or sending it to others. (Of course, do this on a copy of your presentation if you're sending for review before the file is finalized.) This will break the "shortcut" OLE link to the object, leaving you with an image that's easily displayed in your PowerPoint file and that doesn't cause a huge file size hit.

Fonts on Chart Not Visible

THE ANNOYANCE: My Excel chart uses black fonts, which makes it impossible to read when I paste it onto my slide with a black background. Do I have to reformat this stupid chart just so I can see what it says?

THE FIX: Relax, you don't have to reformat your chart. Instead, recolor the chart to make it more readable.

Choose View→Toolbars→Picture to display the Picture toolbar. Select the chart and click the Recolor Excel Chart button (see the left side of Figure 4-16). Specify whether to recolor the entire chart, recolor only the text and background colors of the chart, or do nothing (see the right side of Figure 4-16).

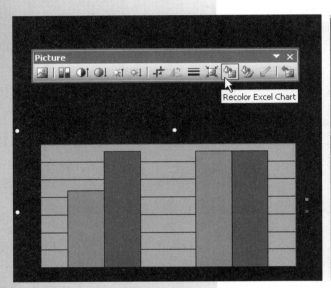
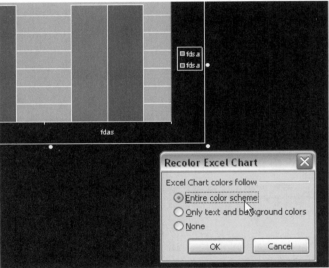

Figure 4-16. The Recolor option on the Picture toolbar (left) lets you recolor portions of your Excel chart or the entire thing (right).

> **NOTE**
>
> *The Recolor tool on the Picture toolbar is also great for working with clip art. It lets you recolor clips without having to deconstruct them by ungrouping a million times, selecting individual pieces and changing the colors, and then regrouping.*
>
> *PowerPoint also has a hidden feature that lets you recolor slide background images (see www.indezine.com/products/powerpoint/cool/recolorimages.html for specifics).*

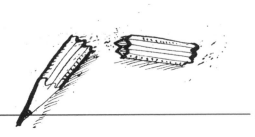

Excel Headers and Footers Don't Transfer

THE ANNOYANCE: How do I import headers and footers from an Excel workbook onto a slide? I can get the Excel workbook onto the PowerPoint slide without any trouble.

THE FIX: Headers and footers don't actually show up in Excel until you print the file. If you must transfer your headers and footers to the PowerPoint slide, add text boxes to the Excel worksheet, enter the appropriate header and footer text, and take a screenshot. You can hit the Print Screen button on your keyboard and Ctrl+V to paste the image onto the slide. Crop as desired using the Crop tool on the Picture toolbar in PowerPoint. Alternatively, you can add the headers and footers by adding text boxes to the PowerPoint slide itself.

> **NOTE**
>
> *Print Screen will capture your entire monitor display. Holding the Alt key while you hit Print Screen will limit the capture to the active window.*

CLIP ART

Clip Art Task Pane Doesn't Show Clips

THE ANNOYANCE: All my clip art shows up as "dglxasset." How can I see pictures of the clips?

THE FIX: Clear out your Temporary Internet Files folder, and the problem should resolve itself. Clip Gallery and Clip Organizer need space in the Temporary Internet Files folder to display clips.

Open Internet Explorer, choose Tools→Internet Options, click the General tab, and click the Delete Files button (see Figure 4-17).

Figure 4-17. Emptying your Temporary Internet Files folder can help with Clip Organizer issues.

Clip Gallery Versus Clip Organizer

Microsoft introduced Clip Organizer with Office XP. This upset users who had invested a lot of time in their clip art collections because Clip Organizer cannot import clip art complete with its keywords and image catalogs from Clip Gallery.

Clip Gallery 3.0, 4.0, and 5.0, which are the clip applications for Office 95, 97, and 2000 respectively, can still access Microsoft Office Online and download clips using the CIL download format. Clip Organizer, which is included with Office XP and 2003, downloads clips in the MPF format. CIL and MPF files are a little like WinZip or CAB files—they package up the clips along with keyword search terms and such into one nice little file.

When you go to Office Online (*http://office.microsoft.com/en-us/default.aspx*), search for clip art and click the Download button, you may be prompted to choose between the CIL and MPF file formats. The page explains the two formats fairly well. Select one, click the Download Now button, and then choose Open or Save.

If you choose Open, the clips should automatically load in Clip Gallery or Clip Organizer. If you choose Save, make sure you note where you save the file, and then double-click the file to install the clips.

Clips Take Forever to Load

THE ANNOYANCE: It takes too darned long to search online for clip art. How do I turn this off?

THE FIX: In the Clip Art task pane, uncheck the Web Collections box in the "Search in" drop-down menu (see Figure 4-18).

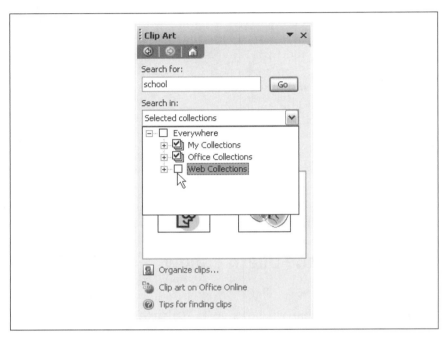

Figure 4-18. Deselecting Web Collections in the "Search in" section of the Clip Art task pane will restrict your search to your hard drive.

Newer versions of Microsoft Office don't include a lot of clip art. Instead, you'll find it on the Office web site (*http://office.microsoft.com*), which is why the Web Collections box is checked by default. You may want to uncheck it if you have a slow Internet connection. To turn it off permanently, select Tools→Options, click the General tab, click the Service Options button, click Online Content in the Category pane, and uncheck the "Show content and links from Microsoft Office Online" box.

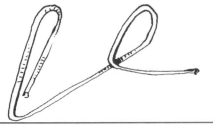

Recolor a Clip

THE ANNOYANCE: I found a really cool piece of clip art I want to use. It perfectly suits my needs, except for the color. Can I recolor the clip easily?

THE FIX: Sure. Select the clip and click the Recolor Picture button on the Picture toolbar. In the Recolor Picture dialog box, change the colors of the clip by clicking the arrows to expand the drop-down boxes and choose new colors (see Figure 4-19).

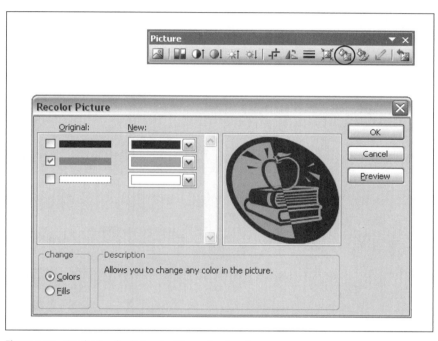

Figure 4-19. Use the Recolor Picture tool to recolor clip art.

Search Just Black and White Clips

THE ANNOYANCE: I used to be able to search for just black and white clip art. This was really handy when I created my organization's newsletter because I could be sure the clips would print correctly with the black and white page. It seems that Microsoft removed this option from its clip gallery site. Will they bring it back?

THE FIX: Actually, the Black and White search option is still available on the site (*http://office.microsoft.com/clipart/default.aspx?lc=en-us*). In the "Browse Clip Art and Media Categories" section, click the "Black & White" link and type your keywords in the search box (see Figure 4-20).

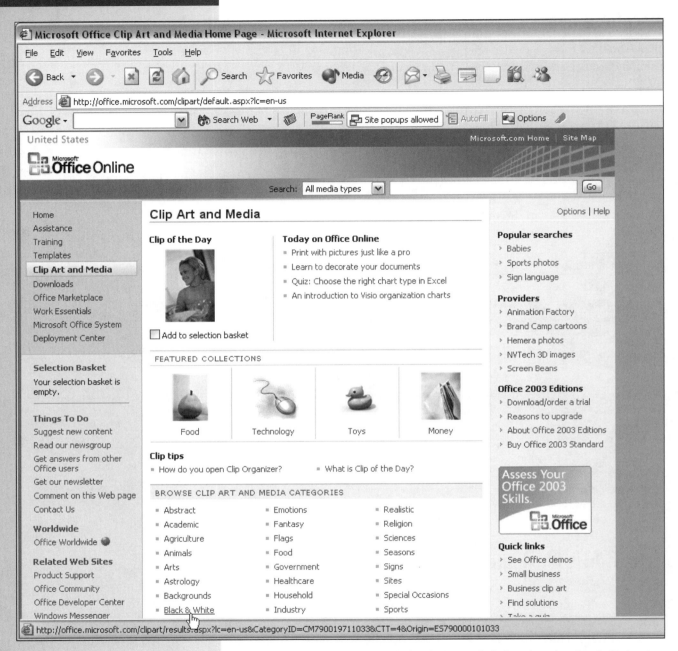

Figure 4-20. Many users bemoaned the fact that Microsoft eliminated search options for black and white clip art when it revamped the Clip Art and Media web site. However, you can still find the black and white search option if you know where to look.

Inserted Clips Look Fuzzy

THE ANNOYANCE: I inserted some clips onto my slide, but they look really nasty—they're all fuzzy, not crisp at all. What happened? They looked fine on the Web.

THE FIX: Import the clip into your Clip Organizer or Clip Gallery instead of copying and pasting the clip's thumbnail from the Web.

The fuzziness occurs because Microsoft uses small thumbnails for the clips so the Clip Art and Media site loads quickly, even for users without a fast Internet connection—they're not meant to be used as the clip art on the slide. Use the options to download the clip from the Web instead of right-clicking the small thumbnail and selecting "Save Target As" or "Save Picture As."

Usually, when you hover your cursor over any clip on the Clip Art and Media pages, you'll see a drop-down arrow. Click the arrow and choose whether to copy the image to the clipboard, add the clip to your selection basket, or see the properties of the clip (see Figure 4-21).

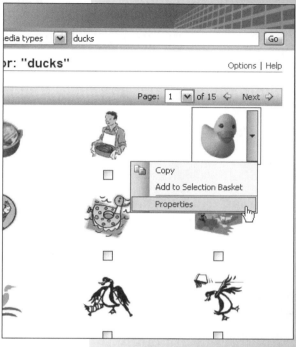

Figure 4-21. Choose whether to copy the clip art, add the clip art to your selection basket, or see the properties of the clip.

Nothing Happens When I Click Properties in an Online Clip

THE ANNOYANCE: I'm on the Microsoft Office Clip Art and Media pages, and I want to see more information about a particular piece of clip art. I clicked Properties in the drop-down box on the clip art, but nothing happened. Should a window or something open with the clip properties?

THE FIX: You probably have a pop-up blocker enabled. You'll have to allow pop-ups on the Clip Art and Media pages to be able to view clip properties. The Help files for your pop-up blocker should explain how to do this, as each one is a little bit different.

Can I Use This Clip Art in My Project?

Users often ask if the clip art from Microsoft (*http://
office.microsoft.com/clipart/default.aspx?lc=en-us*) costs
anything to use. The answer is no. You can use the clips
on the Microsoft Office Clip Art and Media pages for
free, even in commercial projects.

However, you do want to be aware of what the End-User
License Agreement for the clips says. You can find it here:
http://office.microsoft.com/en-us/tou.aspx. If you're
unsure about the use of a clip, consult a lawyer.

WORD, PDFS, AND STUFF FROM THE WEB

Change the Default Paste Action

THE ANNOYANCE: I pasted some text from Word into PowerPoint 2002. I see the paste option to "keep source formatting," but how can I make this the default behavior?

THE FIX: Unfortunately, you can't change the default paste behavior, which formats the text based on the slide template.

Figure 4-22. When you paste an object onto a slide in PowerPoint 2002 and 2003, a Paste Options button should appear. Click it to see the various paste options available for the object.

In PowerPoint 97 and 2000, pasted text is formatted based on PowerPoint's default AutoShape and font settings, or it conforms to the slide placeholder formatting if pasted into a placeholder. You don't have a choice about how that works.

The default is the same in PowerPoint 2002 and 2003, but in those versions, you can at least choose from some paste actions. After you paste something onto your slide, a Paste Options button will appear (see Figure 4-22). Click the button to see the paste actions available for that particular object.

Use Animations from the Web

THE ANNOYANCE: I found this cool animation on the Web and pasted it into my presentation, but it doesn't animate. Why?

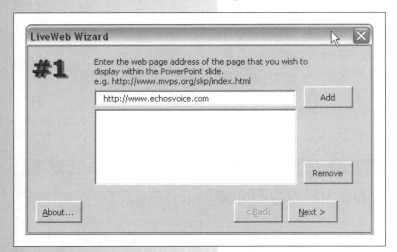

Figure 4-23. The free LiveWeb add-in lets you place a web page on a slide and refreshes the page automatically throughout your presentation.

THE FIX: You probably pasted in a Java applet. Not to mention that you probably violated every copyright law in the book. Anyway, PowerPoint doesn't support Java applets, so it will be just a pretty picture on your slide.

As an alternative, you can use Microsoft PowerPoint MVP Shyam Pillai's free LiveWeb add-in (*http://skp.mvps.org/liveweb.htm*) to run the web page in your PowerPoint file. LiveWeb lets you insert web pages into a PowerPoint slide and refreshes the pages in real time during the presentation. Just make sure you can access the web page during your presentation. Select Insert→Web Pages to insert a LiveWeb page onto your slide (see Figure 4-23). LiveWeb uses an ActiveX control, so it does not work in PowerPoint Viewer 97 or PowerPoint Viewer 2003.

What Does the Little Blue Circle with a Question Mark Mean?

THE ANNOYANCE: Sometimes when I paste an object into PowerPoint, I get a little blue circle with a question mark inside it.

THE FIX: This icon shows up when the Office clipboard hasn't been activated or has lost its focus to another application. To activate the clipboard and maintain its focus, open PowerPoint before you copy whatever it is you're copying, and after you've copied it, go directly to PowerPoint and paste. Don't stop anywhere on the way.

Pasted Buttons Don't Work

THE ANNOYANCE: I copied some buttons and drop-down boxes from a web page into PowerPoint, but they don't work.

THE FIX: PowerPoint is not designed to use HTML in this manner. If you really need the buttons from the web site, consider using LiveWeb, a free add-in from Microsoft PowerPoint MVP Shyam Pillai (see "Use Animations from the Web").

Use Animated GIFs

THE ANNOYANCE: I used Insert→Picture→From File to insert an animated GIF, but it doesn't animate. What gives?

THE FIX: Well, if you're using PowerPoint 97, you're stuck because Microsoft added animated GIF functionality in PowerPoint 2000. However, the company still managed to get it wrong. PowerPoint 2000, 2002, and 2003 all play animated GIFs differently. Go figure.

You'll have to edit the loop flag on the GIF so it plays correctly in your version of PowerPoint. A loop flag is a setting in the GIF header. When set to 0, it causes an animated GIF to animate indefinitely in most web browsers. However, in PowerPoint it can cause different behavior:

- In PowerPoint 2000, all animated GIFs animate indefinitely, regardless of the loop setting.

- In PowerPoint 2002, a loop flag setting of 0 causes the GIF to animate just once.

- In PowerPoint 2003, a loop flag setting of 0 causes the GIF not to animate at all.

To change this setting, open the GIF in a utility such as the $24 GIF Construction Set (*http://www.mindworkshop.com/alchemy/gifcon.html*).

Double-click the 1:Header to edit it. Check the Loop box and set the number of iterations somewhere between 1 and 99 (see Figure 4-24).

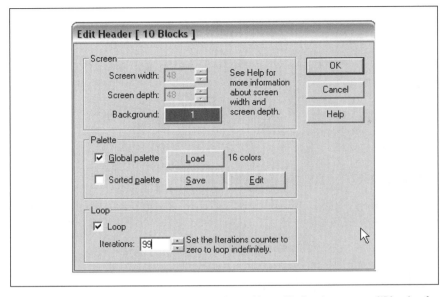

Figure 4-24. Use a utility like GIF Construction Set from Alchemy Mindworks to correct GIF headers for playback in PowerPoint.

Import a Word Outline

THE ANNOYANCE: When I use Insert→Slides→From Outline or simply open a Word document in PowerPoint, I get, like, one line of text per slide and it takes me forever to set it right. I even tried using File→Send to→PowerPoint in Word, but it does the same thing. How can I import a Word document more easily?

THE FIX: If you spend some time in Word applying styles to your text, it will import more easily into PowerPoint.

PowerPoint reads anything using Word Heading 1 style as a slide title. It reads anything using Word Heading 2 style as a primary bullet. It reads anything using Word Heading 3 style as a secondary bullet. And so on. Anything using Normal style in Word will not transfer to PowerPoint.

Insert a Gantt Chart from Microsoft Project

THE ANNOYANCE: I want to insert a Gantt chart from Project into PowerPoint, but I can't figure out how to do it.

THE FIX: In Project, click the camera icon on the toolbar to take a snapshot of the open view in Project and save the image. In PowerPoint, select Insert→Picture→From File to insert the saved image.

Import PDFs into PowerPoint

THE ANNOYANCE: How in the world do I import PDF content into PowerPoint? When I use Alt+PrintScrn and paste into PowerPoint, everything just looks fuzzy.

THE FIX: In Adobe Acrobat or the Acrobat Reader, use the Snapshot tool on the Basic toolbar to drag a marquee around the area you want to copy (see Figure 4-25); this copies the selected area to the clipboard. Then press Ctrl+V to paste the content onto the PowerPoint slide.

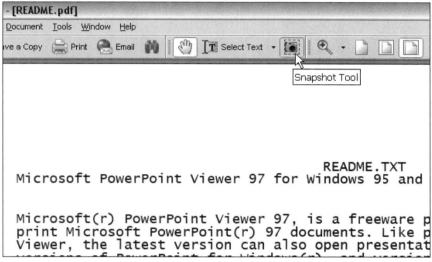

Figure 4-25. Use the Snapshot tool in Acrobat to copy content in the PDF to the clipboard. From there, you can paste the content into PowerPoint.

If the text in the pasted screen grab is fuzzy, zooming in on your selection will sometimes help. Once you've used the Snapshot tool to select the area you want to copy, type in a larger zoom percentage in the zoom box on the Reader toolbar, which increases the resolution of the selected area. Right-click and choose Copy Selected Graphic to copy this new, larger image. Press Ctrl+V to paste it onto the PowerPoint slide. (Don't go too crazy with that zoom percentage—if it's too big, you can lock your computer! Start with 200% and move your way up in increments of 100% until you get what you want.)

Once it's on the slide, you can drag the image of the text on the slide so it's a bit smaller. This, in effect, increases the resolution of the image (pixels-per-inch), which makes it look a bit crisper on the slide.

Adobe added the Snapshot tool to Adobe Reader in Version 6.0. In older versions, you'll have to use the Graphics Select tool. It works the same way as the Snapshot tool, except it doesn't make the copy automatically—you'll have to press Ctrl+C to copy the area to the clipboard.

If you have the full version of Adobe Acrobat, not just the free Reader, you can also export your PDF as a series of images, and then import those images into your slides using Insert→Picture→From File or one of the batch import tools (see "Batch Import Images"). In Acrobat, select File→Save As and choose an image type from the "Save as type" drop-down list (see Figure 4-26). The *.png* file type generally works well if your PDF includes text.

You can protect PDFs from opening and/or copying and editing and/or printing. If you're working with a protected file, many of these techniques won't work.

You can also use screen capture tools such as the $40 SnagIt (*http://www.techsmith.com/*) to take a snapshot of the content and create an image. Finally, use Insert→Picture→From File to insert it onto your slide. SnagIt has a handy "scrolling window" option for copying entire pages when you're already zoomed in on them.

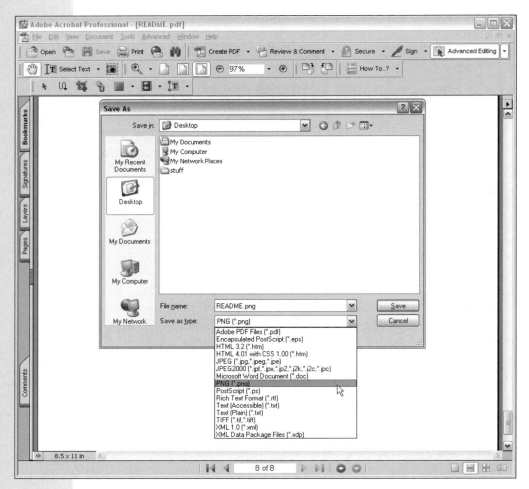

Figure 4-26. In the full version of Adobe Acrobat (but not in the free Adobe Reader), you can choose an image type to save the pages of the PDF as individual images.

Organization Charts, Diagrams, and Drawing Tools

5

PowerPoint helps explain complex concepts visually using organization charts and diagrams of all sorts. However, many of these tools can be inflexible and frustrating to use at times.

This chapter shows you how to minimize annoyances associated with creating, editing, and formatting organization charts and diagrams. It also looks at PowerPoint's drawing functions, and solves the most vexing problems you encounter when you use its AutoShape and alignment tools, transparency and shadow options, 3D objects, and watermarks.

ORGANIZATION CHARTS

Edit Existing Org Charts

THE ANNOYANCE: I have a bunch of organization charts in an old PowerPoint file. I'm now using PowerPoint 2003, and when I try to edit the org charts, I get an error message that says "server application, source file, or item can't be found." How can I edit these org charts?

THE FIX: PowerPoint 2002 and 2003 use a new diagramming applet to create org charts rather than relying on the OLE Organization Chart objects PowerPoint 97 and 2000 used. This error message just means that Organization Chart 2.0 isn't available, so PowerPoint can't edit the organization chart.

You need to download and install Organization Chart 2.0 (*http://support. microsoft.com/default.aspx?scid=kb;en-us;826835*), which lets you edit old-style organization charts in your PowerPoint files. Installing Organization Chart 2.0 also lets you create more "old-style" org charts in PowerPoint 2002 and 2003 by selecting Insert→Object→MS Organization Chart 2.0.

Alternatively, you can ungroup an existing org chart (Draw→Ungroup) and edit it using PowerPoint's AutoShapes and smart connectors on the Drawing toolbar (see Figure 5-1). Ungrouping an organization chart turns it into PowerPoint drawing objects, so you don't need Organization Chart 2.0 to manipulate the individual pieces.

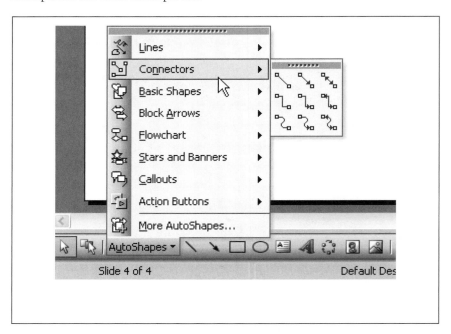

Figure 5-1. PowerPoint's drawing tools include smart connectors, which gives you another option for creating and editing organization charts and other diagrams. Smart connectors "lock" their ends to other AutoShapes.

If you see this particular "server not found" error when you attempt to create or edit an org chart in PowerPoint 97 or 2000, the issue is probably the Norton AntiVirus Office Plug-In. It wreaks havoc with OLE embedded objects (usually graphs, tables, and org charts) in Office files. If you double-click a graph or an org chart on your slide and see the "server not found" error, you should disable the Norton Office Plug-In. (Don't worry, you'll still be protected by Norton's regular email and file scanning processes.)

To disable the Norton Office Plug-in, close all Office programs and open Norton AntiVirus. Click on Options, and in the left pane, click on Miscellaneous. In the right pane, uncheck Enable Office Plug-in under "How to keep Microsoft Office documents protected."

Out-of-Memory Errors

THE ANNOYANCE: I'm trying to add an organization chart on my slide in PowerPoint 97, but I keep getting an error message that says I'm out of memory. I have tons of memory on this system, so what's the problem?

THE FIX: Believe it or not, having too many fonts installed on your system causes this error message in Org Chart 2.0: "There isn't enough memory available to read MS Org Chart." Move some of your fonts out of your *C:\Windows\Fonts* folder. This effectively uninstalls them and should fix the error you're seeing with Organization Chart.

Organization Chart 2.0

PowerPoint 97 and 2000 rely on an application called Organization Chart 2.0 to create organization charts. To add an org chart in these versions, select Insert→Object→MS Organization Chart 2.0 or use the Organization Chart slide layout and double-click in the placeholder.

Because Organization Chart 2.0 actually inserts an OLE embedded object onto the slide, the application must be available if you need to edit the organization chart. This is sometimes a problem, especially on computers that have never had Office (or PowerPoint) 97 or 2000 installed. If you open a presentation created in PowerPoint 97 or 2000 in PowerPoint 2002 or 2003 and receive a "server application, source file, or item can't be found" error when you try to edit an organization chart, download and install Organization Chart 2.0 from Microsoft

(*http://support.microsoft.com/default.aspx?scid=kb;en-us;826835*). Also remember, because Organization Chart 2.0 objects are OLE embedded objects, spellcheck ignores them.

Microsoft introduced a new diagramming applet in PowerPoint 2002 that does not rely on OLE. These new diagrams (organization charts and cycle, radial, pyramid, Venn, and target diagrams) are actually native to PowerPoint, not an OLE embedded object. To help with formatting, a specialized Diagram toolbar appears when you select a diagram on your slide. You can also use PowerPoint's typical formatting tools to adjust fonts, fill and line colors, line widths, etc., in these diagrams. Spellcheck does check text in PowerPoint 2002 and 2003 diagrams.

There's no magic number of fonts that will clear the error. Usually 500 or more will cause the error, but sometimes you'll see the error with as few as 300 fonts. Just keep moving them out of the folder a few at a time until Org Chart starts working again.

However, make sure you keep the fonts Office and other programs rely on to run properly. These include Arial, Courier New, Marlett, Symbol, Times New Roman, Tahoma, and WingDings.

Fonts use up memory, so you're generally better off not having too many installed at once. To be on the safe side, move the fonts to another folder on your computer so you can reinstall them when you're ready to use them.

Add More Lines to a Box in an Org Chart

THE ANNOYANCE: Some of the people in my organization have really long titles, so I need more than four lines in the organization chart boxes in PowerPoint 2000. Is there a way I can do this?

THE FIX: Select one of the subordinate boxes and click the Elongated Box on the Styles menu (see Figure 5-2). Click the Subordinate icon, and then click on the elongated box (see Figure 5-3). Click the new subordinate box again and drag it to the elongated box just above. Make sure the white directional arrow appears before you let go (see Figure 5-4).

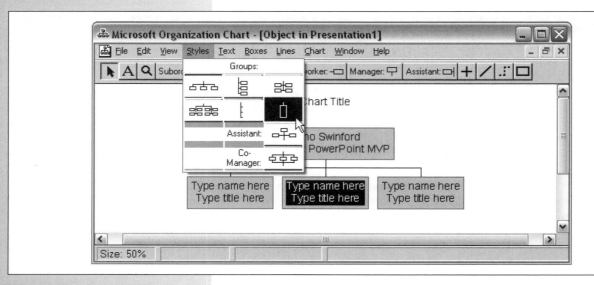

Figure 5-2. Click the Elongated Box style to begin adding more lines to a box in an organization chart.

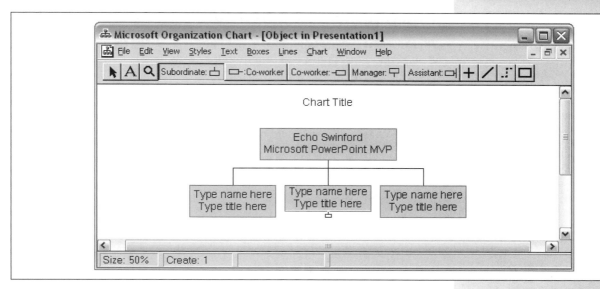

Figure 5-3. Click the Subordinate icon and then click on a box in the window to add subordinates.

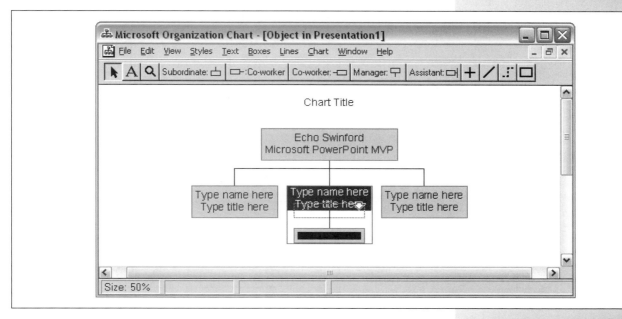

Figure 5-4. Click and drag the subordinate into the upper part of the elongated box to finish adding more lines to a box.

Add Another Head Honcho

THE ANNOYANCE: I need to add more than one boss to the top of an org chart in PowerPoint 2002, but I can't figure out how to do it.

THE FIX: In PowerPoint 97 or 2000, you'll have to use PowerPoint's AutoShapes and connectors to draw the org chart on the slide because there's no way to have two bosses in an Organization Chart 2.0 object. Or, you can create the org chart with only one boss and select Draw→Ungroup to ungroup the chart. This allows you to duplicate and move the individual pieces as necessary.

In PowerPoint 2002 and 2003, it's a bit more complicated.

To add another box to the top level in the organization chart, follow these steps:

1. Select Insert→Diagram and choose the Organization Chart icon in the Diagram Gallery dialog box (see Figure 5-5). Or, you can apply the "Title and Diagram or Organization Chart" layout from the Slide Layout task pane and double-click the placeholder on the slide to open the Diagram Gallery dialog box. You can also single-click the Diagram icon on any of the slide layouts that include "Content" (see Figure 5-6).

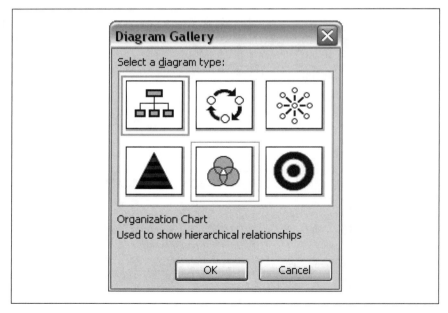

Figure 5-5. Select Insert→Diagram and choose a diagram type from the Design Gallery.

2. In the Organization Chart toolbar, select Layout→AutoLayout to turn off the AutoLayout option, which allows you to move objects in the org chart. Next, drag the box representing the boss a little to the left in the org chart. Click AutoShapes on the Drawing toolbar, select Basic Shapes, and choose Rounded Rectangle (see Figure 5-7). Then click in the organization chart and drag to draw a rectangle that matches the existing "boss box."

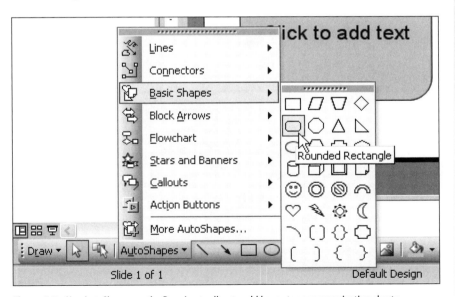

Figure 5-7. Use AutoShapes on the Drawing toolbar to add boxes to your organization charts.

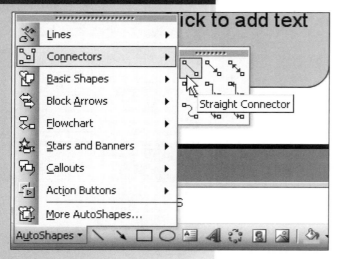

Figure 5-8. Find connectors in AutoShapes on the Drawing toolbar. Connectors latch onto other objects and stay connected to the objects even when you move things around.

3. Add a connector to connect the two boss boxes. Connectors also live on the AutoShapes toolbar (see Figure 5-8), and they travel along with their connected AutoShape, expanding and shrinking when you move the AutoShape around.

   Select the connector and then click and drag your mouse from one box to the other; when you see red on either end of the connector, it has properly "latched" itself to both boxes (see Figure 5-9). If either end of the connector is green, it is not connected to the AutoShape and will not move when you move the AutoShape.

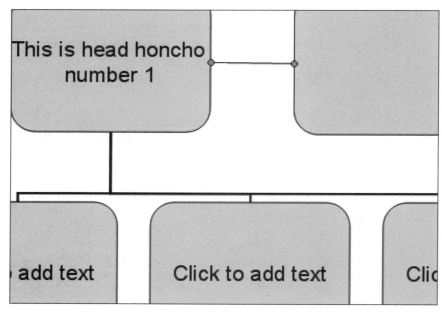

Figure 5-9. When the ends of the connector turn red, it has properly hooked to both AutoShapes.

4. Reposition any of the connectors as necessary by dragging the yellow diamond (see Figure 5-10), and watch out! If you delete a connector, its attached shape will also disappear. To hide a connector, right-click it, choose Format AutoShape, and select No Line in the Line Color area (see Figure 5-11). Add lines or connectors—or even other AutoShapes—as necessary to complete the organization chart to your satisfaction.

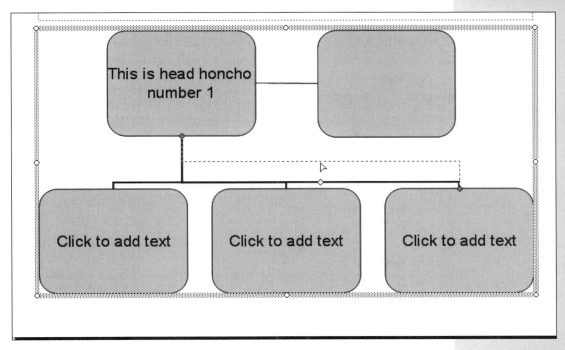

Figure 5-10. Use the yellow diamonds to change dimensions on certain AutoShapes, including connectors.

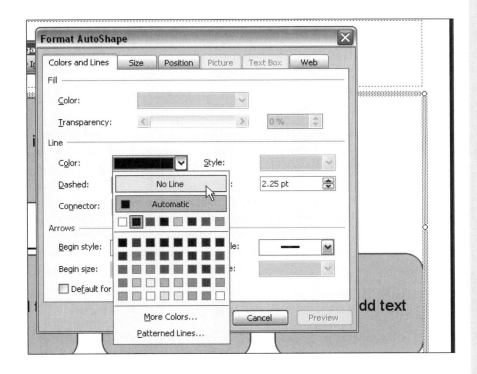

Figure 5-11. If you delete a connector in an organization chart, its associated AutoShape will disappear as well. To hide the connector, choose the "No Line" option on the Colors and Lines tab of the Format AutoShape dialog box.

Organization Chart Exceeds Limit

THE ANNOYANCE: While editing an organization chart in PowerPoint 97, I got the following error message: "Your chart would exceed the MS Organization Chart size limit (22×17 inches)." Huh?

THE FIX: Amazingly, this error message actually means what it says: you've exceeded the maximum allowable size for Organization Chart objects.

The error sometimes occurs because of the font size used in the organization chart. Try decreasing the font size in the chart to see if it resolves the error message. If not, create two smaller organization charts, place them side by side on the slide, and use PowerPoint's drawing tools to connect the two as necessary.

DIAGRAMS

Change Fonts and Other Formatting

THE ANNOYANCE: I made a Target diagram in PowerPoint 2003, and I want to change the font and colors of some of the rings, but it won't let me do anything. Aaaarrrrrgggghhhh!

THE FIX: I can't say it enough: turn off AutoLayout on the Organization Chart toolbar (select Layout→AutoLayout). You should now be able to format fonts to your heart's content using PowerPoint's typical text formatting tools.

If you turn off AutoLayout but still can't recolor objects, right-click an object in the organization chart and choose "Use AutoFormat" to toggle the AutoFormat styles off (see Figure 5-12).

AutoFormat is a kind of style gallery for diagrams. Choose AutoFormat on the Organization Chart or Diagram toolbar to apply a style to your diagram, and then right-click and select "Use AutoFormat" to toggle it off so that you can recolor the objects. When you toggle "Use AutoFormat" off, the basic style remains, and you can then make changes to it. But beware! If you apply a different AutoFormat style to your diagram after making changes to it, you *will* lose all of the customized color formatting you may have done on the objects in the previous style. You won't lose your font formatting or color changes, however.

Figure 5-12. If your fill color options appear grayed out, right-click an object in the organization chart and choose "Use AutoFormat."

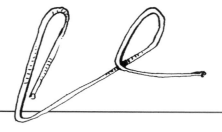

Ungroup Objects in Your Diagram

THE ANNOYANCE: I tried to ungroup my diagram in PowerPoint 2002, but the ungroup option appears grayed out.

THE FIX: You can't ungroup the new diagrams in PowerPoint 2002 and 2003, but you can create a metafile from a diagram and ungroup that. Press Ctrl+X to cut your diagram, and then delete the diagram placeholder. Next, select Edit→Paste Special, choose "Picture (Enhanced Metafile)" or "Picture (Windows Metafile)" to paste a metafile of your diagram (see Figure 5-13). Select the image and choose Draw→Ungroup. You will see a warning saying, "This is an imported picture, not a group. Do you want to convert it to a Microsoft Office drawing object?" Click the "Yes" button. With the object still selected, choose Draw→Ungroup again.

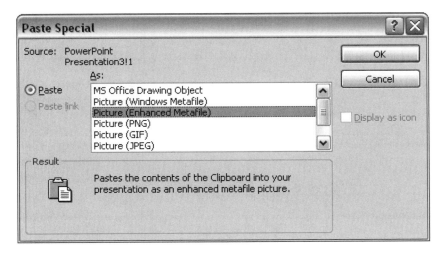

Figure 5-13. If you need to ungroup a diagram in PowerPoint 2002 or 2003, paste it onto your slide as a picture.

Ungrouping twice is necessary only in PowerPoint 2002 and 2003. Microsoft introduced the ability to select and make changes to individual graphics inside a group in these versions of PowerPoint, and this added functionality applies a second "layer" of grouping to grouped objects.

> ── **NOTE** ──
>
> *Enhanced Metafile (EMF) and Windows Metafile (WMF) are graphics formats native to Windows. The word "Metafile" signifies that the file is a vector format, but it can contain both raster and vector data (e.g., a drawn line, as well as an actual photograph). WMFs are 16-bit files, while EMFs are 32-bit files, but for most purposes either one is fine.*

Diagram Change Erases Customizations

THE ANNOYANCE: I changed my diagram from a Venn diagram to a Pyramid and I lost all my coloring changes. What'd I do wrong?

THE FIX: You didn't do anything wrong—this behavior is by design. That doesn't necessarily mean it's a *good* design.

Seriously, make sure you've decided what type of diagram you want to use before you spend a lot of time customizing it because you *will* lose your changes if you apply a different diagram type. When you apply a different diagram type from the Diagram toolbar, PowerPoint reminds you it has to turn on AutoLayout and AutoFormat (see Figure 5-14). If you click the Yes button, PowerPoint applies the default diagram style for the new diagram type, overwriting the modifications you made to the old diagram. If you don't want to lose your customization work, click No.

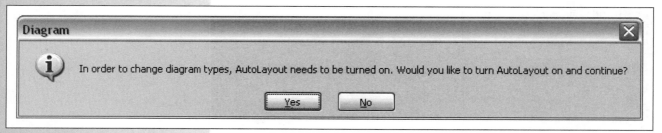

Figure 5-14. PowerPoint actually warns you that it needs to turn on AutoLayout and AutoFormat when you change diagram types.

Move Text Boxes in a Diagram

THE ANNOYANCE: I made a Venn diagram and I want to move the text boxes onto the circles themselves. PowerPoint won't let me move the text boxes.

THE FIX: Once again, turn off AutoLayout on the Diagram toolbar (select Layout→AutoLayout). If there's ever anything you can't move in a diagram, it's probably AutoLayout's fault!

Add Arrows to the Cycle Diagram

THE ANNOYANCE: The Cycle diagram icon shows arrows on it in PowerPoint 2002, but the diagram itself doesn't have arrows. How do I add arrows?

THE FIX: Select one of the wedges in the diagram. Select Draw→Change AutoShape→Block Arrows and choose the "Circular Arrow" (see Figure 5-15). Repeat for the other objects as necessary.

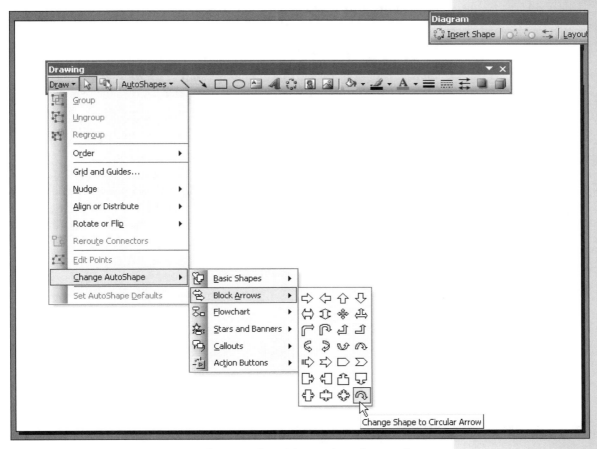

Figure 5-15. A handy but little-known tool is Change AutoShape. It lets you change from one shape to another without losing formatting such as color or line width.

OTHER DRAWING TOOLS

Connect Connectors

THE ANNOYANCE: I like the connectors on PowerPoint's AutoShape menu, but I can't always get them to connect at the right place. Any suggestions?

THE FIX: It would be nice if we could specify anchor points for connectors, but that's not possible. One workaround is to create an invisible shape and anchor to it.

First, you need to understand the anatomy of a connector. When you select a connector from the AutoShapes menu, the available anchor points show up when you move your mouse over objects on the slide (see Figure 5-16). These anchor points are automatically generated based on the object in question.

Figure 5-16. Connection points show up as little blue dots when you hover your mouse over an object while you have a connector selected in the AutoShapes menu.

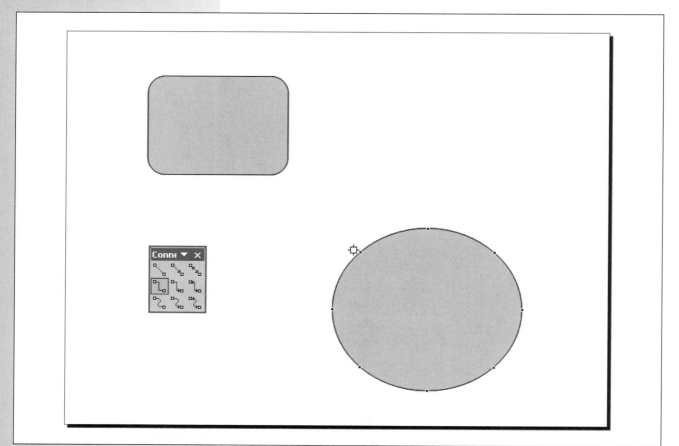

When you click on one of the blue dots, one end of the connector is anchored. Anchor the other end by clicking on another blue dot.

But what if there's no anchor point where you need it to be? One solution is to create a "dummy" AutoShape and connect to it. Move the dummy shape into place so it "connects" where you want it to on the real object (see Figure 5-17).

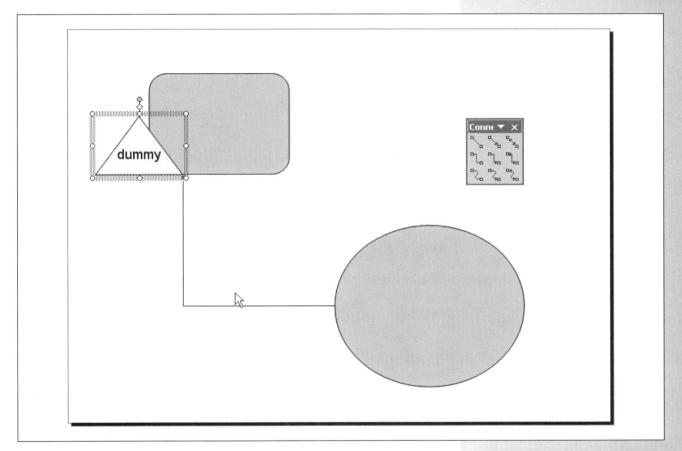

Once in place, right-click the dummy shape and choose Format AutoShape. In the Fill section, choose No Fill from the Color drop-down menu, and in the Line section, choose No Line from the Color drop-down menu (see Figure 5-18). The dummy object will be invisible, and the connector will seem as if it connects to the visible shape on the slide. To keep your connector connected, select the dummy shape and the visible shape and select Draw→Group so that the dummy shape moves with the visible shape when you move it around on the slide.

Figure 5-17. Move the dummy shape into place so it looks like the connector connects to the real object instead.

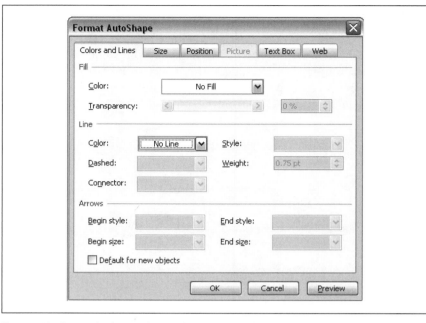

Figure 5-18. Format the dummy shape with no line and no fill to make it invisible on the slide.

Make Selected Tool "Sticky"

THE ANNOYANCE: I have to draw about a million oddball shapes on this slide, and I'm getting cramps in my hand from choosing AutoShapes→Lines→ Freeform so many times. Please tell me an easier way!

THE FIX: Any tool or menu you see with dots at the top can be dragged so it floats in your workspace (see Figure 5-19), which usually makes it *much* easier to get to. You can also dock these "tear away" menus in the same areas where you dock toolbars.

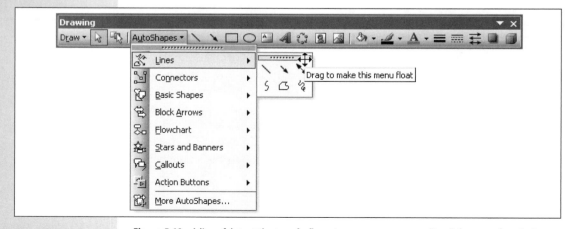

Figure 5-19. A line of dots at the top of a fly-out menu means you can "tear" the menu from its base and place it wherever is convenient.

In addition, double-clicking a tool's icon lets you use it repeatedly until you click the tool icon again or hit the Esc button on your keyboard to toggle it off.

Draw a Half-Circle

THE ANNOYANCE: How in the heck do I draw a half-circle in PowerPoint? Is there a half-circle AutoShape or something?

THE FIX: PowerPoint does have a half-circle AutoShape, but it's really hard to find. Choose "More AutoShapes" from the AutoShapes menu on the Drawing toolbar. The Clip Art task pane will open, displaying more AutoShapes to choose from. Type **chord** in the Search box at the top of the pane and click the "Go" button to perform the search. Click on the chord AutoShape (see Figure 5-20) to place it on your slide. To get rid of the shadow, select the Shadow Style button on the Drawing toolbar and click "No Shadow" (see Figure 5-21).

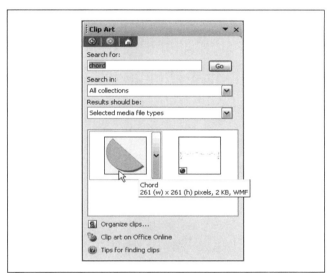

Figure 5-20. Search for "chord" in the Clip Art task pane to find PowerPoint's semicircle shape.

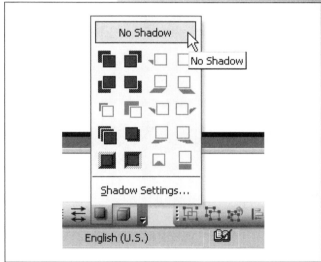

Figure 5-21. You can add or remove shadows to objects using the Shadow Style options on the Drawing toolbar.

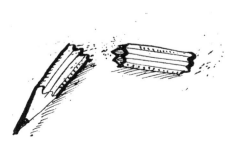

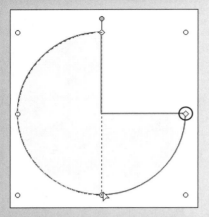

Figure 5-22. Many AutoShapes have yellow diamond handles to help you proportion the AutoShape. Just click and drag the diamond and let go when the dotted line indicates the desired shape.

Actually, you can create semicircles in PowerPoint in several different ways. One fairly easy way is to use the Pie Slice shape. On the Drawing toolbar, select AutoShapes→More AutoShapes. Scroll down the list until you see the Pie Slice, and click it to insert it on your slide.

Drag a yellow diamond handle on the pie slice shape and let go when the dotted line is in the proper position (see Figure 5-22). Turning off the shadow on the pie slice shape may help as you create the half circle.

Another slick way to create a half circle is to use the Arc AutoShape (select AutoShapes→Basic Shapes and choose the Arc icon). Hold down your Shift key as you click and drag to create a perfect quarter circle. Copy the quarter circle, paste it, and select Draw→Rotate or Flip→Flip Vertical or Flip Horizontal. Drag the flipped arc into place to form a 180° arc. Add a straight line to complete the half circle (see Figure 5-23).

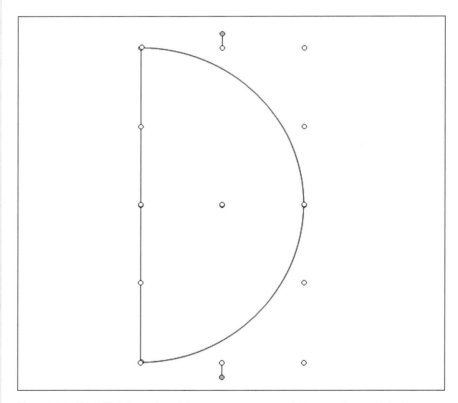

Figure 5-23. This half circle consists of three parts: two quarter-circle arcs and one straight line.

If you need to add a fill color to this half circle, select the three shapes (two quarter-circle arcs and a straight line) and choose Draw→Group. Add a fill color by clicking the Fill tool (paint bucket icon) on the Drawing toolbar. Or, you can right-click the grouped shape, choose Format Object, and add or change fill and line colors in the Colors and Lines tab of the dialog box.

Edit Points Refines Drawings

THE ANNOYANCE: I'm trying to trace my company logo to create an object shaped like the logo, but none of the line drawing tools—Curve, Freeform, or Scribble—gives me enough control. Is there a way to edit a line after I've drawn it on a slide?

THE FIX: Draw your line, right-click it, and select Edit Points to access PowerPoint's version of Bezier curves.

PowerPoint actually gives you six line tools to draw with: Line, Arrow, Double Arrow, Curve, Freeform, and Scribble. The first three are pretty straightforward to use: just select one by clicking on AutoShapes→Lines and click and drag on your slide to draw the line between a start and end point (see Figure 5-24).

NOTE

Developed by Pierre Bézier in the 1970s, Bezier curves are mathematically defined lines with end points and control points. When you drag a control handle on a Bezier curve, it changes the underlying equations, which in turn changes the shape of the curve.

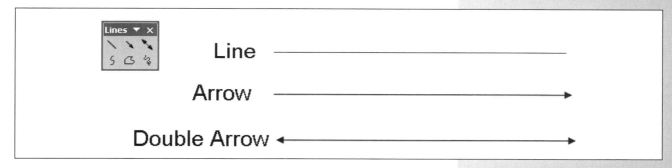

Figure 5-24. Tools to draw lines, arrows, and double-headed arrows are available on the AutoShapes menu.

To use the Curve tool, select it (AutoShapes→Lines→Curve) and click on the slide to start the line. Continue clicking at every location where the line should bend and create a point. Double-click to finish drawing your curved line. You can also create a closed shape by clicking near the line's point of origin—the end of the line will snap to the beginning point, and a closed AutoShape with a fill color will appear.

The Freeform tool (AutoShapes→Lines→Freeform) is similar to the Curve tool in that you click to begin the line; you click every time you want to change direction or add a "corner point;" and you double-click to finish the line. The difference is that the Freeform tool draws with straight line segments, while the Curve tool draws, predictably, with curves.

The Scribble tool (AutoShapes→Lines→Scribble) works a bit differently. To draw with it, hold down the mouse button while you drag on the slide. Let go of the mouse button to complete the line.

Don't worry if you have trouble drawing exactly the line or shape you want because you can right-click and choose Edit Points to refine the form after you've finished drawing it. Once you're in "Edit Points Mode," you can click one of the black points (Microsoft calls them "vertexes") and drag to reform your object (see Figure 5-25). Right-click the line itself to add or delete vertexes as necessary, or Ctrl-click a vertex to delete it. Left-clicking and dragging on the line will also add a vertex, but it's difficult to do without inadvertently changing the shape of your line. Click outside of the selected area to deactivate "Edit Points Mode."

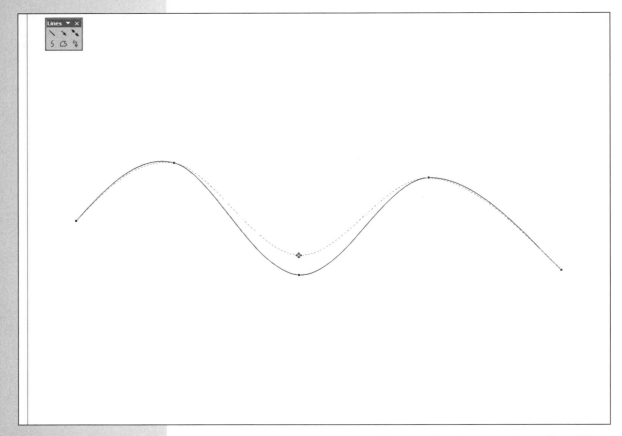

Figure 5-25. Turn on Edit Points with a right-click and then drag the points to change a line or object.

You can also right-click directly on the vertexes to change them to smooth, straight, or corner points. This activates Bézier Curves, which are represented by the blue lines and white handles you see in Figure 5-26. Click and drag the white handle at the end of a blue Bézier control to further refine your line or object.

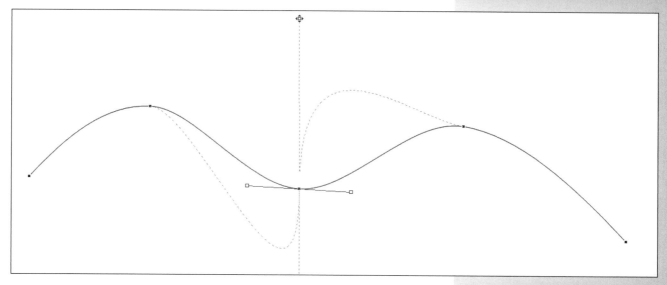

Figure 5-26. Click and drag a Bezier Curve control line to further refine your object. The further away from the object you drag, the more dramatic the change to the object.

Edit Points Not Available

THE ANNOYANCE: Okay, okay, you've convinced me that Edit Points are cool and useful. Problem is, they're grayed out on this AutoShape, so I can't use 'em. Now what?

THE FIX: You must convert the AutoShape to a "drawing object" before you can use Edit Points.

Copy or cut the AutoShape. Select Edit→Paste Special and choose "Picture (Enhanced Metafile)" or "Picture (Windows Metafile)" from the list of options. Select the picture and choose Draw→Ungroup. Click Yes when prompted with "This is an imported picture, not a group. Do you want to convert it to a Microsoft Office drawing object?" Select Draw→Ungroup one more time. Now when you right-click the object, Edit Points should be available.

Alignment Tools Are Grayed Out

THE ANNOYANCE: I'm trying to align an object on my slide, but the alignment tools are grayed out. How do I make them available again?

THE FIX: The alignment tools will be available, depending on what you've selected. Generally speaking, you need to have more than one object selected for the alignment tools to work. Think about it—if you've selected only one item, there's nothing to align your selected object *to*. The exception is if you choose "Relative to Slide" from the Align or Distribute menu (see Figure 5-27). Relative to Slide lets you position one object relative to the edges of the slide, so if it is selected, all alignment tools will be available even if you have only one object selected.

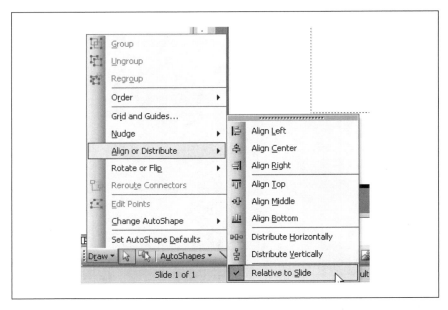

Figure 5-27. If the alignment tools are grayed out, make sure you have more than one object selected on the slide. Alternatively, elect to align just one selected object relative to the edges of the slide.

Use Alignment Tools to Distribute Objects

THE ANNOYANCE: I need to arrange some text boxes so they're evenly spaced on the slide. What's the best way to do this?

THE FIX: Select the text boxes, and then click Draw→Align or Distribute and choose Distribute Horizontally or Distribute Vertically on the Drawing toolbar. Make sure you've selected "Relative to Slide" so the text boxes are placed in relation to the slide itself (see Figure 5-28).

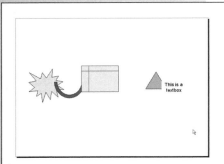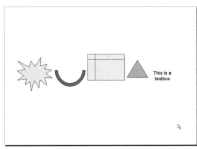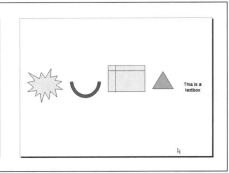

Figure 5-28. Use Distribute Horizontally and Vertically to quickly arrange objects on your slide. The image on the left shows the original slide with five objects. The middle image shows these objects distributed horizontally, and the image on the right shows the objects distributed horizontally "Relative to Slide."

If you do not use "Relative to Slide," you must select at least three objects in order for the Distribute options to be available. In this case, the objects are distributed in relation to the two objects on the outside edge.

Rotate Objects with Precision

THE ANNOYANCE: I need to rotate a shape 60 degrees clockwise. What's the easiest way for me to do this?

THE FIX: You can rotate objects in PowerPoint in a lot of ways. Probably the most precise method is to double-click the object to open the Format AutoShape dialog box and type the degrees of rotation on the Size tab (see Figure 5-29).

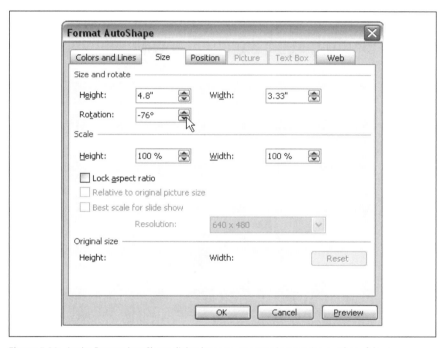

Figure 5-29. In the Format AutoShape dialog box, you can type in a precise number of degrees to rotate an object. Type positive numbers to rotate clockwise and negative numbers to rotate counterclockwise.

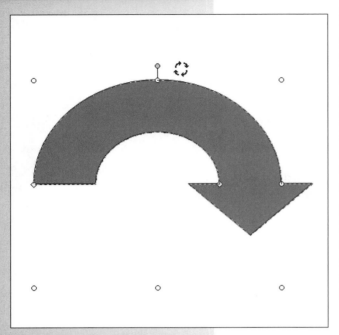

Figure 5-30. Use the green handle to rotate objects. The mouse cursor will turn into a four-headed arrow; then just drag to rotate the object.

Rotate Objects on the Fly

THE ANNOYANCE: I'm terrible at geometry, so I never know how many degrees to type in the rotation box. Can I just drag to rotate until it looks good?

THE FIX: Sure, you can simply drag the green rotation handle on an object (see Figure 5-30) to rotate it. Hold down the Shift key while dragging if you want to constrain the rotation to 15-degree increments. Hold down the Ctrl key while dragging to rotate the object around its middle, bottom point (see Figure 5-31).

If your object lacks a green handle, you can select Draw→Rotate or Flip and choose Free Rotate. The white selection handles will turn green so you can rotate the object. The Rotate or Flip tool also includes options to rotate 90 degrees (clockwise or counterclockwise) and flip (horizontally or vertically).

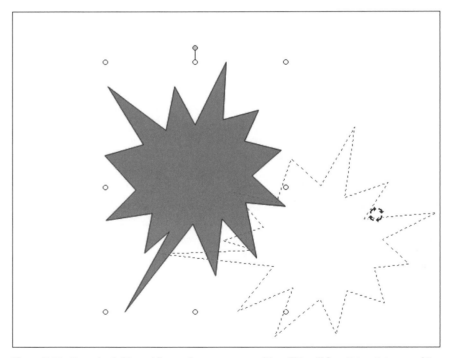

Figure 5-31. Press the Ctrl key while you drag to rotate an object. This will force it to rotate around its middle, bottom point. Otherwise, the object rotates around its center.

Format One Object in a Group

THE ANNOYANCE: I grouped a bunch of stuff, animated the group, and now I need to change the color on one line. If I ungroup everything, I'll lose all the animation. Is there anything I can do?

THE FIX: Click the group, and then click again on the specific object in the group. The typical selection handles will become filled selection handles (see Figure 5-32). When you see that type of selection handle, it means that an individual object is selected in the group, and any formatting changes you make will apply only to that object, and not to the group as a whole (see Figure 5-33). You can't resize the object (e.g., make a line longer), though.

The ability to format one object in a group was introduced in PowerPoint 2002. In PowerPoint 97 and 2000, you can't format an individual object in a group. If you ungroup so you can edit an object, you can use a third-party add-in, such as Animation Carbon or Effects Library, to reapply an animation sequence after you make your edits and regroup (see Chapter 7 for more information on these add-ins).

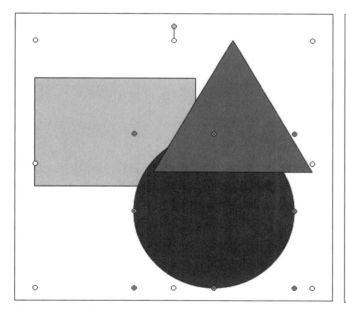

Figure 5-32. Filled selection handles indicate that an individual object is selected within objects that have been grouped.

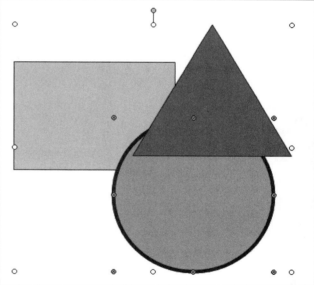

Figure 5-33. In PowerPoint 2002 and 2003, you can select just one object in a group, which allows you to apply formatting to only that object. In this picture, the fill color and line weight have been changed on the circle.

Spellcheck WordArt Objects

THE ANNOYANCE: I used some Word Art in my presentation, but when I gave the presentation, I noticed that I misspelled one of the words. Can you spellcheck WordArt objects?

THE FIX: No, spellcheck will not check WordArt (see Table 5-1).

Table 5-1. What can you spellcheck?

	Spellchecked?	Notes
WordArt	No	
Pictures	No	
OLE embedded and OLE linked objects	No	For example, data from an Excel spreadsheet pasted as an Excel workbook; a PDF inserted via Insert→Object→Create From File; Word text pasted with Edit→Paste Special→Word Document Object; etc.
Organization Chart 2.0 objects	No	Primarily an issue with PowerPoint 97 and 2000.
PowerPoint Graphs	No	
Excel Graphs	No	
Pasted Word tables	No	Generally only an issue with PowerPoint 97, which doesn't convert Word tables to PowerPoint tables by default.
Text inserted via View→ Header and Footer	No	
Text inserted on the Slide Master	Yes	
Text in PowerPoint Notes Pages	Yes	
Text in placeholders and text boxes	Yes	
Diagrams	Yes	Venn Diagrams, Pyramids, Organization Charts, etc., created in the PowerPoint 2002 and 2003 Diagram applet.
PowerPoint tables	Yes	

How do you know for sure if the type of object you're working with will be spellchecked? Open a new, blank presentation and insert or create your object and include an intentionally misspelled word. Select Tools→Spelling or press F7 and see if spellcheck catches the error. If you see the dialog box indicating "The spelling check is complete," but you've not been prompted to change or ignore the misspelled word, then the object is not included in the spellcheck.

Where Are Outlined Fonts?

THE ANNOYANCE: I want to use outlined fonts in my presentation. How do I do this?

THE FIX: You can use WordArt to create outlined text in PowerPoint, but regular PowerPoint text doesn't have an outline option. To create outlined text in WordArt, select Insert→Picture→WordArt and choose the first style in the WordArt Gallery (see Figure 5-34). Choose your font (a heavy font face, such as Impact or Arial Black, is usually a good choice), enter your text, and select the font size. Click OK to place your text on the slide.

Right-click the WordArt object and choose Format→WordArt Object (or click the Format WordArt icon on the WordArt toolbar) to change the line weight and color or add a fill color. Double-click the WordArt object or click the Edit Text button on the WordArt toolbar to change the text. Click the WordArt Same Letter Heights, Vertical Text, Alignment, or Character Spacing icon on the WordArt toolbar to make further adjustments (see Figure 5-35).

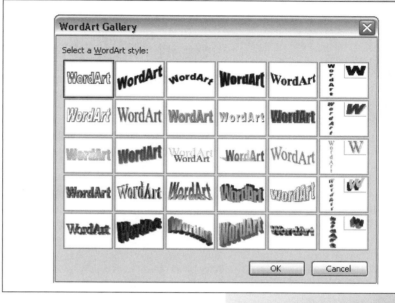

Figure 5-34. Select the first style in the WordArt Gallery to create outlined fonts.

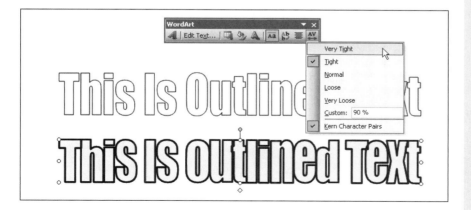

Figure 5-35. The WordArt toolbar includes tools to adjust letter height, create vertical text, change the text alignment, and fine-tune character spacing.

You can also use programs such as Adobe Illustrator to create outlined text, and then export it into PowerPoint as a *.png* file. To insert the text onto your slide, select Insert→Picture→From File. Of course, you'll need to do any subsequent text edits in the original Illustrator file and re-export and import the *.png* file as necessary.

Both of these methods are rather tedious, so you may want to reconsider using outlined text in your presentation or reserve it for small bits of text only.

Create Mirrored Text

THE ANNOYANCE: There should be a way to create mirrored text. I tried dragging the right side of the text box over the left edge, but all it did was move my text box.

THE FIX: You'll have to use WordArt to create mirrored text. Or you can copy or cut your text box, select Edit→Paste Special, and choose one of the image formats from the list. You can then drag one edge of the image over the other edge, and it will create a mirror image.

Interestingly enough, you can drag the bottom and top edges of a text box over each other to create vertically mirrored text. You only have to resort to WordArt or Paste Special for horizontally mirrored text.

Word Wrap Around an AutoShape

THE ANNOYANCE: I want to wrap my text around a diamond-shaped object. This is easy to do in Word, but I can't figure it out in PowerPoint.

THE FIX: PowerPoint doesn't have a word wrap feature like Word does (see Figure 5-36), but you can always copy the text and object in Word, and then in PowerPoint select Edit→Paste Special and choose Microsoft Office Word Document Object or one of the picture options to paste the words and shape onto your slide.

Another option is to add manual line breaks in appropriate spots to the text in PowerPoint. Press Shift+Enter to create "soft" line breaks, which moves your text to the next line but keeps it as part of the same paragraph (see Figure 5-37). This usually helps with any line spacing issues caused by using "regular" Enter.

This is a block of text, and I want to arrange an autoshape inside it. In other words, I want these words to wrap around the autoshape. Microsoft Word has this ability, and most page layout programs also have this ability.

Using Shift+Enter creates a "soft return" instead of the typical "hard return" you get when you hit just the Enter button on the keyboard.

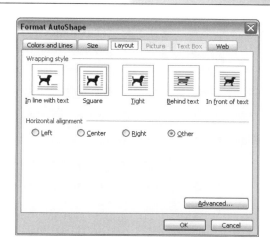

Figure 5-36. To use the Word Wrap feature in Word, right-click the object and select Format AutoShape (or Format Picture, Format Object, etc.). Set the wrapping style on the Layout tab.

This is a block of text, and I want to arrange an autoshape inside it. In other words, I want these words to wrap around the autoshape. Microsoft Word has this ability, and most page layout programs also have this ability.

Soft returns

Hard return

Using Shift+Enter creates a "soft return" instead of the typical "hard return" you get when you hit just the Enter button on the keyboard.

Figure 5-37. Press Shift+Enter to create "soft returns," also known as "soft line breaks," in most applications. PowerPoint is no exception.

Change the Color of a Shadow

THE ANNOYANCE: I know how to add a shadow to text, but how do I change the color of the shadow? I tried changing the shadow color in the slide color scheme, but it didn't help.

THE FIX: PowerPoint actually has two shadow tools: one on the Formatting toolbar near the other text formatting icons like bold, italic, and underline, and one on the Drawing toolbar next to the 3D settings.

The shadow tool on the Formatting toolbar works on text only, and it applies the shadow color automatically, based on the colors you've used for your slide background and font. This shadow is almost always black, white, or a shade of gray, although you'll occasionally see a color like steel blue. The point is that you can't control this shadow color.

If you need to control the shadow color on your object or text, use the shadow tool on the Drawing toolbar. Select the text box or object, click the Shadow Style icon on the Drawing toolbar, and choose a type of shadow from the fly-out menu (see Figure 5-38).

Figure 5-38. The type of shadow available in the Shadow Style list depends on the type of object you've selected. Only five shadow styles are available to apply to text.

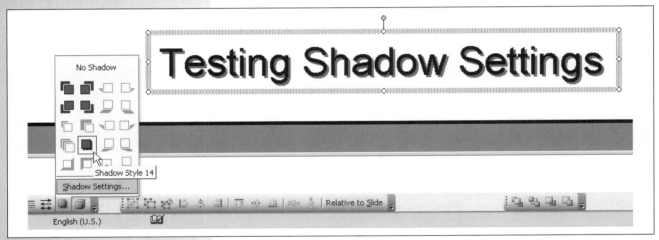

To change the color or other attributes, click Shadow Settings on the fly-out menu to open the Shadow Settings toolbar. You can use these tools to nudge the shadow closer to or farther away from the text or object, or to select different colors for the shadow (see Figure 5-39).

Figure 5-39. The Shadow Settings toolbar includes the tools to change the shadow color and to adjust the distance of the shadow from the original object.

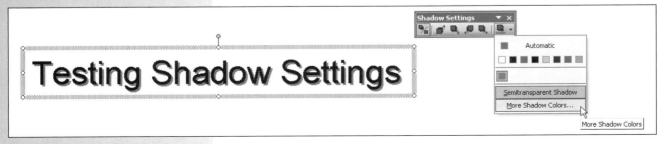

If you click the Semitransparent Shadow option and then click the More Shadow Colors option, you'll see that the shadow transparency setting has automatically been moved to 50%. In PowerPoint 2002 and 2003, you can further refine the transparency by dragging the transparency slider: move it to the right for a more transparent shadow or to the left for a more opaque (less transparent) shadow (see Figure 5-40). Click the Preview button to see how the transparency slider affects your object.

A couple of caveats: if your text box has a fill color, any shadows you apply using the Shadow Style tool on the Drawing toolbar will apply to the text box, not to the text itself. Also, the Semitransparent Shadow option does not work on text, even though you can select it and make transparency adjustments when working with Shadow Styles on a text box. If, however, the text box has a fill, the Semitransparent Shadow option will be applied to the fill.

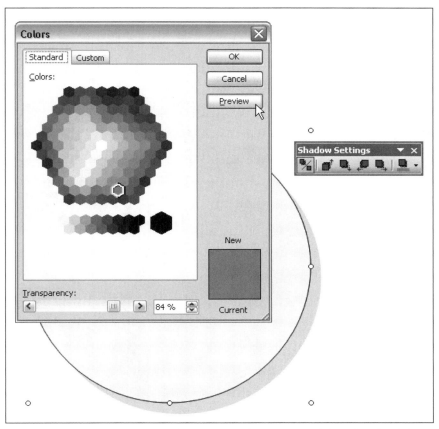

Figure 5-40. Control the transparency of a shadow with the transparency slider in the Colors dialog.

Give a Photo Soft Edges

THE ANNOYANCE: When I insert pictures onto slides, I'd like to soften the edges so they blend into the background a little. Can I do this in PowerPoint, or do I have to use an image editor?

THE FIX: One way to simulate soft edges in PowerPoint is to create rectangles with semi-transparent gradients to cover the picture's edges.

To create the semitransparent gradient, double-click the rectangle to open the Format AutoShape dialog box. On the Colors and Lines tab, choose Fill Effects from the Color drop-down menu in the Fill area. Click the Gradient tab, choose the "One color" option, and elect to follow the background color scheme (see Figure 5-41). Set the transparency to an appropriate amount, and choose the direction of the gradient. If you check the "Rotate fill effect with shape" box, you can create just one rectangle and then copy and resize it to cover the other three edges.

How successful you are with this technique often depends on your slide background and the image in question, but it will often do in a pinch.

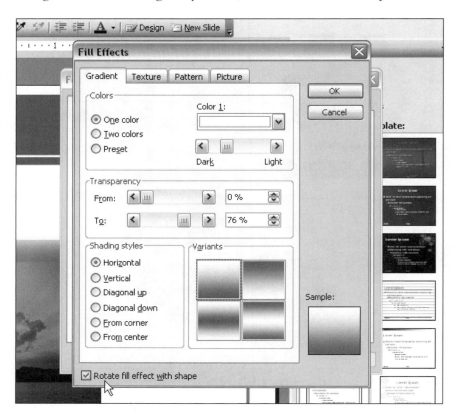

Figure 5-41. You can use rectangles filled with semitransparent gradients to soften the edges of photos.

Add a Watermark to a Slide

THE ANNOYANCE: I want to add a watermark to my slide, but I can't figure out how.

THE FIX: How you do this really depends on what you want to use for the watermark. If you need to use a picture as a watermark, insert your picture or clip art as usual. In PowerPoint 2002 and 2003, click Color on the Picture toolbar and choose Washout (see Figure 5-42). In PowerPoint 97 and 2000, click Image Control on the Picture toolbar and choose Watermark.

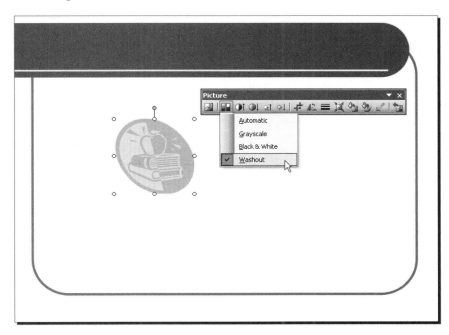

Figure 5-42. The Color tool on the Picture toolbar gives you a quick and easy method to change pictures into watermarks.

WordArt can also make good watermarks. Select Insert→WordArt, choose one of the styles in the WordArt Gallery, type your text, and click OK. Click the Format WordArt icon on the WordArt toolbar to further refine the watermark (see Figure 5-43). Here, you can change the fill color to an appropriate color or increase the transparency of the object. Drag the edge of the WordArt object to resize it, and use the yellow diamond to reshape as necessary (see Figure 5-44). Finally, you can select Draw→Order→Send to Back so the watermark is behind other objects on the slide.

Fill Text with Pictures and Other Cool Stuff

You can do a lot more with PowerPoint's drawing tools and WordArt than you may realize. One very cool technique that can spice up a presentation is using pictures as text fills.

Insert a WordArt object on your slide, and then click the Format WordArt button on the WordArt toolbar. On the Colors and Lines tab, choose Fill Effects from the Color drop-down menu in the Fill area. Click the Picture tab, click the Select Picture button, navigate to an appropriate picture, and click OK twice to close the dialog boxes. Your text will be filled with the picture. You can then use the various options on the WordArt toolbar to tweak the text size, shape, and spacing.

Microsoft PowerPoint MVP TAJ Simmons has a gallery of very slick text tricks at *http://www. presentationpictures.com/ powerpoint-wow.htm*.

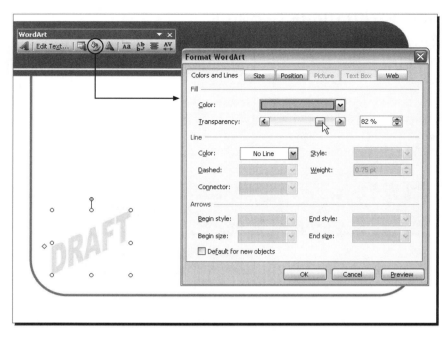

Figure 5-43. Use the options in Format WordArt to refine your WordArt object just as you would any AutoShape.

Figure 5-44. Most WordArt objects have the same yellow diamond you see with many AutoShapes. Dragging it reshapes the WordArt.

Create a 3D Object

THE ANNOYANCE: My boss wants to make a diagram that looks like a food pyramid. Any suggestions?

THE FIX: You can use PowerPoint's 3D tools to create objects such as pyramids, cubes, and cones.

To create a pyramid, for example, draw a triangle AutoShape on the slide. Then click the 3D button on the Drawing toolbar and select one of the options (see Figure 5-45). The triangle will become pyramidal, and the 3D Settings toolbar will appear. If the toolbar doesn't appear, click the 3D button and choose 3D Settings.

Use the 3D Settings toolbar to refine the look and position of your object (see Figure 5-46). The AutoShape's original fill color will determine the color of its face, and the color options at the end of the 3D Settings toolbar control the color of the 3D object's sides. The lighting intensity and direction selected on the 3D toolbar will also affect these colors somewhat.

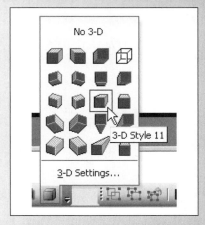

Figure 5-45. Click the 3D button on the Drawing toolbar and choose a setting.

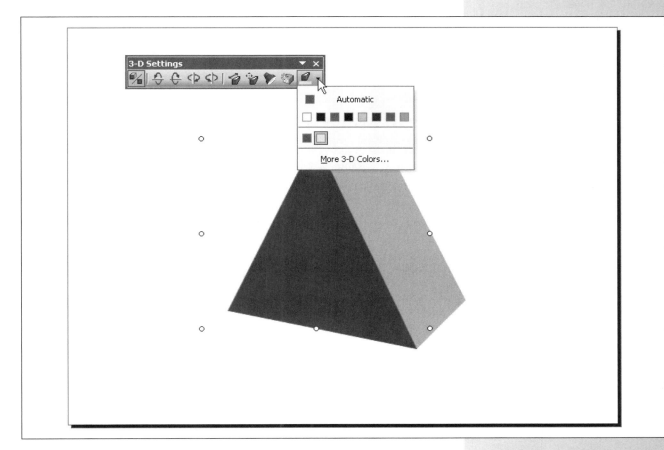

Figure 5-46. The 3D Settings toolbar lets you change the depth, lighting, color, and other characteristics of your 3D object.

Shadow Options

You can't apply both a 3D style and a Shadow style to an object. So what do you do if you need to add a shadow to a 3D object on a slide?

You could create an AutoShape—or multiple AutoShapes—that mimics your object, fill it with black or another appropriate color, and set the fill transparency to about 50% or 60%. On the Drawing toolbar, select Draw→Order→Send to Back to position the shadow behind the object. This can be tedious and time consuming, but it can be done.

Another way is to copy the object and paste it into your image-editing software. Use the tools in the software to create a shadow for the object. Save the image and select Insert→Picture→From File to reinsert it into PowerPoint.

By far, the easiest and fastest way is to use the $50 SoftShadow add-in from pptXTREME (*http://www. pptxtreme.com/softshadow. asp*). This tool installs easily and creates elegant drop shadows with the click of a button.

If you need more control when you create 3D objects for your slides, you can buy Perspector (*http://www.perspector.com/index.cfm?*), a slick, $69 3D graphics add-in for PowerPoint. In addition to making it easy for you to create your own 3D objects, Perspector has a very nice library of existing 3D objects you can use.

Fill an AutoShape with the Slide Background

THE ANNOYANCE: I used a square AutoShape to cover some text on my slide. It was fine as long as I used a background with one color, but when I switched to a gradient background, the square became obvious. (I intend to apply an entrance animation to the square to cover the text because PowerPoint 2000 doesn't have exit animations.) Is there anything I can do?

THE FIX: PowerPoint has a little known option to add a background fill to an AutoShape. However, the option is available only when you select Format→AutoShape or right-click the AutoShape and choose Format AutoShape. If you click the Fill Color icon on the Drawing toolbar, you will not see the background fill option. Go figure.

Applying a background fill to an AutoShape lets it disappear against the slide background. It works extremely well with gradients, and it's also useful with picture backgrounds in PowerPoint 2002 and 2003.

Save Drawings for Later

THE ANNOYANCE: I made this really cool drawing on my slide. How can I save it so I can use it later?

THE FIX: Select the objects that make up the drawing, right-click, and choose Save as Picture. PowerPoint will automatically opt to save the picture in the "Sample Pictures" folder on your hard drive (generally located under My Documents→My Pictures→Sample Pictures). If you want to edit the drawing later, choose *.emf* for *.wmf* in the Save as Picture dialog box. (You can ungroup *.emf* and *.wmf* files on your slides.)

If you want to save so you can, for example, use your drawing as a fill for WordArt text (see the sidebar, "Fill Text with Pictures and Other Cool Stuff"), choose one of the following image formats: *.png*, *.jpg*, *.tif*, *.gif*, or *.bmp*.

Whichever way you decide to save the drawing, you can later add it to a slide using Insert→Picture→From File.

Make Overlapping Pieces Transparent

THE ANNOYANCE: I've drawn a bunch of circles to simulate a Venn diagram in PowerPoint 2000, but the areas where they all overlap aren't the right colors. How can I make my Venn diagram look better?

THE FIX: True transparency for objects isn't available in PowerPoint 97 or 2000. Although you can check the semitransparent box in the More Colors dialog box (see Figure 5-47), this selection does not give you any control over the amount of transparency, and it does not blend colors in semitransparent objects.

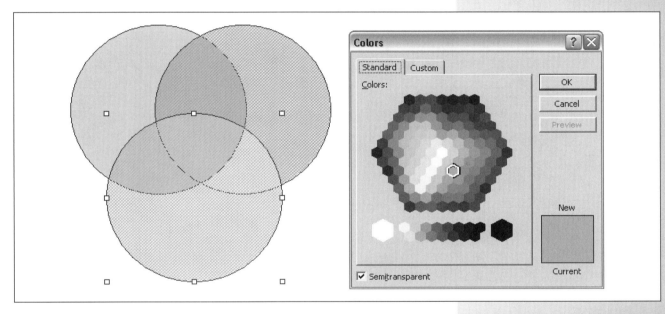

For true transparency, create the transparent or semitransparent objects in an image editing program (see Chapter 4 for a list of image editors), or upgrade to PowerPoint 2002 or 2003, which has a transparency slider in its various More Colors dialog boxes (see Figure 5-40). These versions of PowerPoint also offer decent semitransparent Venn diagrams in the Diagram Gallery.

Figure 5-47. PowerPoint 97 and 2000 have a semitransparent color option, but it's an all-or-nothing choice with no way to control the level of transparency.

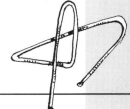

Charts and Graphs

If you use PowerPoint for any length of time, sooner or later you'll come face to face with Microsoft Graph, PowerPoint's charting engine. Microsoft Graph is a scaled-down subset of Excel that charts based on data in a datasheet. Graph does not do calculations, nor can it handle formulas. It just charts the data as is. If you need something more robust, you can always create your charts in Excel and import those charts into your presentation.

This chapter tackles some of the more annoying issues you may run into when working with charts in PowerPoint, whether they're created in Microsoft Graph or Excel. We'll deal with some of the bizarre text and formatting issues Microsoft's graphing programs bring your way. You'll also learn how to resize your charts without distorting the fonts, create user-defined charts, and solve other tricky issues.

TEXT ISSUES

Y-Axis Titles Truncated

THE ANNOYANCE: The last letter of my Y-axis title text is cut off. I tried making the font smaller, but it didn't help. How can I make PowerPoint show the whole title?

THE FIX: Unfortunately, you can't resize the Y-axis title box on the chart. You can, however, replace the Y-axis title with a regular text box.

You can also try adding two spaces followed by a period to the Y-axis title box to extend it. Format the period as the background color so it won't print.

This is a sporadic issue possibly related to video drivers and display settings. The truncated Y-axis title on the chart will usually print fine, even if it doesn't display properly.

Control Axis Label Line Breaks

THE ANNOYANCE: I have some really long category descriptions on my X-axis, but the lines break in strange places. How can I control the line breaks on chart axes?

THE FIX: You'll have to add regular text boxes if you need to control line breaks on chart axis labels in MSGraph.

If you create the chart in Excel, you can press Alt+Enter to add line breaks to text in a cell. You can also input the axis text in Excel, using Alt+Enter to create the line breaks, and then copy the cell and paste it into the PowerPoint graph datasheet.

Unfortunately, pressing Alt+Enter in MSGraph in PowerPoint 97, 2000, 2002, or 2003 does not create line breaks on chart axis labels. (If you remember doing this in PowerPoint graphs, you were using PowerPoint 95!) You can, however, use Alt+Enter or Shift+Enter to create line breaks on chart and axis *titles* and data labels in all versions of PowerPoint and MSGraph.

Axis Labels Missing

THE ANNOYANCE: My chart only shows every other X-axis label. What happened to the other labels?

THE FIX: Microsoft Graph tries to maintain the default font size settings on your chart and must hide some of the axis labels (see Figure 6-1). To resolve this issue, decrease the size of the font on the X-axis or increase the size of the plot area on the chart.

To increase the size of the plot area, simply click to select the plot area on the slide and drag. If you have a hard time selecting the plot area of the chart—which often seems to be especially difficult in pie charts—select Plot Area from the Chart Objects drop-down menu on the Standard toolbar.

To decrease the size of the font, select the axis, choose Format→ Selected Axis, and click the Font tab. Select a smaller font size and uncheck the "Auto scale" box (see Figure 6-2). Some fonts work better than others at small sizes, so experiment.

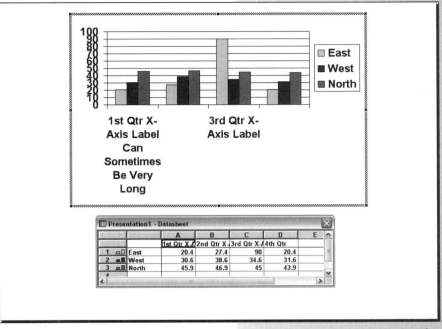

Figure 6-1. Is your chart missing some of its X-axis labels? Increase the plot area of the chart or decrease the font size.

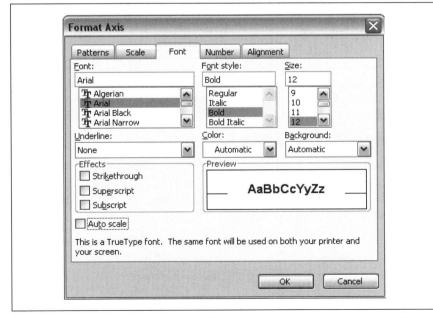

Figure 6-2. To open this dialog box and adjust the font, choose Format→Selected Axis and click the Font tab, or double-click the axis.

Align Axis Labels

THE ANNOYANCE: Is it possible to right-align the axis labels on my horizontal bar chart?

THE FIX: You'll have to create regular text boxes and put the axis label text in them. Unfortunately, neither MSGraph nor Excel offers any way to set the right or left justification of axis label text. You can select a chart or axis title and justify it, but the justification will show up only in titles longer than one line (see Figure 6-3).

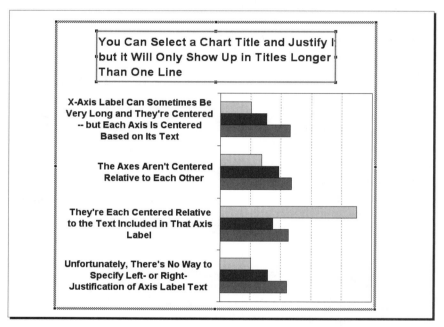

Figure 6-3. To align axis titles and chart titles in a chart, select the title box and click the appropriate justification icon on the toolbar. Selecting the text itself will make the justification tools unavailable.

Fonts Appear Distorted I

THE ANNOYANCE: When I create a PowerPoint chart, the fonts become distorted after I click on the slide to deactivate the chart. I checked the aspect ratio of the chart by right-clicking it and choosing Format Object—and it's set to 100% × 100%. So what's the problem?

THE FIX: You're using a wide-screen display (such as 1280×800), aren't you? You'll need to update the video drivers or set the screen display to a non–wide-screen format (e.g., 1024×768, 1280×1024, etc.).

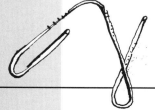

Fonts Appear Distorted II

THE ANNOYANCE: I'm not using a wide-screen display, but the text in my chart is all out of whack. It looks like it's been stretched or something.

THE FIX: Always resize your chart by dragging the herringbone borders while the chart is activated (see Figure 6-4). If you click on the slide to deactivate the chart, and then click on the chart and drag one of the edges to resize, everything gets squished and stretched relative to the original proportion of the graph. If you adjust the size while the chart is activated, the fonts on the chart will maintain their proportion.

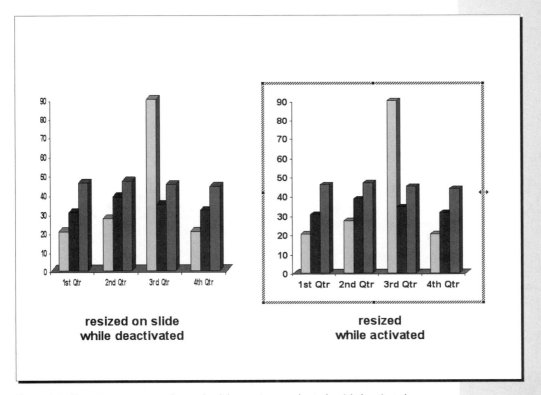

resized on slide
while deactivated

resized
while activated

Figure 6-4. If you drag a corner or edge on the slide to resize your chart when it's deactivated, the text will look distorted (left). If you resize your chart using the herringboned borders when it's activated (right), the text will look normal.

If your chart proves especially difficult to fix, right-click the chart on the slide and choose Format Object. On the Size tab, uncheck the "Lock aspect ratio" box and set the height and width both to 100%, which fixes the font distortion (see Figure 6-5). If you need to make the chart smaller or larger after resizing it to 100% × 100%, double-click to activate the chart and drag the herringboned borders to adjust it. When you finish and click on the slide to deactivate the chart, the chart will be set to a new 100% × 100% size, and the fonts will not be distorted.

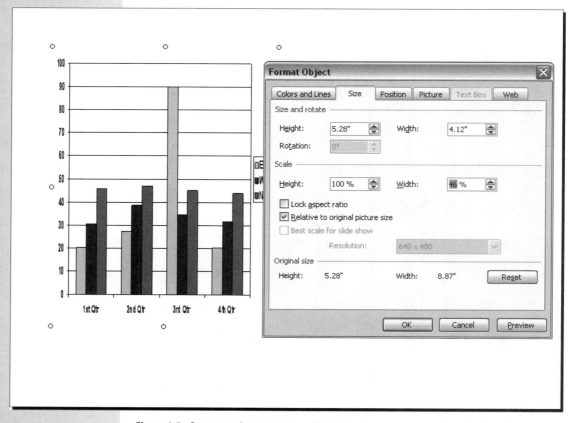

Figure 6-5. Reset your chart to 100% × 100% as the first step to deal with especially distorted text. Don't click the Reset button—it doesn't always reset the chart the way you expect. Double-click to activate the chart and drag the herringboned handles to readjust the size without distorting the fonts.

Keep Chart Font Sizes the Same

THE ANNOYANCE: Our corporate template specifies Arial 14-pt Bold on all charts and graphs, but when I look at the slides, all the font sizes look different. What did I do wrong?

THE FIX: You need to select the chart, choose Format→Font, and uncheck the "Auto scale" box (see Figure 6-2). If you leave Auto scale on, the fonts in charts will resize when you resize the chart by clicking and dragging on an edge (see Figure 6-6). This is why your chart font sizes are not the same throughout your presentation—they're resizing when you resize your charts.

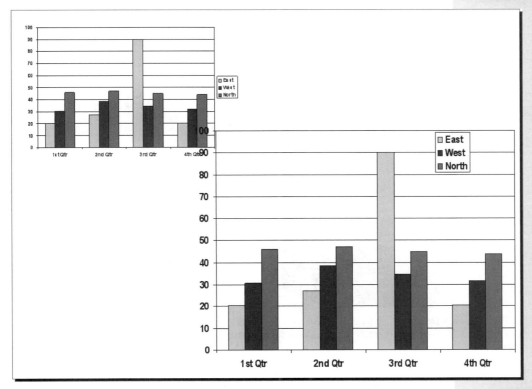

Figure 6-6. If you leave Auto scale on, the font will resize when you resize the chart. You can see this effect here—the smaller chart in the upper left has a much smaller font than the larger chart on the right. Interestingly, because the smaller chart was resized by dragging the edge of the deactivated chart on the slide, its font size is 14 point, the same as the font size listed in the larger chart. Obviously, that's not really the case.

Resizing a chart with Auto scale turned on often causes strange font sizes (e.g., 15.75, 28.25 pt, etc.), and these can cause problems for some printers. Turn off Auto scale, and your font size will remain the size you specified in the Font tab, even when you resize the chart.

Pie Charts Appear Jagged

THE ANNOYANCE: My pie charts look horrid! They're all jagged. I can't present these! What do I do?

THE FIX: Nothing totally resolves this issue, as it's difficult to render smooth arcs on a computer display consisting of square pixels. Nevertheless, you can do a few things to make the pies look a bit better.

1. Remove the border on the pie pieces.

   Double-click the chart to activate it, right-click a pie piece, and select Format Data Series. On the Patterns tab, choose None for the Border (see Figure 6-7). Repeat for additional pie pieces as necessary.

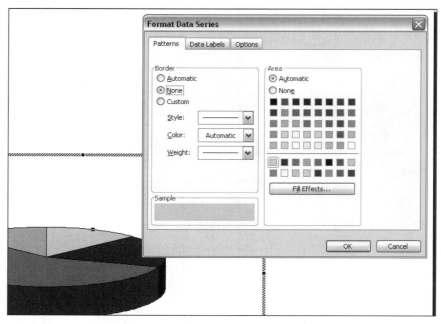

Figure 6-7. Click a data point in a chart to select the data series. Choose Format→Selected Data Series, and make fill and line color and style adjustments on the Patterns tab.

2. Increase the angle of the pie.

Double-click the chart to activate it, and select Chart→3D View. Click the arrows or type a new value in the Elevation box (see Figure 6-8), and click the Apply button to preview the change. Click OK to close the dialog box.

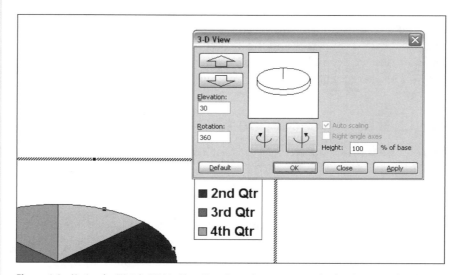

Figure 6-8. Notice the "Height XX % of base" setting, where you can make the pie more or less thick. The Rotation setting specifies where the first pie slice starts.

3. Draw an oval over the outside edges of the pie.

In PowerPoint 2002 and 2003, select Draw→Grid and Guides and uncheck Snap to Grid (Draw→Snap→to Grid in PowerPoint 97 and 2000). Select an oval from the Drawing toolbar and drag to draw it on top of the chart on the slide. Drag the white handles to adjust the oval, and set the line color and thickness using the line color and style buttons on the Drawing toolbar.

Copy the oval and select Draw→Order→Send to Back to create the bottom oval. Use your mouse and the arrows on your keyboard to nudge it into place (see Figure 6-9).

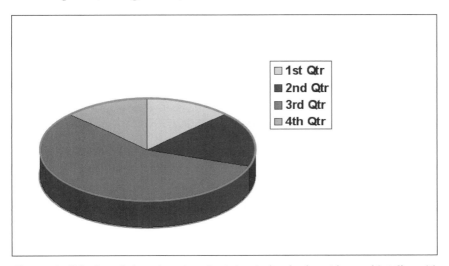

Figure 6-9. If they're entirely too jagged, mask existing pie chart borders with an oval AutoShape. It's easier to add these on the slide, because you can use the arrows on your keyboard to nudge the oval into place. The ovals in this picture are thick so you can see them more easily.

4. Remove Gradient Fills.

2D pie charts will sometimes become jagged when a gradient fill is applied. Changing back to a solid color fill will often resolve it.

5. Change Print Options.

If the pie chart prints jagged edges, select Tools→Options, click the Print tab, and check the "Print objects at printer resolution" box.

Fonts Appear Jagged

THE ANNOYANCE: The fonts in this presentation are the scruffiest, jaggediest, most raggedy things I've ever seen. I thought PowerPoint was a *presentation* package. These fonts sure present badly.

THE FIX: There's no good resolution for this problem. It seems worst on animated text, so if your text is animated, remove the animation.

If that isn't an option, right-click the text box, choose Save as Picture, and save the text as a *.png* file. Select Insert→Picture→From File, insert the *.png* file of the text, and animate it. Of course, delete or move your text box off the edge of the slide where it won't show in the presentation.

The ragged edges are usually also worse in presentations with dark text on light backgrounds. If you have the luxury of changing your presentation to light text on a dark background, the text may not look as jagged.

Some fonts are also worse about the jaggies than others. Changing to a basic font like Arial may help.

Change the Datasheet Font

THE ANNOYANCE: I'd really like to change the font in the chart datasheet so I can see more text while I'm typing.

THE FIX: You can change all the type in the datasheet. Select View→Datasheet to open the datasheet, click a cell in the datasheet, and select Format→Font. Change any of the attributes in the Font dialog box.

This is an all-or-nothing setting; you can't change the text on just one cell (or row or column) in the datasheet, so don't waste your time trying.

Font Changes on a Pasted Excel Chart

THE ANNOYANCE: I pasted a chart onto my slide, and the font changed to Times New Roman! I hate TNR—help me get rid of it!

THE FIX: This sometimes happens in PowerPoint 2000 when you paste an Excel chart or cells using a font smaller than 8 points onto your slide. Increasing the size of the font in Excel resolves the issue, as does applying Service Release 1/1a (SR-1/SR-1a) for Office 2000 (*http://support.microsoft. com/kb/245025/EN-US/*).

This also happens occasionally when you print. To fix it, choose Tools→ Options, click the Print tab, and check the "Print inserted objects at Printer Resolution" box.

Default Chart Font Is Wrong

THE ANNOYANCE: I created a new default chart style, but when I insert new charts onto my slide, the font still looks wrong. Any ideas?

THE FIX: Select Tools→Options, click the Edit tab, and uncheck the "New charts take on PowerPoint font" box. This should force the font to show up in the chart's default font face rather than the font you're using in the PowerPoint file itself.

CREATING AND FORMATTING CHARTS

Use Dates on the X-Axis

THE ANNOYANCE: I want the X-axis of my chart to be a bunch of dates. What do I do?

THE FIX: Right-click the X-axis and choose Format Axis. Click the Number tab, and choose Date in the Category list (see Figure 6-10). If you don't see the date style you want in the Type list, choose Custom in the Category list and create what you need. For example, to display your dates as Friday, August 30, 2002, select Custom and input **dddd, mmmm d, yyyy** in the Type area.

If, for some reason, the date in your chart does not show up properly even after you've selected the date format on the Number tab, select Chart→ Chart Options, click the Axes tab, and choose the Category or Time-scale option under Category (X) axis (see Figure 6-11).

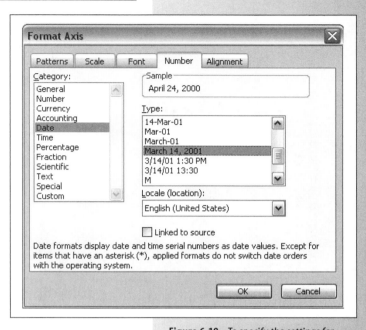

Figure 6-10. To specify the settings for numbers on your chart, choose from a variety of categories on the left: percentages, time, date, number (where you can set the number of decimal points), etc., and make category-specific adjustments on the right.

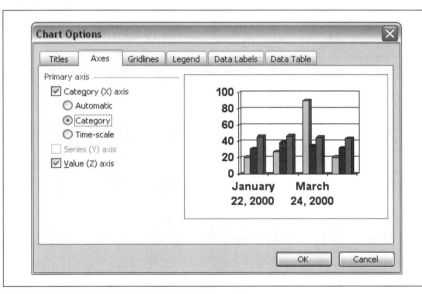

Figure 6-11. Occasionally your axis won't behave correctly even after you've formatted the numbers. In that case, select Chart→Chart Options and choose either the Category or Time-scale option on the Axes tab.

Create a Combination Chart

THE ANNOYANCE: I need to make a combination column and line chart. That is, I need to have a column chart, but I want one of the data series to be a line. I can't find this kind of chart in the available choices. Did I just miss it?

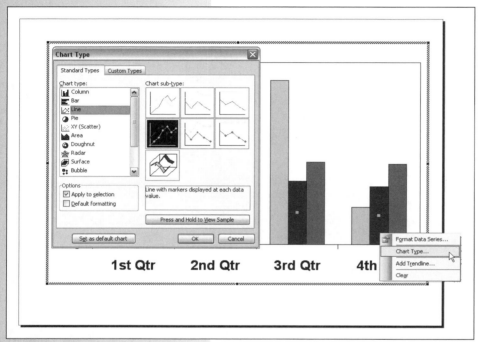

THE FIX: To create a combination column-line chart in PowerPoint, create a column chart using all your data series. Right-click the "line" series and choose Chart Type (see Figure 6-12). Select a line chart from the dialog box, make sure the "Apply to selection" box is checked, and click OK; the data series will become a line (see Figure 6-13).

The possible combinations depend on the types of charts with which you're working. For example, you can't combine many 3D charts with each other, and you also can't combine 2D and 3D charts.

Figure 6-12. To create a combination column-line chart, right-click a column data series, choose Chart Type, and select a line chart type from the list on the left.

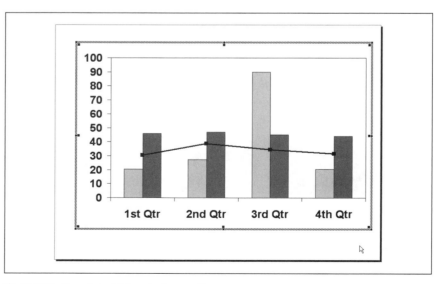

Figure 6-13. The selected data series is now a line.

Create a Secondary Axis

THE ANNOYANCE: I have a bunch of wildly disparate data I'd like to plot on two different axes, but I can't figure out how to add another axis and tie some of the data to it.

THE FIX: Right-click a data series, choose Format Data Series, click the Axis tab, and choose the Secondary axis option (see Figure 6-14). Repeat for any other data series you want to tie to the secondary axis.

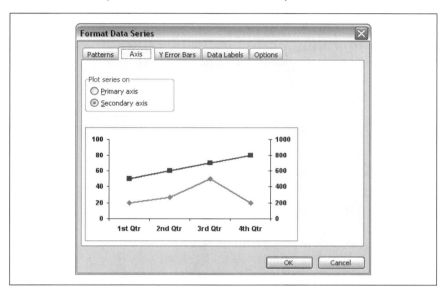

Figure 6-14. Choose the Secondary axis option to plot data on a secondary axis.

Add Error Bars to Data Points

THE ANNOYANCE: I need to add error bars to all the points on my data series, but the values are different for each point. Do I have to draw these in manually? This will not only be incredibly tedious, but also very inaccurate. Is there a better way?

THE FIX: You can either create your chart in Excel, where you can input a range of values for your error bars, or you can use the Stock chart type in PowerPoint. It's best to use Excel for these charts, as Excel offers much more flexibility than the Stock chart type in PowerPoint.

To add error bars in Excel, create your chart, right-click a data series, and choose Format Data Series. On the Y Error Bars tab, click the "Custom +" button (see Figure 6-15). Click and drag on the spreadsheet to select the

Figure 6-15. In Excel, you can add a range of values for custom error bars. PowerPoint does not have this option. Simply click the button to the right of "Custom +" or "Custom –" to add values for the error bars.

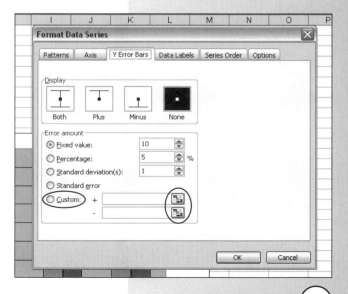

range of data representing the positive side of the error bars for the series—the data will be added to the "Custom +" area of the dialog box. Click the button on the right (see Figure 6-16) to expand the dialog box and repeat the process for the "Custom –" values. If the positive and negative error bar values are the same, you can input the same data range.

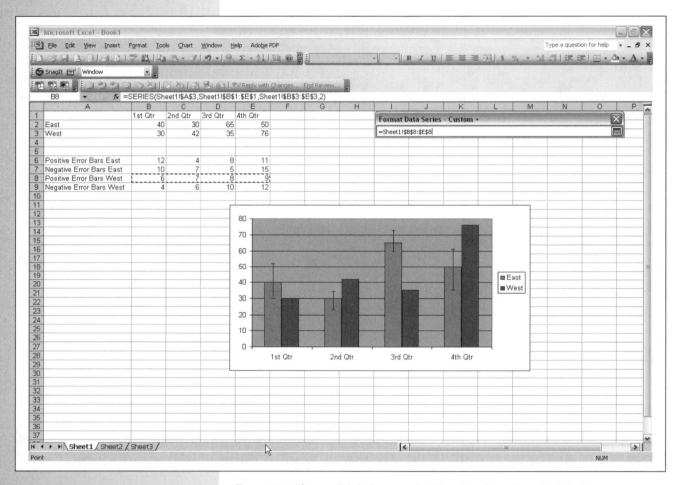

Figure 6-16. After you click the button on the Y Error Bar tab to collapse the dialog box so you can select data, your screen will look something like this. Click and drag across the data range on the spreadsheet; it will be added automatically to the custom range area. Click the Select button to expand the dialog box.

To format the error bars, right-click one (which selects all error bars in the series) and choose Format Error Bars. Change the marker, line weight, color, and style on the Patterns tab.

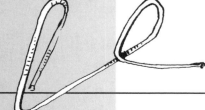

To manipulate the Stock chart type in PowerPoint to display error bars, use the following steps:

1. Create a chart based on the Stock Chart Type.

   Select Insert→Chart, and with the chart activated, choose Chart→ Chart Type, choose Stock (High-Low-Close) from the list, and click OK (see Figure 6-17). You will start with this chart based on PowerPoint's default dummy data.

   Select View→Datasheet and change the dummy data to your actual data. East represents the high point of the error bar, West represents the low point of the error bar, and North represents the data point itself (see Figure 6-18).

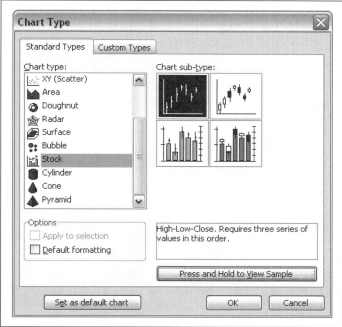

Figure 6-17. Start with a Stock chart to add individual error bars in PowerPoint.

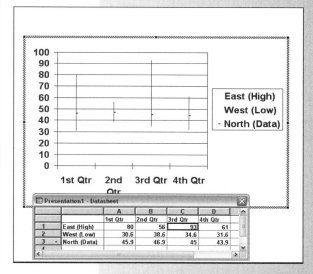

Figure 6-18. Replace dummy data with your own data. In a High-Low-Close Stock chart, the first data series represents the top point of the high-low lines, and the second data series represents the bottom point. The third data series is the actual data point.

3. Format the North (Data) points into columns.

   Right-click the little dash representing the North (Data) series and choose Chart Type. Select Column from the Chart Type list, make sure the "Apply to selection" box is checked, and click OK (see Figure 6-12).

4. Format the error bars.

Right-click one of the high-low lines, choose Format High-Low lines, and change the line style, weight, and color as desired. Note that high-low lines don't have the "T" caps. If you need your error bars to have caps, you'll need to create the chart in Excel.

Create an Axis Break

THE ANNOYANCE: I can't add a break to the Y-axis labels. Since the values of my data are so different, I need to show 0 to 25, a break, and then 80 to 100. Any suggestions?

THE FIX: Honestly, it's easiest to just draw a couple of hash marks to represent a break on the Y-axis. You can add AutoShapes to create breaks for the columns, too, if you wish.

Neither Excel nor PowerPoint includes a "break-axis" option, although Microsoft Excel MVPs Tushar Mehta (*http://www.tushar-mehta.com/ excel/newsgroups/broken_y_axis/tutorial/index.html*), Jon Peltier (*http:// peltiertech.com/Excel/Charts/BrokenYAxis.html*), and Andy Pope (*http:// www.andypope.info/charts/brokencolumn.htm*) have all posted techniques for displaying broken axes.

Use the following steps to create a chart with a broken Y-axis in PowerPoint:

1. Make a copy of your chart.

Because this technique requires changing the data in your datasheet, you'll want to keep a copy of your actual chart in case you need to revisit the data later. Select the chart on the slide, press Ctrl+C to copy it, and press Ctrl+V to paste it. Right-click the copy, choose Format Object, click the Size tab, and set the scale to 5%×5%. Drag this off the edge of the slide where it won't show during a presentation.

2. Change the data.

Change the uppermost data value so it's closer to the smaller data values. You'll replace the upper Y-axis numbers later (see Figure 6-19). Select View→Datasheet to open the datasheet if it's not already open.

3. Change the axis scale.

Right-click the Y axis, choose Format Axis, click the Scale tab, and change the maximum value to something lower than it was, but still high enough to exceed your largest data point (see Figure 6-20).

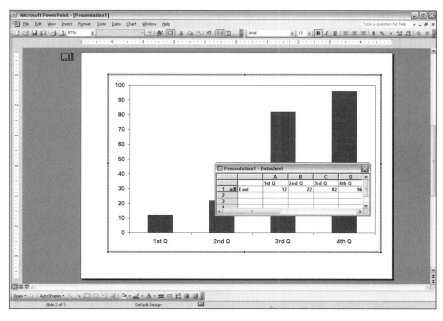

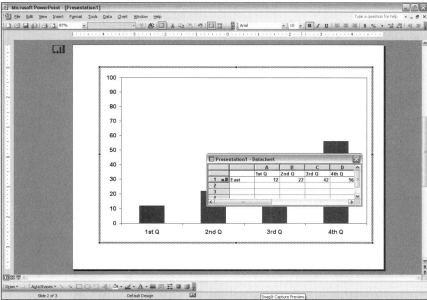

Figure 6-19. The original data and chart is shown in the top screenshot. In the bottom screenshot, we subtracted 40 from each of the large data points to make them closer to the smaller data point.

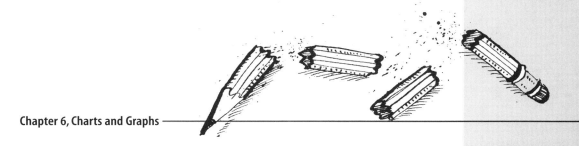

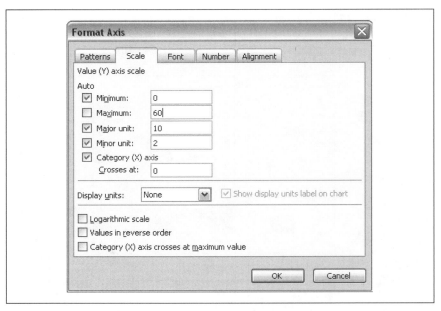

Figure 6-20. After changing the data, the largest point is 56. Thus, 60 is a good point to use for the Y-axis scale maximum.

4. Draw the axis break.

Click the slide to deactivate the chart, select AutoShapes→Basic Shapes→Parallelogram, and draw a parallelogram on the slide. Size and rotate it appropriately along the Y-axis. Draw a line on the top edge of the parallelogram, copy it, and position it at the bottom edge of the parallelogram (see Figure 6-21).

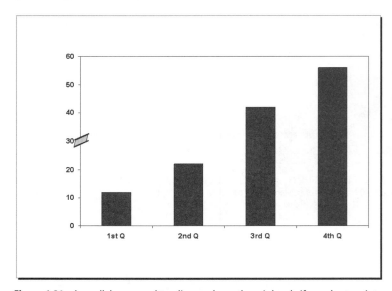

Figure 6-21. A parallelogram and two lines make up the axis break. If you plan to print the chart, check the black and white settings to make sure the "break" objects will print the way you want.

Double-click the parallelogram, and on the Colors and Lines tab, choose Background from the Color drop-down menu in the Fill area. Next, choose No Line from the Color drop-down menu in the Line area and click OK to exit the dialog. Select the parallelogram and the two lines and choose Draw→Group to group the three items.

5. Add new Y-axis labels.

    Create text boxes on your slide to represent the old Y-axis values. Select Draw→ Align or Distribute→Align Right to align the labels (see Figure 6-22).

6. Remove existing Y-axis labels.

    Right-click the chart and choose Chart Object→Edit to activate it. Click the Y-axis, choose Format→Selected Axis, and click the Patterns tab. Remove the Y-axis labels by selecting None in the "Tick mark labels" section (see Figure 6-23).

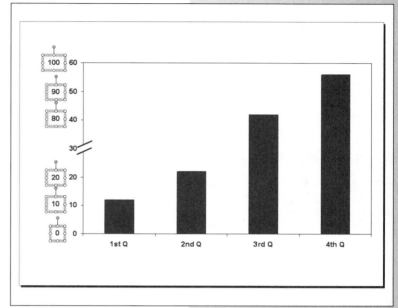

Figure 6-22. Add new Y-axis values in text boxes on the slide. Press the arrows on your keyboard to nudge them, and choose Draw→Align or Distribute to align them.

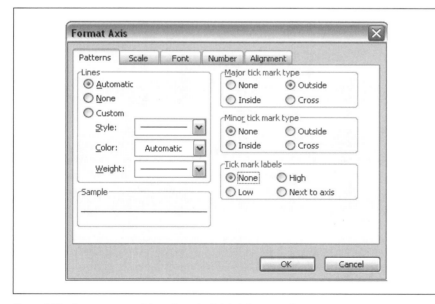

Figure 6-23. You can remove tick marks and axis labels from an axis.

7. Make final adjustments.

Click outside the chart to deactivate it. If you wish, add parallelograms to "break" the tall columns (see Figure 6-24). Adjust the placement of the axis-label text boxes and axis break lines as necessary.

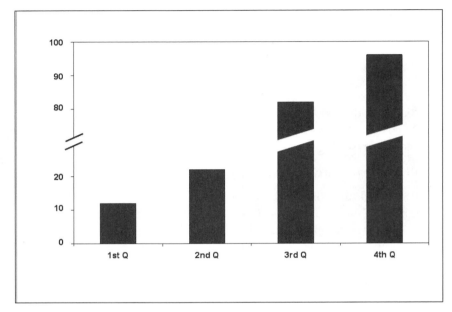

Figure 6-24. This is the final chart showing the axis break. Parallelograms were also added on top of the columns to more clearly represent the break in the data.

Get Rid of Chart Junk

As much as Edward Tufte frustrates me with his whole "Cognitive Style of PowerPoint" invective, he's still the godfather of displaying data. Take his advice and eliminate the extraneous clutter on your charts wherever you can: tick marks, axis labels coupled with data point labels, unreadable fonts, etc. And include a reference for the data on the slide.

Remove Percent Markers from Y-Axis

THE ANNOYANCE: Our corporate style specifies that we use the word "Percent" in the Y-axis title and not put "%" on the Y-axis label numbers. That's fine, but all the charts I receive are already plotted as percentages. Is there an easy way around this?

THE FIX: There's no perfect way around this issue. The best way is probably to copy the data into Excel, multiply by 100, and paste it back into the PowerPoint datasheet. Of course, you must select Format→Number to change the data's number format to "number" or "general" instead of "percentage."

You can also remove the Y-axis labels. Select Format→Selected Axis, click the Patterns tab, choose None in the "Tick mark labels" section (see Figure 6-23), and then add text boxes with just the numbers.

Or you can draw a rectangle to cover the existing axis labels, select Format→AutoShape, click the Colors and Lines tab, and choose Background from the Color drop-down menu. Next, choose No Line from the Color drop-down menu in the Line area to make the cover blend into the background. Finally, add text boxes with the new axis labels.

Add Percent Markers to the Y-Axis

THE ANNOYANCE: Can I add a % symbol to the Y-axis labels without having to redo all the data? My chart looks almost exactly the way I want it to right now, and I'd really rather not have to reformat it.

THE FIX: Activate the chart, right-click the Y-axis and choose Format Axis. Click the Number tab, choose Custom from the Category list, and enter **0.0"%"** in the Type box. The quotation marks tell MSGraph to add the percent sign as a text character without replotting the values as percents (see Figure 6-25).

Reverse Order of Categories

THE ANNOYANCE: My chart is plotted backward! How can I change the order?

THE FIX: Activate the chart, select the category axis, choose Format→Selected Axis, click the Scale tab, and check the "Categories in reverse order" box (see Figure 6-26).

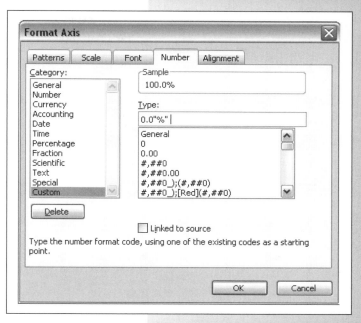

Figure 6-25. You can add text to the numbers on your value axis by enclosing the text in quotation marks.

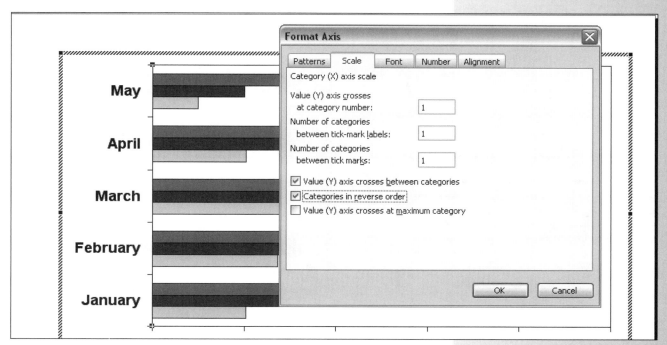

Figure 6-26. Check the "Categories in reverse order" box to reverse the plot order of categories.

Insert Picture Fills

THE ANNOYANCE: Can I use a picture or clip art for my data points?

THE FIX: Sure! Select your data series, choose Format→Selected Data Series, click the Patterns tab, click the Fill Effects button, and click the Picture tab. Select an appropriate picture, check the settings you want (see Figure 6-27), and click OK.

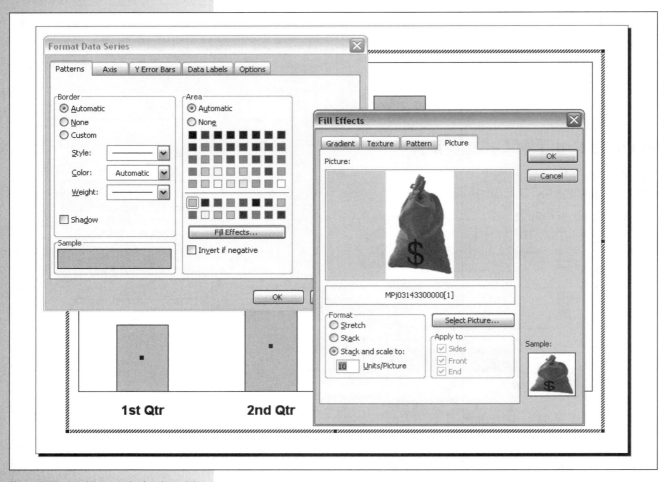

Figure 6-27. In addition to the familiar solid colors, you can fill chart data points with pictures, patterns, gradients, and textures.

Change Chart Colors

THE ANNOYANCE: I don't like the colors on the chart in this template. How can I change the colors so I don't have to hand-format every single one?

THE FIX: The colors in a chart are actually tied directly to the slide color scheme. To change the colors in the chart, you must change the colors in the slide color scheme.

In PowerPoint 2002 and 2003, select Format→Slide Design, click Color Schemes in the task pane, and then click Edit Color Schemes at the bottom of the task pane. In PowerPoint 97 and 2000, select Format→Slide Color Scheme and click the Custom tab. The first data series will take the color assigned to "Fills," the second series will use "Accent," the third will use "Accent and hyperlink," and the fourth, "Accent and followed hyperlink" (see Figure 6-28).

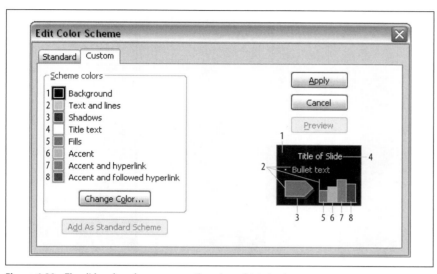

Figure 6-28. The slide color scheme governs the colors of data in charts.

Or create your charts in Excel. Select Tools→Options, click the Color tab, and then click the Modify button to change any of the colors in any of the available swatches. Next, select File→Save and save the worksheet to your hard drive. You can then use it as a color master. Open another Excel workbook, create your chart, choose Tools→Options, click the Color tab, and choose the color master file from the "Copy colors from" drop-down menu. The menu lists only open Excel files, so make sure your color master file is open when you're ready to copy colors into a new file.

Create a Default Chart

THE ANNOYANCE: Every single time I create a chart, I have to change the chart type from that stupid 3D column chart. Can I use a different chart type as the default?

THE FIX: Absolutely! Go find or create a chart you want as your default, choose Chart→Chart Type, click the Custom Types tab, choose the User-defined option, and click the "Set as default chart" button. When asked if you're sure, click Yes, and then fill in the dialog box to add the chart to the list of user-defined charts (see Figure 6-29).

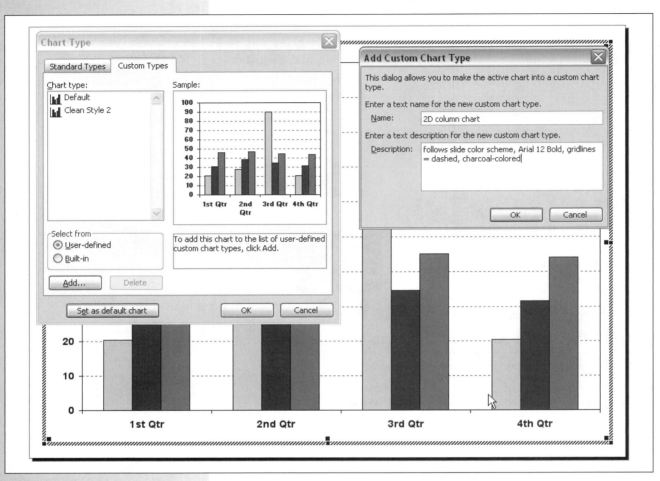

Figure 6-29. Click the "Set as default chart" button to set a default chart style. Unfortunately, these user-defined and default charts are specific to a computer, not to a presentation or template file.

If you would just like to add a chart style to your arsenal to save some formatting time, simply click the Add button. This adds the chart to your user-defined chart style list, but it does not replace the default chart style. When you create default and user-defined charts, you should be aware of the following:

• If your default chart follows your slide color scheme, when you create a new chart on a slide with a different color scheme, the chart will follow the new slide's color scheme.

• User-defined charts are machine-specific settings. That means these chart styles do not travel with the template or the presentation.

• The file *GRUSRGAL.GRA* contains your user-defined and default chart settings. If you want to try replacing another user's *GRUSRGAL.GRA*

    Creating and Formatting Charts

file with your own, you can usually find this file in the following folder: *C:\Documents and Settings\[UserName]\Application Data\Microsoft\ Graph*. Replacing someone's *GRUSRGAL.GRA* file will delete any user-defined chart styles he may have created.

- You cannot *globally* change the fill color swatches on the Patterns tab (see Figure 6-30). You can, however, modify these swatches (select Tools→Options, click the Color tab, and click the Modify button) for an *individual* graph, but the swatches reset to their original colors each time you create or insert a new chart on a slide.

- If you need more colors for your charts, modify the 40 fill color swatches. Select Tools→Options, click the Color tab, and click the Modify button. Next, create a chart using those colors and include it on a slide. Instruct your users to paste that slide and change the data in the chart to create more charts.

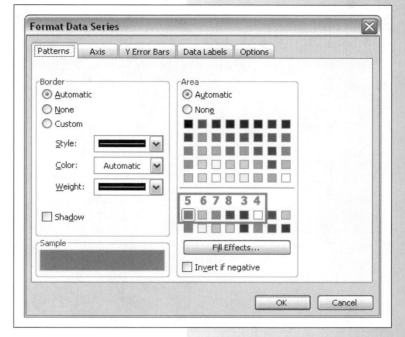

Figure 6-30. The colors you see on the Patterns tab reset to these default colors each time you create a new chart. However, the colors indicated do change according to the slide color scheme.

Reset the Default Chart Style

THE ANNOYANCE: I tried to create a new default graph style, but I messed up. How do I get the old default chart back?

THE FIX: Just delete the current default chart type and it will reset to the original. Select Chart→Chart Type, choose the User-defined option, choose Default from the list, and click the Delete button.

Charts Recolor When Pasted into Presentations

THE ANNOYANCE: When I paste my chart into a different presentation, it changes colors.

THE FIX: Before you paste the slide or chart into the new presentation, select it and choose View→Toolbars→Picture. Click the Recolor Chart button and choose None from the options (see Figure 6-31). You may want to experiment with selecting the recolor "only text and background" option as well (see Figure 6-32).

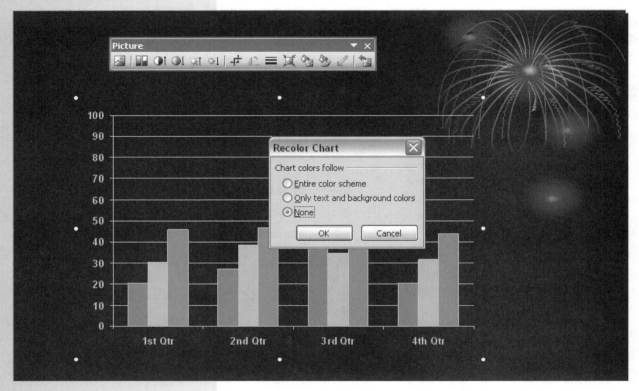

Figure 6-31. Click the Recolor Chart button on the Picture toolbar to specify what happens to the chart colors when you paste the chart onto a slide using a different color scheme.

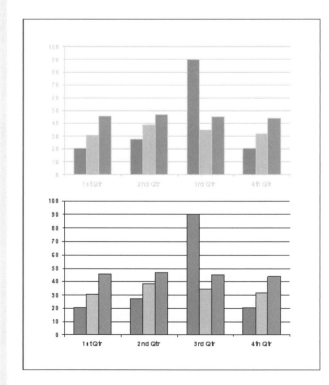

Figure 6-32. The top chart shows what happens when you paste the chart after choosing None in the Recolor Chart options. The chart on the bottom shows the results of choosing to recolor "only text and background."

Creating and Formatting Charts

Alternatively, you can select the chart *after* you've pasted it into the new presentation and choose the Recolor Chart button on the Picture toolbar. This technique also works well on Excel charts imported into PowerPoint, and is a fantastic way to leverage Excel's color management (in Excel, choose Tools→Options, click the Color tab, and make a selection from the "Copy colors from" drop-down list) on charts in PowerPoint.

Change Settings for Printing in Black and White

THE ANNOYANCE: I have a chart with a bunch of data points, and I can't tell them apart when I print to a black and white printer—all the different shades of gray are too close. What should I do?

THE FIX: Specify pattern fills for some of the data points or series. Right-click a data series, choose Format Data Series, click the Patterns tab, click the Fill Effects button, and click the Pattern tab (see Figure 6-33). For maximum contrast, choose black for the Foreground and white for the Background colors. Of course, do this type of thing on a copy of the slide or presentation so you don't mess up the colors on the real presentation files. You may also need to change the actual color of some of the data points to black, white, medium gray, and light gray.

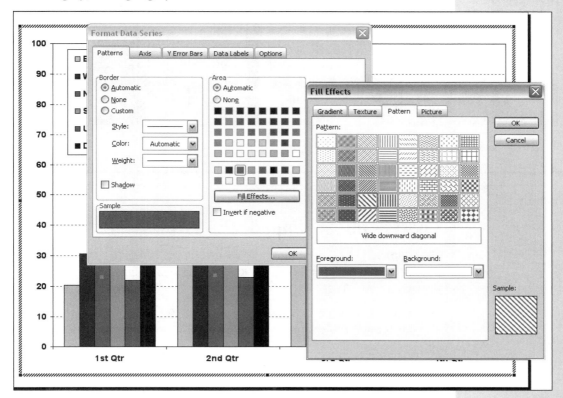

Figure 6-33. Adding a pattern fill to a data point or data series makes it easy to identify in black-and-white prints.

Don't forget to check the Black and White settings for the chart. Click the slide to deactivate the chart and select View→Color/Grayscale→Grayscale or Pure Black and White. (In PowerPoint 97 and 2000, select View→Black and White.) Next, right-click the chart, select the Grayscale or Black and White setting, and choose another option from the list (see Figure 6-34).

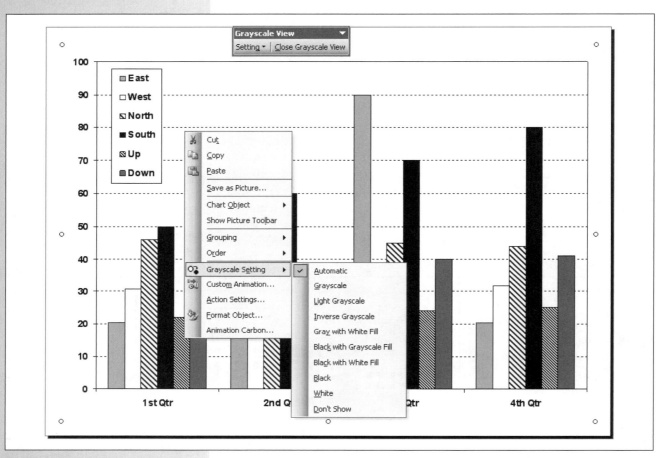

Figure 6-34. Black and White or Grayscale settings also have some bearing on how a chart looks when printed in black and white. Unfortunately these settings apply to the chart as a whole and cannot be applied to the individual elements of the chart.

Charts Appear Flipped

THE ANNOYANCE: My office upgraded to PowerPoint 2002, but when I view the charts I created in PowerPoint 2000, they appear flipped. Do we have to downgrade to 2000?

THE FIX: Open the file in PowerPoint 97 or 2000, select the chart, choose Draw→Rotate or Flip to rotate it appropriately, and save the presentation.

Unfortunately, you can't reset charts to their original orientation in PowerPoint 2002 or 2003.

Charts Resize When Opened

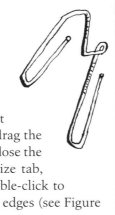

THE ANNOYANCE: When I double-click my chart and open it, it's not the same size as on the slide.

THE FIX: This is because you dragged the edges of the chart when you were looking at it on the slide. And you didn't drag the edges proportionately (that is, drag the corner). To fix it, close the chart, right-click it, choose Format→Object, click the Size tab, specify 100% in the Scale area, and click OK. Then double-click to open and resize the chart by dragging the "herringbone" edges (see Figure 6-4 earlier in this chapter).

Resize a chart only when it is activated. If you *must* resize a chart when it's not activated, maintain its aspect ratio by dragging a corner.

Other Charting Options

If compatibility is not a huge issue for you, there are a number of charting programs available aside from Excel and PowerPoint's Microsoft Graph. Some do extensive statistical functions and analysis, others are best at making pretty charts from the data. Most of the heavy-duty statistical programs will at least export images, which you can then insert into PowerPoint. Others will insert into slides as OLE linked or embedded objects. Some even convert graphs to Flash and other formats, which often allows for sophisticated animations.

- PowerPlugs: Charts (*http://www.crystalgraphics.com/presentations/charts.main.asp*) costs $99.

- MekkoGraphics (*http://www.mekkographics.com/*) Basic Edition costs $99 and the Professional Edition costs $499.

- Swiff Chart (*http://www.globfx.com/products/swfchart/*) costs $149.

- XcelsiusXL (*http://www.infommersion.com/index.html*) costs $195 for the Standard version and $495 for the Professional version.

- KaleidaGraph (*http://www.synergy.com/*) costs $200 but the company offers a discount for academic institutions.

- Delta Graph (*http://www.rockware.com/catalog/pages/deltagraphw.html*) costs $295, but the company offers a discount for academic institutions.

- Grapher (*http://www.goldensoftware.com/products/grapher/grapher.shtml*) costs $299.

- Prism (*http://www.graphpad.com/prism/Prism.htm*) costs $371.25 for qualified students, $495 for commercial enterprises, and $445 for academic institutions.

- Miner3D (*http://miner3d.com/index.html*) Basic Edition costs $495 and the Professional Edition costs $875.

- Adobe Illustrator (*http://www.adobe.com/products/illustrator/main.html*) costs $499.

- SigmaPlot (*http://www.systat.com/products/*) costs $499 for academic institutions, $579 for government organizations, and $699 for commercial enterprises.

- Origin Lab (*http://www.originlab.com/*) is available to individuals and academic, government, and commercial clients. Check its web site for prices.

- S-Plus (*http://www.insightful.com/products/splus/default.asp*). Email a company sales person for a price quote.

- SPSS Base (*http://www.spss.com/*) costs $1,599.

- While not a true graphing program, Perspector (*http://www.perspector.com/*) is a fantastic 3D business graphics creator for PowerPoint. The Standard version costs $69 and the Professional version costs $199.

DATA

Pie Chart Totals Less Than 100%

THE ANNOYANCE: The data labels on my pie chart only add up to 98.7%. Is PowerPoint stupid or what?

THE FIX: Assuming your data does indeed add up to 100%, what you're seeing is a rounding issue. Occasionally, when PowerPoint calculates the pie slice percentages, rounding errors force the numbers to add to slightly more or less than 100%.

You can right-click one of the data labels, choose Format Data Labels, and increase the number of decimals on the Number tab. Or you can manually edit individual data labels to display the number you want. Click a data label once (which selects the series), and then click it again to select the individual label.

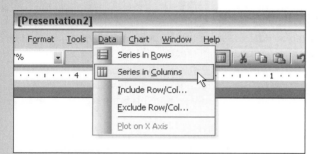

Figure 6-35. Opting to plot data by column instead of by row can save you from having to reenter data.

Change Data Plot from Rows to Columns

THE ANNOYANCE: I think my data should have been set up in rows instead of columns. Can I fix the chart without having to retype all the data?

THE FIX: Just choose Data→Series in Columns (see Figure 6-35) to tell Graph your data is set up in columns, not the usual rows. By default, PowerPoint's MSGraph plots series by row.

Hide Data on Your Datasheet

THE ANNOYANCE: I have a bunch of data that I don't want to plot, but I want to keep it available in case my boss decides to plot it later. What should I do?

THE FIX: Just double-click at the beginning of the row or the column with the data. The text in the datasheet will become gray, indicating that the data is hidden (see Figure 6-36). Double-click again to unhide the data.

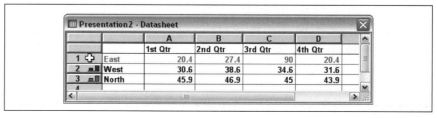

Figure 6-36. Double-click a row or column to hide its data on the chart. Double-click again to unhide.

Interpolate Lines with Missing Data

THE ANNOYANCE: I made a scatter chart, but some of the data points are missing, so my chart lines look discontinuous. What should I do? I don't want to have fake data just to make the lines appear on the chart.

THE FIX: Select Tools→Options, click the Chart tab, and choose the Interpolated option (see Figure 6-37). Interpolation basically means "filling in the missing pieces." When you use interpolation, MSGraph applies an internal algorithm (often a simple average of surrounding data) to estimate missing data and fill in gaps.

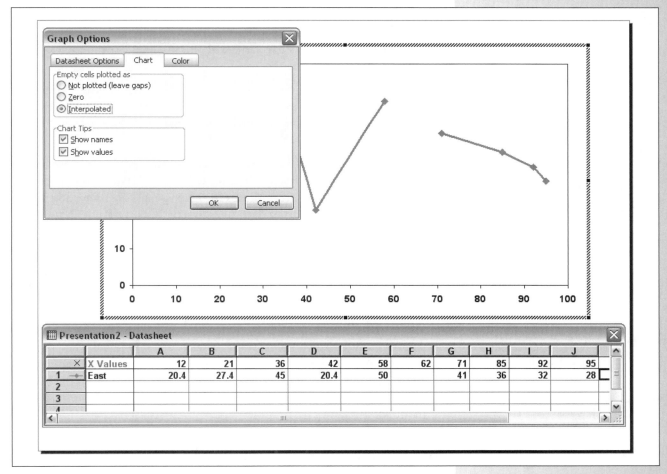

Figure 6-37. To fill gaps in data, choose the Interpolated option.

The Datasheet Is Just a Datasheet

THE ANNOYANCE: I want to add one column of data in my graph spreadsheet and include the sum as a column in my graph.

THE FIX: You'll have to add the data manually, using a calculator, or in Excel. The datasheet in MSGraph is solely a datasheet to input existing data into; it doesn't do any calculations or formulas at all.

EXCEL CHARTS

Import Excel Charts

THE ANNOYANCE: I can create charts in Excel, no problem. How in the world do I get them into PowerPoint?

THE FIX: Copying the chart in Excel and using Edit→Paste Special in PowerPoint is probably the best way. This process gives you the widest variety of formats to choose from when pasting or linking your chart to the slide.

If you choose Microsoft Office Excel Object from the Paste Special list, your entire Excel workbook will be pasted into your PowerPoint presentation file. This option severs all ties to the original Excel file and enables you to work on the chart and its data directly in PowerPoint.

If you've pasted your entire workbook into your presentation, you may want to right-click the chart and choose Grouping→Ungroup to remove the background data from the chart before finalizing the file or sending a copy to anyone. You cannot get the data back once you've ungrouped the chart, so you probably want to do this on a copy of the presentation file, not the actual working file.

Alternatively, in PowerPoint, you can select Insert→Chart, click the cell in the upper-left corner of the datasheet, and choose Edit→Import File. Navigate to the saved Excel file and click the Open button. In the Import Data Options dialog box, choose the appropriate chart or datasheet (see Figure 6-38).

Figure 6-38. In an activated chart, select Edit→Import File to import Excel data or charts into PowerPoint's MSGraph.

Pasted Charts Cause File Size Increase

THE ANNOYANCE: I pasted a couple of charts from Excel into my PowerPoint presentation, and my PowerPoint file size ballooned! What happened?

THE FIX: When you paste charts from Excel into PowerPoint, the entire workbook is pasted into the presentation by default. If you're pasting from a large Excel file, your PowerPoint file will get big, too.

If this is an issue for you, you can choose from a few different options:

- Select Edit→Paste Special and choose *.emf* or *.wmf* to paste a picture of the chart on your slide. It behaves like a picture, not a chart; it is completely divorced from the data used to create it. Double-click the "chart" on the slide to bring up a picture formatting dialog box. (In PowerPoint 2002 and 2003, you can choose this option from the Paste Options button when you do a plain ol' paste.)

- Select Edit→Paste Special, choose the "Paste link" option, and select Microsoft Office Excel Chart Object. This pastes a picture of the chart on your slide with a link to the original Excel workbook. Double-click the chart to open it in Excel, and any changes you make will actually be made to the Excel file. The thing you should know about linking is you must keep the Excel workbook available to the PowerPoint file—if you move the workbook, the link to the data will be severed, and the chart will act like a picture.

- Go ahead and paste the entire workbook. This allows you to work on the chart as usual inside PowerPoint, although it does increase the file size. When you're finished working on the chart and no longer need the data, select the chart and choose Draw→Ungroup. This separates your chart from the data and knocks the file size back down to normal. The pieces of the chart will become individual objects on the slide.

Update Links Automatically

THE ANNOYANCE: I linked some data from an Excel spreadsheet to my PowerPoint graph spreadsheet by copying the data in Excel and using Edit→Paste Link on the graph datasheet. When I close the PowerPoint file and reopen it, the data links don't update.

THE FIX: You can open each graph to update its link. Or you can use the free Chart Update add-in from Microsoft PowerPoint MVP Shyam Pillai (*http://skp.mvps.org/ download.htm*).

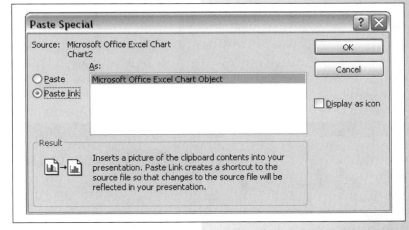

Figure 6-39. If you choose the Paste link option, any updates to the data or chart must be made in the Excel file, not in PowerPoint. Be sure to keep your Excel and PowerPoint files in the same locations, or the link will break. Best practice is to place both files in the same folder before creating the link so you can easily move the folder to another computer without breaking the link.

These links don't update because you've introduced MSGraph into the mix and MSGraph has to be activated before the links will update. You can eliminate this issue by creating and copying your charts in Excel. In PowerPoint, select Edit→Paste Special, choose the Paste link option, and then choose Microsoft Office Excel Chart Object (see Figure 6-39). This removes MSGraph from the mix and relies solely on OLE links to Excel workbooks.

Prevent Linked Charts from Updating

THE ANNOYANCE: I have a bunch of linked Excel charts in my presentation file. Every time I open the file, it spends forever updating the links. Is it possible to update the links when *I* want—like just before I go get a cup of coffee?

THE FIX: Select Edit→Links to specify the link behavior for OLE linked objects (see Figure 6-40). Press the Shift or Ctrl key while clicking to select more than one linked object from the list, and then choose the Manual option.

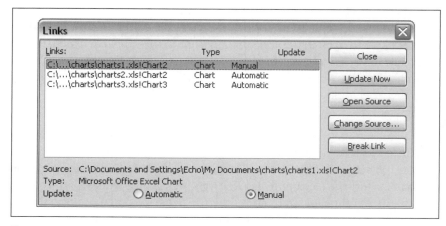

Figure 6-40. The Links dialog box lets you control the link behavior of OLE linked objects.

N O T E

Did you know the PowerPoint team at Microsoft doesn't "own" Microsoft Graph? The Excel team is actually responsible for it. Makes sense when you think about it, since Microsoft Graph is pretty much a calculation-free subset of Excel's graphing engine.

How to Animate a Chart

To animate a chart in PowerPoint 2002 or 2003, add an animation to the chart, click the animation in the task pane, and choose Effect Options. On the Chart Animation tab, choose "By series" or "By category" from the "Group chart" drop-down list. (See Chapter 7 for more information on animations.)

In PowerPoint 97 and 2000, select Slide Show→Custom Animation and click the Chart Effects tab. Next, choose your animation and select an option from the "Introduce chart elements" drop-down menu.

In all versions, if the only option is to group the chart "as one object," apply a less complicated animation—like a wipe or appear—to the chart. The level of grouping available depends on a combination of the type of chart and the actual animation effect used.

Animations, Action Settings, and Hyperlinks

7

PowerPoint is all about making things move, so animations and transitions are extremely important. Animations control the movement on an individual slide, while transitions control the movement between slides. Action settings and hyperlinks are equally important—you can click them to initiate a transition and move yourself around in a presentation.

All this moving and shaking can be challenging. This chapter aims to get you into the groove by making movement easier. You'll learn about using various settings on the Animation task pane, creating complex animations, using action settings and hyperlinks to jump to other slides, and troubleshooting the most common annoyances.

ANIMATIONS AND TRANSITIONS

Animation Plays Differently in Different Versions

THE ANNOYANCE: I made this really cool presentation at home using PowerPoint 2002. When I brought it to the office, the objects with motion-path and exit animations just appear dormant on the slide.

THE FIX: Most likely, you're using an earlier version of PowerPoint at the office. PowerPoint 97 and 2000 don't support the new animations and transitions introduced in PowerPoint 2002 and 2003. To show the presentation as you intended it to look, download the free PowerPoint Viewer 2003 from Microsoft (*http://www.microsoft.com/downloads/details.aspx?FamilyID=428d5727-43ab-4f24-90b7-a94784af71a4&DisplayLang=en*).

PowerPoint Viewer 2003 lets you show presentations created in newer versions of PowerPoint on computers either running older versions of PowerPoint or without PowerPoint installed. Microsoft also offers PowerPoint Viewer 97, which lets you display presentations created in PowerPoint 97 or 2000 on machines without those versions installed (*http://www.microsoft.com/downloads/details.aspx?FamilyID=7C404E8E-5513-46C4-AA4F-058A84A37DF1&displaylang=EN*). Make sure you read the download pages to understand the limitations of the viewers. For example, neither viewer supports VBA—this means no macros will run in the PowerPoint Viewer. PowerPoint Viewer 2003 will run on Windows 98 SE (Second Edition), ME, XP, 2000 SP3, and 2000 Server. It will not run on Windows NT or 98. You can read more about the limitations of PowerPoint Viewer 97 (*http://www.soniacoleman.com/FAQs/FAQ00021.htm*) and PowerPoint Viewer 2003 (*http://www.soniacoleman.com/Tutorials/PowerPoint/powerpoint_2003_viewer.htm*) from Microsoft PowerPoint MVP Sonia Coleman.

After you install PowerPoint Viewer 2003, select Start→Programs to open the viewer. Next, select File→Open and navigate to your presentation. If you just double-click the presentation file on a computer with both PowerPoint Viewer and a full version of PowerPoint installed, the file will more than likely open in the full version of PowerPoint.

Of course, you can also simply turn off the new features in PowerPoint 2002 and 2003. Select Tools→Options, click the Edit tab, and uncheck the "New animation effects," "Multiple masters," and "Password protection" boxes.

> **NOTE**
>
> *What's the difference between an animation and a transition? You use animations on a slide, and you use transitions between slides. Transitions, or rather the lack of a transition effect, can sometimes be used to fake animations.*

Animate Individual Bullet Points

THE ANNOYANCE: I have a bunch of bullet points on this slide, but I want to give them different entrance animations. A whole list of fly-ins is just too boring.

THE FIX: If you want the text to have different animations in PowerPoint 97 and 2000, create separate text boxes for each bullet point and animate each one. An easy way to do this without having to reformat each bullet point is to type all the text into the text placeholder ("Click to add text"), copy the placeholder, paste onto the slide, and delete the extraneous text. Repeat for each bullet point. Once you've created separate text boxes for each bullet point, select all the text boxes and use Draw→Align or Distribute to left-align and vertically distribute the text boxes. Right-click and choose Custom Animation to add an animation effect and specify the order of animation for each text box.

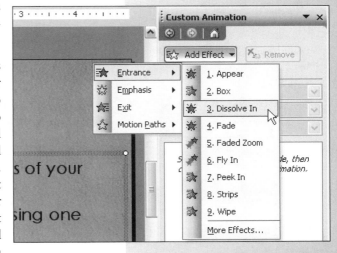

Figure 7-1. To add an animation, select the object on the slide, click the Add Effect button on the Custom Animation task pane, and choose the animation you want to apply.

In PowerPoint 2002 and 2003, click the top of the task pane and choose Custom Animation to open the Custom Animation task pane. With the text placeholder selected on the slide, click Add Effect→Entrance, and choose an animation effect from the list (see Figure 7-1). This applies the animation effect to all of the text in the selected placeholder.

Click the downward-pointing chevron to expand the animations so you can see each one (see Figure 7-2). In the task pane, select the animation you want to change. The Add Effect button becomes a Change button. Click the Change button, choose Entrance, and select a new entrance animation effect from the list. Repeat as desired for each bullet point.

Make the First Bullet Visible

THE ANNOYANCE: I have a bunch of bullet points on this slide. My boss wants the first one to be visible when the slide initially appears, and then the rest to come in when he clicks. Can I choose not to animate the first bullet?

THE FIX: In PowerPoint 97 and 2000, create a separate text box for the first bullet point and remove the animation from it (see "Animate Individual Bullet Points").

In PowerPoint 2002 and 2003, apply the animation to the placeholder (see Figure 7-1), click to expand the contents (see Figure 7-2), select the first bullet point in the Custom Animation task pane, click the arrow to the right, and choose Remove to un-animate the first bullet point (see Figure 7-3). You can also simply select the animation in the Custom Animation task pane and press Delete on your keyboard.

Figure 7-2. To apply different animation effects or tweak the settings on individual elements, click the chevron to expand the contents so you can select the individual pieces.

Figure 7-3. Click the arrow next to an animation in the Custom Animation task pane to open a panel with further options.

Apply Options to Animation Effects

THE ANNOYANCE: I set up animations on some bulleted text. I want to click to start some of the animations but have others come in automatically.

THE FIX: In PowerPoint 97 and 2000, you would have to create separate text boxes and animate each individually. In those versions of PowerPoint, animations applied to a text box are all or nothing.

In PowerPoint 2002 and 2003, you can apply different settings to individual bullet points. Apply the animation to the placeholder (see Figure 7-1) and click to expand the contents (see Figure 7-2). In the Custom Animation task pane, select the bullet point you want to change. Click the drop-down arrow in the Start area and choose to start the animation on mouse click, With Previous, or After Previous (see Figure 7-4).

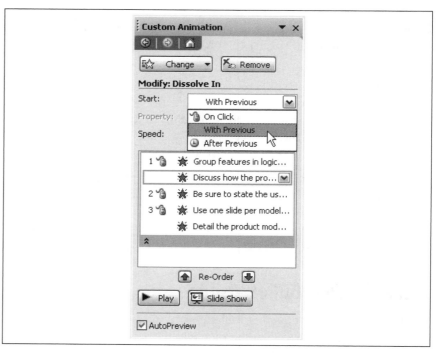

Figure 7-4. With an object selected in the Custom Animation task pane, click the pull-down arrow in the Start area to change the start behavior of an object.

If you choose "With Previous," the animation starts automatically at the same time the object before it in the task pane *starts* its animation. Selecting "After Previous" starts the animation automatically when the object before it in the task pane *stops* its animation.

You may want to start an animation a few seconds after another object begins animating, but before it stops animating. In that situation, set the Start value to "With Previous," and double-click the object in the Custom Animation task pane to open the Effect Options dialog box. Select the Timing tab and use the arrows to adjust the time in the Delay area (see Figure 7-5).

You can also set a delay on animations starting with "on mouse click" and "After Previous." The delay will begin when you click the mouse or when the previous animation is complete.

Animate Text by Levels

THE ANNOYANCE: A colleague told me that it's possible to animate a primary bullet and all its secondary bullets so they fly in at the same time. How?

THE FIX: In PowerPoint 2002 or 2003, select the text box on the slide, right-click, and choose Custom Animation. On the Custom Animation task pane, click Add Effect→Entrance, and choose an animation effect from the list (see Figure 7-1) to apply an entrance animation. Double-click the animation in the Custom Animation task pane. (Do not click the chevron to expand the contents unless you want to apply this setting to just one set of bullets.) In the Effect Options dialog box, click the Text Animation tab (see Figure 7-6), where you can opt to animate the text all at once or by paragraph levels. To force the primary bullet to come in with all of the bullets underneath it, choose "1st Level Paragraphs." To have the first bullet come in, and then the second one follow with all the rest of the bullets below, select "2nd Level Paragraphs."

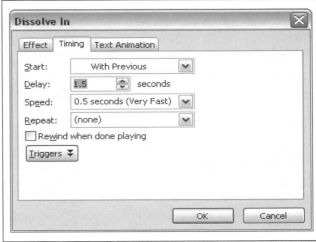

Figure 7-5. Set delay times for your animated objects on the Timing tab in the Effect Options dialog box. Use the arrows or just type in the number of seconds you want to delay.

50 Ways to Open the Effect Options Dialog

Okay, okay, so it's not really 50. But you can still open the Effect Options dialog in the Custom Animation task pane in several different ways.

- Double-click the name of the item in the Custom Animation task pane.

- Right-click the name of the item in the Custom Animation task pane and choose Effect Options or Timing.

- Click the arrow to the right of the name in the Custom Animation task pane and choose Effect Options or Timing from the drop-down list.

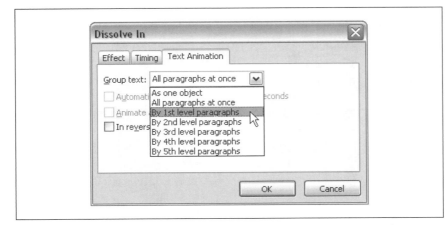

Figure 7-6. You'll find the options to group text by bullet level for animation purposes listed in the Text Animation tab of the Effect Options dialog box.

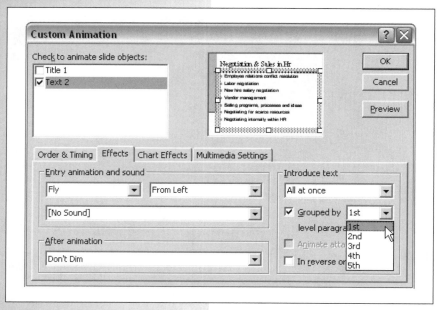

Figure 7-7. Set the "Grouped by" level of
text on the right side of this dialog box.

Of course, you can set the individual
bullets manually as well using the
techniques described in "Animate
Individual Bullet Points."

In PowerPoint 97 and 2000, select
the text box, choose Slide Show→
Custom Animation, click the Effects
tab, and set the "Grouped by" level
for text (see Figure 7-7).

Apply More Than One
Animation to an Object

THE ANNOYANCE: I want to have some
text move across the slide and change
colors at the same time. Is this possible to do in PowerPoint?

THE FIX: Simultaneous animation is only possible in PowerPoint 2002 and
2003.

Select the text box on the slide, and in the Custom Animation task pane,
click Add Effect→Entrance→Fly In. If you don't see the Fly In animation on
the list, click More Effects and choose it from the Basic section of the list
(see Figure 7-8).

Figure 7-8. Choose Fly In from the Add
Effects menu (left). If not available, choose
More Effects and select it from the resulting
list (right).

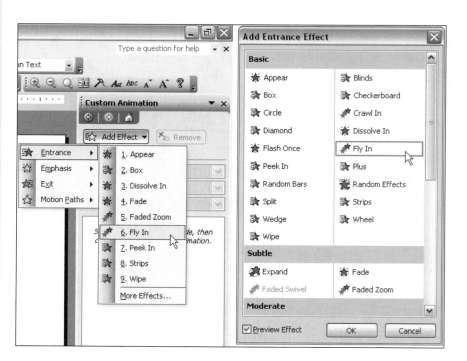

Set this animation to begin on mouse click and change its speed to Medium
(see Figure 7-9).

Repeat the steps to add the second animation: select the object on the slide,
click Add Effect→Emphasis→Change Font Color. In the Custom Animation
task pane, set the animation to begin With Previous (see Figure 7-10).
Change its speed to Medium, and choose a color for the text. Setting the
speed of both objects to "Medium" forces them to play for the same two-
second duration.

Click the Slide Show button at the bottom of the Custom Animation task
pane to test the animation. Remember, the first animation effect begins "On
Click," so click your mouse once you're in Slide Show view.

The key to adding more than one animation effect to an object is to select
the object on the *slide*, not in the Custom Animation task pane. Selecting
the object in the Custom Animation task pane converts the Add Effect button to a Change button. The Change button changes an animation effect
you already applied to an object.

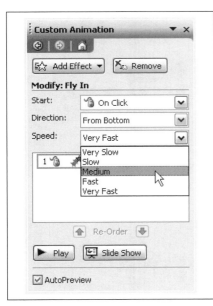

Figure 7-9. Control basic aspects of animations
in this section of the task pane.

Figure 7-10. Control the animation start
and other basic attributes in this area of the
Custom Animation task pane.

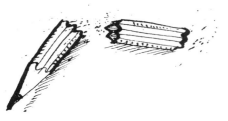

Objects with Motion Paths Animate Twice

THE ANNOYANCE: Several objects on my slide have motion path animations applied. I want each object to appear on the slide one after the other. However, when I run the presentation, the slide appears with all the objects on at first, and then each one is removed and reenters and animates one by one. How do I get them to behave and not enter twice?

THE FIX: Think of it this way: a motion path is not an entrance animation. It may seem like one, especially if you start with the object off the edge of the slide, but that object is really sitting there the whole time—you just can't see it in Slide Show view because it's not on the slide itself.

With objects that *are* on the slide, you have to add an entrance animation if you want them to be invisible until you're ready for them to move along the path. An Appear entrance is usually the entrance animation of choice in that situation. Select the object on the slide, click Add Effect→Entrance→ Appear, and drag the Appear animation so it begins at the same time the motion path animation begins (see Figure 7-11). Don't forget to change the start behavior of the motion path animation so it begins immediately after (or with) the Appear entrance animation (see Figure 7-12).

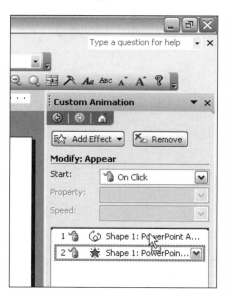

Figure 7-11. Drag and drop in the Custom Animation task pane to reorder animations. Or use the Re-Order buttons at the bottom of the task pane.

Figure 7-12. If you use an Appear entrance animation along with a Motion Path animation, make sure to change the start behavior of the Motion Path animation. Because Appear entrances happen so quickly, Start With Previous and Start After Previous seem to behave the same way in this situation.

Edit Motion Paths

THE ANNOYANCE: I have to make an animation of a train "moving" along its tracks. I know I can choose, like, a million different motion path animations, but none of them go exactly where I want. I'm screwed!

THE FIX: Nah, you're fine. Just draw your own motion path or edit a similar one to fit your needs.

To draw your own motion path, select an object in the slide area and click Add Effect→Motion Paths→Draw Custom Path. Choose Line, Curve, Freeform, or Scribble and draw the path on the slide (see Figure 7-13). To edit a motion path, first apply it to the object, and then right-click the path on the slide and choose Edit Points.

For more information about working with the different line drawing tools and edit points, see Chapter 5.

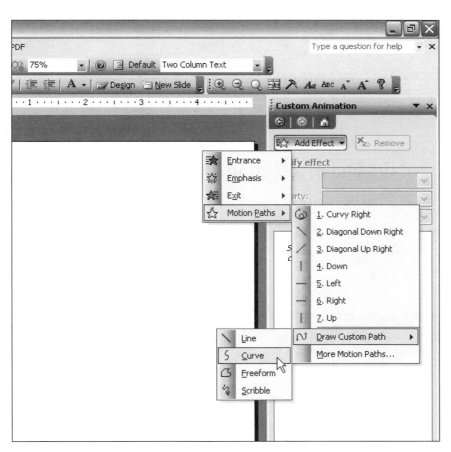

Figure 7-13. You can draw your own animation motion paths by choosing Add Effect→Motion Paths→Draw Custom Path on the Custom Animation task pane.

Object Jumps Before Starting Motion Path Animation

THE ANNOYANCE: I applied a motion path animation to a text box, but it jumps when it starts to animate. I want it to begin from where it is now! How do I make it quit jumping around?

THE FIX: Right-click the motion path and click Edit Points. Drag the starting point of the path to the middle of your text box.

Motion path animations begin at the middle of the object. If the object jumps when the animation begins, it means the start point of the path isn't in the middle of the object.

Unlock a Motion Path

THE ANNOYANCE: I added a motion path animation to a shape on my slide, but when I move the shape, the path doesn't move. Do I have to start all over and add a new motion path?

THE FIX: Your motion path has been set to "Locked" in the Custom Animation task pane. When a path is locked, it stays in place even if you move the object that has the path applied to it (see Figure 7-14). If unlocked, the path moves with the object. Choose Unlocked from the Path drop-down menu.

Find the End of a Motion Path

THE ANNOYANCE: I'm trying to align multiple motion paths for the same object. I want the second motion path to start at the end of the first path, the third motion path to start at the end of the second one, and so on. I can't seem to line up the start of one motion path with the end of another.

THE FIX: There's no easy way to do this with PowerPoint's animation tools—other than simple trial and error.

Figure 7-14. Choose Unlocked from the Path drop-down menu if you want the motion path to move with the object on the slide.

An alternative is to use the free Motion Path Tools add-in (*http://skp.mvps. org/mptools.htm*) from Microsoft PowerPoint MVP Shyam Pillai. This add-in will create a duplicate object at the end of a selected motion path, which will let you easily see the end point of the object. After you download the add-in, select Tools→Motion Path Tools→Motion Path End Position. This add-in will also align and join multiple motion paths applied to one object. See Figure 7-15.

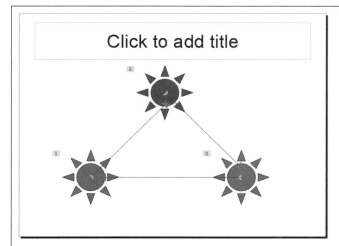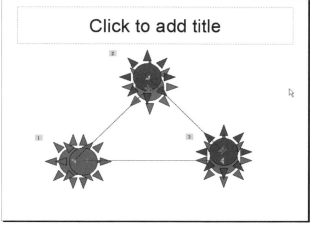

Figure 7-15. It's often difficult to align the start of one motion path with the end of another (left). With the free Motion Path Tools add-in, you can create duplicate objects at the endpoint of a motion path and align the original objects to the duplicates (right). Of course, delete the duplicate objects when you've finished placing everything.

Animate a Chart by Series or Category

THE ANNOYANCE: I want to animate my chart one category at a time, but I can't figure out how to do it.

THE FIX: First, apply an animation to the chart. In the Custom Animation task pane in PowerPoint 2002 and 2003, right-click the chart and choose Effect Options and click the Chart Animation tab. Finally, select "By category" from the "Group chart" drop-down menu (see Figure 7-16). Similar options are available for diagrams and organization charts.

In PowerPoint 97 and 2000, right-click the Chart, choose Custom Animation, and specify an entrance animation type on the Chart Effects tab. Click the drop-down menu in the "introduce chart elements" area to select by series, by category, or by element in a series or category.

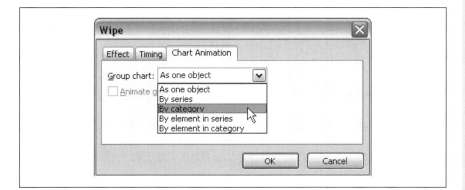

Figure 7-16. You can animate a chart a variety of ways by selecting from the "Group chart" options on the Chart Animation tab.

Series and Category Animations

What groups (series or category) you can animate depends on the combination of the chart type and animations you select. For example, if you use a 3D clustered column chart with a fly-in animation, the only possible grouping level is "as one object." If you change the animation to something simpler, such as Appear or Fade or Wipe, you can animate by series, by category, by element in series, or by element in category.

If you must use the more complex animation—the one that makes the "By series" and "By category" animations unavailable, you'll have to ungroup the chart and animate the individual pieces. If you'll need to update the data or make other changes to the chart, copy the chart and drag the original off the slide where it won't show during a presentation. Right-click it, choose Format Object, and set the scale to 5% x 5% on the Size tab if you don't want it to alter your view of the slide too much in Normal (editing) view.

Limits to Credit Animations

THE ANNOYANCE: My ending credits stop animating before the end of the list. Is there a limit or something?

THE FIX: Yes, credit animations are limited to about the height of the slide. If you have more credits than that, you'll need to use multiple text boxes and apply credit animations set to start "After Previous" or "With Previous," plus some delay time.

The easiest way to tweak the timing for your credit animations is to apply the credit animation to each text box. Next, right-click an animation in the Custom Animation task pane and choose Show Advanced Timeline. Make sure each animation is set to begin "With Previous" on the animation task pane, and drag the orange timeline bars to adjust the start time of the individual animations (see "Show Advanced Animation Timeline," later in this chapter).

The credit animation effect is available only in PowerPoint 2002 and 2003. In PowerPoint 97 and 2000, you can use a crawl animation effect to simulate credits.

Exit Objects in PowerPoint 97 and 2000

THE ANNOYANCE: I want to use exit animations in PowerPoint 2000, but there's no such thing. How can I make an object disappear?

THE FIX: Exiting an animation in PowerPoint 97 and 2000 is really more along the lines of *animating in* a background-colored object to cover up the existing object. Draw an AutoShape, select Format→AutoShape, and choose Background from the Fill Color drop-down menu. Apply an entrance animation to the AutoShape by right-clicking it, selecting Custom Animation, and choosing Appear or Dissolve on the Effects tab. Place the object on the slide so it covers the object you want to exit.

Animate Two Objects at Once

THE ANNOYANCE: So how do I animate two objects at the same time?

THE FIX: In PowerPoint 2002 and 2003, you can simply use the "With Previous" start option so the objects begin animating at the same time (see "Apply Options to Animation Effects"). In PowerPoint 97 and 2000, you must group the objects together using Draw→Group, which means they use the same animation effect, or you have to settle for the objects animating one right after the other.

What Is a Trigger Animation?

Microsoft introduced trigger animations in PowerPoint 2002. They're used when you want to click something and have something else happen on a slide. For example, you might click some text to make a picture disappear. Or you might click a picture to make a movie start playing.

You can use triggers to start animations when you don't know what order you need to animate, which makes them perfect for games. Triggers are different than hyperlinks. Hyperlinks and action settings generally move you to another slide. Triggers are used to trigger an animation effect on the current slide.

To create a trigger animation, add two objects to a slide: a text box that says Sunny and an AutoShape of a sun (AutoShapes→Basic Shapes→Sun). Right-click the sun, choose Custom Animation, and select Add Effect→ Entrance→Fade. This simply adds an entrance animation, Fade, to the sun. Right-click the sun in the Custom Animation task pane and choose Effect Options or Timing. On the Timing tab, click the Triggers button, choose "Start effect on click of," and select Sunny in the drop-down menu (see Figure 7-17). This tells the sun to perform the entrance animation when you click the word Sunny.

This trigger animation technique is also very useful for making objects disappear when you click them. To illustrate this, add a lightening bolt (AutoShapes→Basic Shapes→Lightning Bolt) to the sun slide and apply an exit animation (in the Custom Animation task pane, click Add Effect→Exit→Collapse). Right-click the lightning bolt exit animation in the Custom Animation task pane and choose either Effect Options or Timing. On the Timing tab, click the Triggers button and choose Lightning Bolt from the "Start effect on click of" drop-down menu (see Figure 7-18). Now hit F5 to test the slide in Slide Show view. The lightning bolt should collapse when you click it.

Layering text boxes triggered to exit when you click on them is a great way to set up a *Jeopardy!*-style board game.

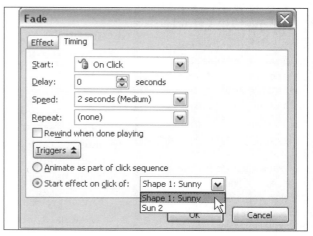

Figure 7-17. Click the Triggers button on the Timing tab and then choose a trigger from the "Start effect on click of" drop-down menu. A "Trigger" designation appears above the animation effect in the Custom Animation task pane to let you know what object you must click to trigger the animation. A finger appears near the animated object on the slide to let you know the object relies on a trigger to animate.

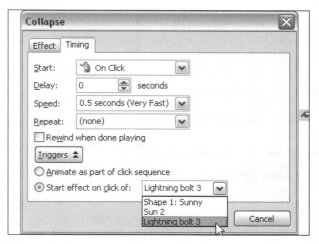

Figure 7-18. An animation effect on an object can be triggered to occur when that object is clicked. This works well for exit animations, but be careful using this technique for an entrance animation—it's pretty hard to click an object to make it appear when it isn't yet on the slide!

Combine Motion Paths with Other Animation Effects

Microsoft introduced motion paths in PowerPoint 2002. To get the most out of motion paths, try combining them with other animations.

For example: select an object on your slide, right-click, and choose Custom Animation to open the Custom Animation task pane. Click Add Effect→ Motion Paths and choose a motion path to apply to your object.

Now, with the object still selected, click Add Effect→ Entrance→Fade. Set both animations to Very Slow in the speed area, and make sure the second animation listed in the Custom Animation task pane is set to Start With Previous.

Now click Play or Slide Show at the bottom of the Custom Animation task pane. Your object should fade in slowly as it moves along the motion path.

Reapply Animations

THE ANNOYANCE: I made a really cool, but complex animation. My boss wants me to animate a different picture now. How can I transfer the animation to the new picture so I don't have to redo all the animation from scratch?

THE FIX: You can't do this with PowerPoint's animation tools, but two add-ins can help: Animation Carbon and pptXTREME Edit. Each add-in will cost you $50.

Animation Carbon (*http://skp.mvps.org/ac/index.html*) makes it easy to save your animation to a library and reapply the animation from the library to other objects. pptXTREME Edit (*http://www.pptxtreme.com/edit.asp*) is a suite of tools and includes an Animation Settings Painter, which lets you pick up animation settings from one object or group of objects and apply them to another.

If you prefer not to use one of these add-ins (both of which have free trial versions available), then be sure to write all the animation steps down because you're sure to forget something when you try to recreate it.

Dealing with Way Too Many Objects on a Slide

THE ANNOYANCE: I need to create a slide that has a ton of information on it. I mean layers and layers and layers of stuff. I don't expect the slide to be legible, I just want to show the audience how many different things my department handles. I'm thinking I can animate a "layer" of images and then another layer, and another, and so on. How should I create this slide?

THE FIX: Simply because of the sheer number of objects on the slide, probably the easiest solution will be to create the last slide—the one with everything on it—first, copy the slide, delete some of the objects, copy that slide, delete more objects, and so on. Don't put any animation on the objects on the slides, and don't put any transition effect on the slides themselves.

This is an example of using multiple slides and no transition effects to mimic animation. Each time you click, you'll move to the next slide, which has even more objects on it. Your audience won't realize you're actually moving to another slide.

As an alternative, download the demo version of the RnR PPT2HTML add-in (*http://www.rdpslides.com/pptools/ppt2html/index.html*) and use the Accessibility Assistant to hide objects while you animate visible objects (see Figure 7-19).

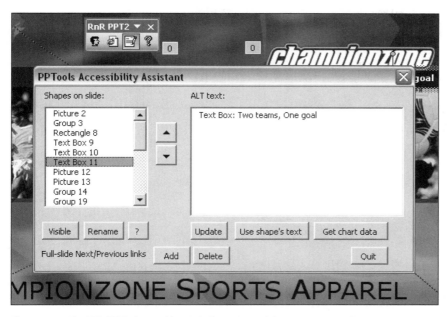

Figure 7-19. The PPT2HTML demo add-in includes an Accessibility Assistant, which comes in handy when animating crowded slides. Use it to make objects invisible while you concentrate on the visible items.

Yet another alternative is PowerPoint's own Select Multiple Objects tool. To add this to your toolbar, select Tools→Customize and click the Commands tab. In the Drawing Category, choose the "Select Multiple Objects" icon and drag it to any toolbar (see Figure 7-20).

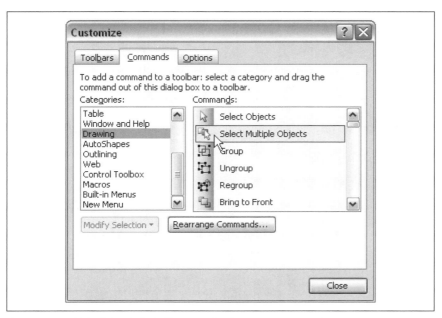

Figure 7-20. Add the Select Multiple Objects tool by dragging it to any toolbar.

If you click the Select Multiple Objects tool, it will open a dialog box listing everything on your slide. If you double-click an object on your slide to open the Format Object dialog, you can add descriptive text in the Web tab, and it will show up in the Select Multiple Objects list (see Figure 7-21). This makes it much easier to determine what you have selected.

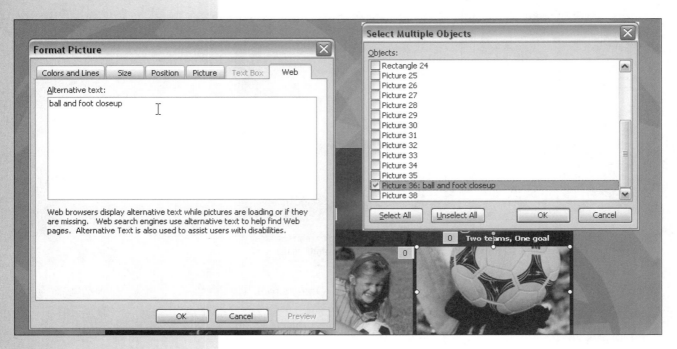

Figure 7-21. Text added in the Web tab will show up in the Select Multiple Objects list. It is also the alternative text that will show up in screen readers and if you save your PowerPoint file as a web page.

Determine Which Objects Are Animated

THE ANNOYANCE: I added descriptive text to my objects using the Web tab in the Format Objects dialog box, but I still can't tell whether those objects are animated. Why are the names in the Custom Animation task pane different?

THE FIX: Unfortunately, this annoyance has no satisfactory workaround. The Custom Animation task pane uses PowerPoint's internal naming scheme, and you can't change it.

However, PowerPoint does give you some hints as to what's been animated. If you insert an image, the name of the image file shows up in the Custom Animation task pane, and if you select an object in the Custom Animation task pane, the number of its animation turns yellow on the slide (see Figure 7-22). Likewise, if you select an object on the slide, its name will be highlighted in the Custom Animation task pane if it has animation.

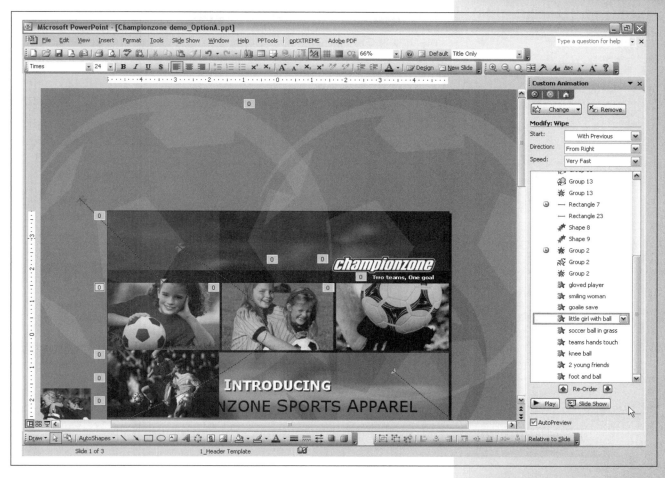

Figure 7-22. When you add an animation to a picture inserted via Insert→Picture→ From File, the name of the picture shows up in the Custom Animation task pane. When you select the picture on the slide, it will also be highlighted in the Custom Animation task pane if it has an animation. If you select the name of the picture in the Custom Animation task pane, the animation number on the slide will turn yellow.

The Select Multiple Objects tool (see "Dealing with Way Too Many Objects on a Slide") also helps determine what objects have animation applied. By exercising discipline and adding alternate web text when adding objects to slides, you can more easily determine what you've selected on a busy slide and add animation to it if it doesn't highlight in the Custom Animation task pane when selected.

Input a Custom Spin Angle

THE ANNOYANCE: When I tried to enter a custom spin angle in the Spin emphasis animation, it just jumped back to 360°.

THE FIX: Make sure you hit the Tab or Enter key after you type in the angle you want. If you just click elsewhere on the slide or animation pane, the number you typed won't "take."

Change the Fulcrum of a Spin

THE ANNOYANCE: I applied a spin emphasis animation to an arrow, but I want it to spin around the point of the arrow, not the center. How can I change the fulcrum of the spin?

THE FIX: In a nutshell, copy the object, group the copy and the original, apply the spin animation, and make the copy transparent.

Because PowerPoint spins all objects around their centers, you basically have to create a new center by grouping the object with another object. To illustrate, use the following steps:

1. Create an arrow on your slide (AutoShapes→Block Arrows→Right Arrow).

2. Select the arrow, copy it, and paste it on the slide.

3. With the copy of the arrow selected, choose Draw→Rotate or Flip→Flip Horizontal.

4. Select both arrows and choose Draw→Align or Distribute→Align Top to align them.

5. Hold down the Shift key and drag the copy of the arrow to the right so its point touches the point of the original arrow.

6. Select both arrows and choose Draw→Group.

7. Right-click the arrows and choose Custom Animation to activate the Custom Animation task pane. In the task pane, choose Add Effect→ Emphasis→Spin.

8. Click one of the arrows again and make it invisible. Select Fill Color→ No Fill and then select Line Color→No Line (see Figure 7-23). You can change these settings in the Format AutoShape dialog box by double-clicking the AutoShape.

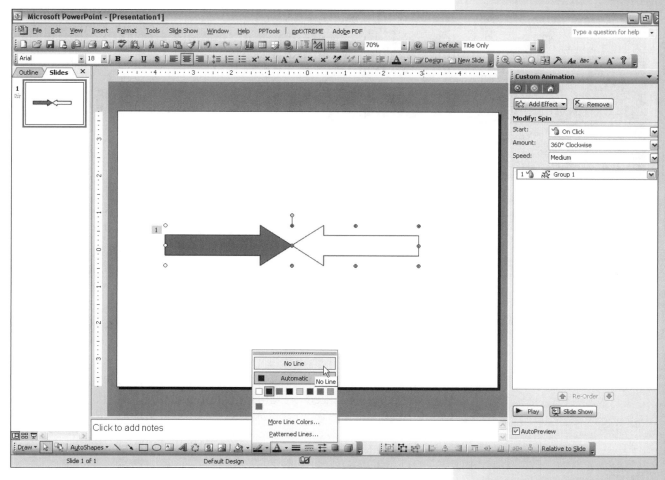

Figure 7-23. Make a copy of an object, group it with the original object, and give it no line and no fill to create a false center point for the Spin emphasis animation.

Animate One Word in a Text Box

THE ANNOYANCE: I have a line of text, and I want one word to change color. Is this possible?

THE FIX: You'll have to create another text box for the highlighted text. PowerPoint's animations apply to the entire text box; you can't animate just one word.

If you're trying to overlay a text box onto another to highlight individual words or phrases, sometimes the text box with just a few words won't line up exactly on top of the text boxes having more text.

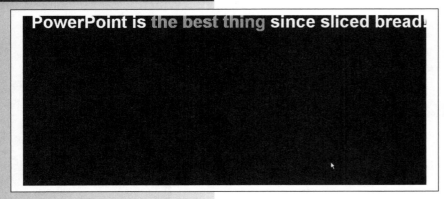

Figure 7-24. PowerPoint tries to be helpful by automatically adjusting text to make it look as good as it can. This can cause problems when you want to overlay one text box on top of another to create a "highlight" animation.

For example, say you're working with a text box that says "PowerPoint is the best thing since sliced bread!" Your goal is to make the phrase "the best thing" turn orange. But when you copy the original text box, change the text to orange, and delete all the extraneous words, the phrase doesn't exactly line up with the phrase in the original text box, so it doesn't *completely* cover the existing text (see Figure 7-24). This is PowerPoint trying to be helpful—it tries to make the text look good in the presentation, so it adjusts the spacing between the letters and words in a text box.

The problem is that the spacing in the one-word (or short phrase) text box is slightly different from the spacing between the letters and words in the "full" text box. As a result, the words no longer align when you layer one on top of the other.

There's no really good fix for this problem. One option is to copy the full text box and animate it. It will work if you can live with an Appear animation, but it may not work well for other animations.

Another option is to split the text into three text boxes–PowerPoint is, the best thing, since sliced bread!–and add a "Change Font Color" Emphasis animation effect to the second text box. And yet another option is to copy the text box, change the color of the appropriate text, and save both the original and the copy as *.png* files (right-click, choose Save As Picture, and select *.png* from the Save As Type drop-down menu). Crop the copy so that only the changed text shows, apply an appropriate animation, and align the two pictures.

A fourth option is to purchase the $50 pptXTREME SoftShadow add-in (*http://www.pptxtreme.com/softshadow.asp*). Set the shadow to 0,0 (i.e., no shadow) to create images of the original text box and the copy. The text images created with this add-in often align better than *.png* files created using PowerPoint's own Save As Picture option.

Show a Formula During a Presentation

THE ANNOYANCE: I want to be able to click on a cell of an Excel spreadsheet and show the Excel formula during my presentation. The spreadsheet is in the presentation already, but I can't get it to show formulas.

THE FIX: With the spreadsheet selected on the slide, click Add Effect→Object Actions→Open in the Custom Animation task pane. Now when you click the spreadsheet during the presentation, Excel will open, and you can show the formula.

You might want to use a trigger effect to start the object action instead of starting it with a "general" mouse-click. Applying a trigger to the spreadsheet itself would be the way to open the spreadsheet when you click it. See "What Is a Trigger Animation?" for information on using triggers to start animations.

You can use Add Effect→Object Actions→Open or Edit on a wide variety of OLE embedded or linked objects in PowerPoint 2002 and 2003.

In PowerPoint 97 and 2000, right-click the embedded object and choose Custom Animation. On the Multimedia Settings tab, select Open from the Object Action drop-down menu to open the object on mouse-click.

Repeat a Sequence of Animations

THE ANNOYANCE: I want a text box to fade in and out continuously until the end of my slide. I've tried everything to make this work, but I can't figure it out.

THE FIX: PowerPoint doesn't provide any way to loop a series of animations.

Microsoft PowerPoint MVP Chirag Dalal's Office One Animations add-in (*http://officeone.mvps.org/anims/anims.html*) adds this functionality to PowerPoint. It's not necessary to have this add-in installed on the computer you use to show the presentation—simply add the animation with the Office One Animation tool when you create the presentation, and it will work as long as you show the presentation in PowerPoint 2002, 2003, or PowerPoint Viewer 2003. The add-in will cost you $50.

Go from Animation to Transition

THE ANNOYANCE: I want this slide to transition to the next slide after I click to start the final animation. I don't think I should have to wait for the animation to end and click again to move to the next slide. It's too confusing.

THE FIX: PowerPoint doesn't have an "animation into transition" setting to combine manual animations with automatic transitions. But you can use the Office One Animations add-in (*http://officeone.mvps.org/anims/anims. html*) from Microsoft PowerPoint MVP Chirag Dalal to get this functionality. You will need to install this $50 add-in on the computer you use to show the presentation.

The Office One Animation's AutoTransitions feature is turned off by default. To turn it on, select OfficeOne Animations→Configure AutoTransitions, check the Enable AutoTransitions box, and click OK.

Alternatively, if you want to combine automatic animations with manual transitions, you can create a "shim" slide following the real slide. The real slide has the first part of the animations along with an automatic transition, which causes the animations to also be automatic. And although the transition *timing* is automatic, the transition *effect* should be set to none. The shim slide has the last animation and its transition is set to manual advance. To see what this looks like in action, and for a downloadable sample file, visit this book's web page (*http://www.oreilly.com/catalog/powerpointannoy/*).

Keep Slide on Screen After Animation

THE ANNOYANCE: I have a bunch of animations and an automatic transition on this slide, but I need the slide to stay put for a couple of seconds so everybody can read all the text before it changes to the next slide. How do I keep a slide on screen after the animation?

THE FIX: Put an extra object, such as a rectangle or oval AutoShape, on the slide and apply an animation to begin a few seconds—or whatever appropriate time as necessary—after the last animation on the slide. Drag this object off the edge of the slide so the audience won't see it during the presentation. This will cause the slide to pause after the last visible animation and before the transition begins.

Slide Transitions Don't Work Right

THE ANNOYANCE: I applied the checkerboard transition to three consecutive slides. The first slide transitions perfectly, but the two remaining slides do not transition correctly—only part of each slide shows the checkerboard transition going across.

THE FIX: This is PowerPoint working as designed. The master elements on a slide may not appear to transition because they don't change from slide to slide.

The first slide transitions through black because there's not a slide in front of it with the same elements to transition from. If you put a black slide with a 00-second automatic transition between each of the "real" slides, you'll get a checkerboard, all right! To add a blank, black slide with an automatic transition, select View→Slide Sorter, click between two slides, select Insert→ New Slide, and choose a Blank slide layout. Click the blank slide to select it, and select Slide Show→Slide Transition. Click "Automatically after" in the Slide Transition task pane (PowerPoint 2002 and 2003) or dialog box (PowerPoint 97 and 2000), and leave the time set to 00:00. Finally, select Format→Background, choose black from the Color drop-down menu, and check the "Omit background graphics from master" box.

Push or cover transitions don't work the same way. The entire slide is displaced in those transitions, so, generally speaking, nothing's transitioning in on top of itself.

Show Advanced Animation Timeline

THE ANNOYANCE: I like to show the advanced animation timeline when I'm animating. Why doesn't the timeline show for all objects?

THE FIX: The advanced animation timeline shows animations that happen based on each mouse click. Only the animations responding to the selected mouse click will show up in the animation timeline (see Figure 7-25). To see the timeline for another object, select a different mouse-click object in the Custom Animation task pane.

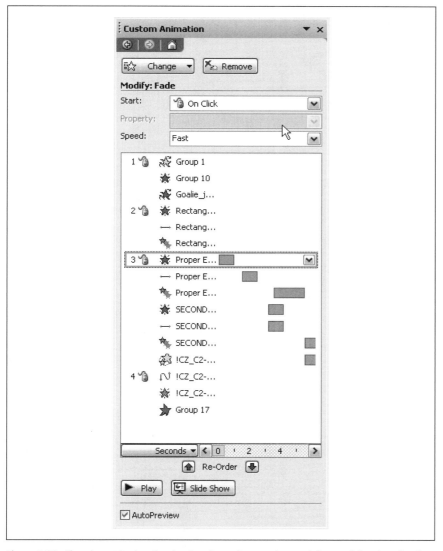

Figure 7-25. The advanced animation timeline shows the start time, end time, and duration of each animation responding to a specific mouse click.

The Advanced Animation Timeline

Double-click any object in the Custom Animation task pane (or right-click and choose Effect Options or Timing) to display a dialog box where you can apply all kinds of different effect and timing options (see Figure 7-26).

Another way to control timing is to right-click an animation in the Custom Animation task pane and choose Show Advanced Timeline and simply drag the orange bars. When your cursor becomes a vertical double-headed arrow (see Figure 7-27), you can drag to change the duration of an animation, which is the same as changing the Speed in the Timing dialog box. When you see a horizontal double-headed arrow (see Figure 7-28), you can drag to change the start time of an animation while maintaining its duration.

Many users find it easier to adjust timing in the advanced timeline, which offers more visual cues as to what's happening than the dialog boxes.

PowerPoint 97 and 2000 only have linear animation options, so the advanced animation timeline is not available in those versions.

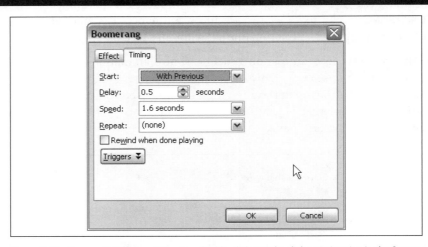

Figure 7-26. To open the Timing dialog box, double-click or right-click an animation in the Custom Animation task pane. Use Delay to adjust the start time of the animation, Speed to adjust the duration, and Repeat to, well, repeat the animation.

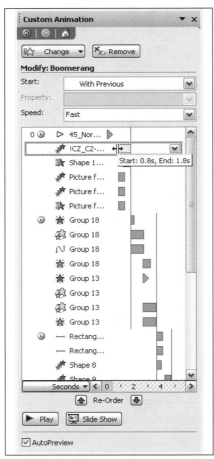

Figure 7-27. When your cursor looks like a double-headed arrow, you can drag it to change the start and/or end time of an animation. Adjusting one without adjusting the other effectively changes the duration of the animation.

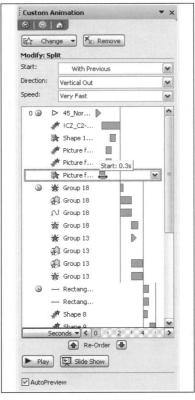

Figure 7-28. When your cursor looks like horizontal double-headed arrow, you can drag the animation to another position on the timeline without changing its duration.

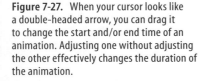

Change After Previous to With Previous

THE ANNOYANCE: I set an animation to begin "After Previous," but I decided I want it to start partway through the previous animation. Problem is, I can't drag the timeline marker where I want it. What do I need to do to adjust my animation settings?

THE FIX: Change the animation start to "With Previous," and then add a delay or drag the animation into place on the advanced timeline.

If you right-click in the Custom Animation task pane and choose Show Advanced Timeline, you'll see a solid line before animations set to start "After Previous." This prevents the animation from starting before the previous animation is complete, which is what start "After Previous" is supposed to do. Changing to start "With Previous" removes that line (see Figure 7-29).

Honey, I Shrunk the Pictures

THE ANNOYANCE: I used a Grow/Shrink animation to enlarge a picture, and it got all pixelated. I need to enlarge my picture to show its details.

THE FIX: The trick here is to insert the image at the largest size you want it to display, make it disappear and shrink, and then enlarge it again. Otherwise, the photo will indeed become pixelated, just as it would if you inserted a small picture and dragged to enlarge it.

Follow these steps:

1. Insert the image at its full size.

   Choose Insert→Picture→From File and navigate to select the picture. If you want the picture to ultimately fill the screen, make sure you insert a picture that fills the screen; otherwise, the picture will become pixelated when it grows to that size.

2. Exit the image immediately.

   Apply an exit animation by selecting the picture on the slide and choosing Add Effect→Exit→Disappear on the Custom Animation task pane. Set the start to "With Previous" so the image doesn't actually show up on the slide while it's shrinking.

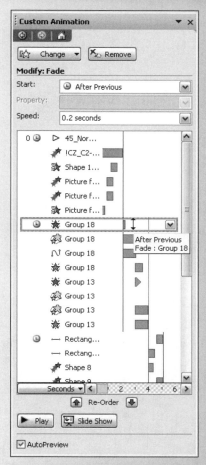

Figure 7-29. Animations set to begin "After Previous" have a solid line in front of them to indicate that they cannot begin earlier. Changing the animation to start "With Previous" allows you to overlap the animation starts.

3. Shrink the animation.

Apply the Grow/Shrink emphasis animation by selecting the picture on the slide and choosing Add Effect→Emphasis→Grow/Shrink on the Custom Animation task pane. Make sure the Start action is set to "With Previous" or "After Previous." Click the Size drop-down menu and type 50 in the Custom size box (see Figure 7-30). Make sure you hit the Tab or Enter key after typing in the new size percentage; otherwise, the size will jump back to 150%. Because you applied an exit animation immediately before the shrink animation, your audience won't see the shrinkage happen.

Figure 7-30. Type a percentage in the Custom Size area of the Grow/Shrink animation effect. Your object shrinks if you type in a number smaller than 100; it grows if you use a number larger than 100.

4. Animate the image when required.

Add an entrance animation by selecting the picture on the slide and choosing Add Effect→Entrance→Appear (or whatever entrance effect you prefer to use) on the Custom Animation task pane. Set the Start action of this animation so that it occurs when you mouse click or automatically ("With Previous" or "After Previous") when you reach the appropriate point in your animation timeline.

5. Grow the image to its original size

Apply a Grow/Shrink animation effect by selecting the picture on the slide and choosing Add Effect→Emphasis→Grow/Shrink on the Custom Animation task pane. Set the Start action so that it occurs "With Previous." Click the Size drop-down menu and type 200 in the Custom size box. Make sure you hit the Tab or Enter key after typing in the new size percentage; otherwise, the size will jump back to 150%.

Because you've decreased the size of the picture before increasing it, to grow the picture back to 100%, you must type a number greater than 100% in the Custom size area of the Grow/Shrink emphasis animation. Use this formula to decide how much to grow the animation after shrinking it:

```
(Target % / Grown %) x 100
```

For example, in the steps above, we "grew" the picture 50%, and now we want to take it back to 100% (100 / 50 = 2, and 2 × 100 = 200). So if we shrink the picture by 50%, we must later grow it by 200% to get back to the original size (see Figure 7-31).

Emphasis animations, including Grow/Shrink, are available only in PowerPoint 2002 and 2003.

Figure 7-31. Your animation settings will look like this if you use the technique to shrink your object out of sight of your audience. This is the way to prevent your image from becoming pixelated when using a Grow emphasis animation.

Zoom In on an Area

THE ANNOYANCE: I was at a conference the other day, and the presenter used a zoom feature or something to quickly enlarge part of her slide. How in the world did she do this?

THE FIX: You can actually enlarge part of your slide in quite a few ways, but they all take a little planning. You'll need close-up pictures of the areas you want to zoom in on.

If you're using PowerPoint 2002 or 2003, you can set up your slides with "hotspots," and set the hotspot to trigger the entrance of a close-up picture. Draw an AutoShape over the area you want to click to make the close-up picture appear. Select Insert→Picture→From File to insert the close-up picture on the slide, select it on the slide, and choose Add Effect→Entrance→ Zoom In on the Custom Animation task pane. Right-click the animation on the Custom Animation task pane, choose Timing, click the Triggers button, and in the "Start effect on click of" drop-down menu, select the hotspot you created (see Figure 7-32).

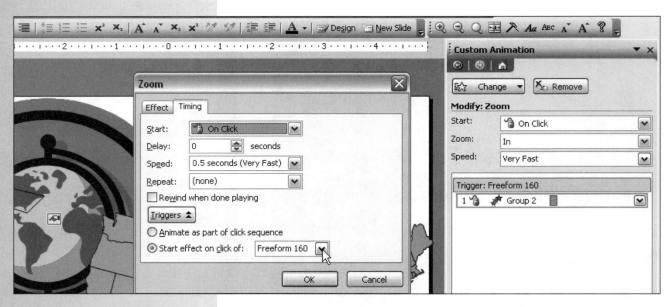

Figure 7-32. Select the object that will trigger the start of an animation when you click it from the drop-down menu.

Finally, make the hotspot transparent by giving it no fill and no line color, or by making the fill and line colors transparent. It's much easier to find the hotspot on the slide while you're working on it if you save this step for last! (If you plan to use PowerPoint Viewer 2003 to display this presentation, see "Hyperlinks Don't Work in PowerPoint Viewer 2003" for further information.)

If you're using PowerPoint 97 or 2000, you don't have any trigger animations to work with. In this case, you can create additional slides with the close-up pictures and use action settings to jump to them. To create an action setting, draw an AutoShape over the area you want to click to make the close-up picture slide appear. Right-click the AutoShape and choose Action Settings. In the Action Settings dialog box, choose the "Hyperlink to" option, select Slide from the drop-down menu, and then choose the close-up slide from the list (see Figure 7-33). When you click the AutoShape with the action setting, you'll jump to the slide with the close-up picture.

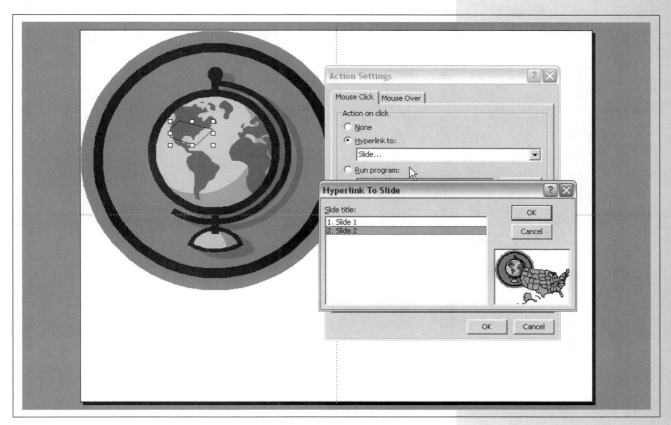

Figure 7-33. To jump to another slide, use the "Hyperlink to" option in the Action Settings dialog box.

Make sure you create an Action Setting button on the close-up slide so you can get back to the original slide. Select AutoShapes→Action Buttons→ Back or Previous and click on the slide to quickly create a Back button. The Action Settings dialog box will open automatically with "Previous Slide" already selected in the "Hyperlink to" area (see Figure 7-34).

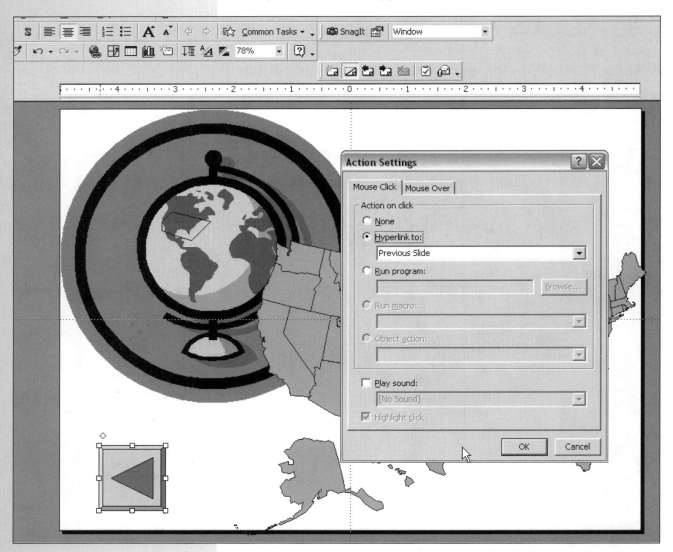

Figure 7-34. You can quickly create action buttons by selecting AutoShapes→Action Buttons. The buttons in this menu have actions such as Hyperlink to Previous Slide already applied.

ACTION SETTINGS AND HYPERLINKS

Remove Underline from Hyperlinked Text

THE ANNOYANCE: Whenever I add a hyperlink to text, it adds an underline. How can I get rid of the underline?

THE FIX: Apply the hyperlink to the *text box*, not to the text itself. To select the text box as opposed to the text, click in the text, and then hit your Esc key. Or just click the "herringboned" edge of the text box instead of clicking the text.

Alternatively, place a no-line/no-fill AutoShape on top of the text and add the hyperlink to it. Click the rectangle AutoShape on your Drawing toolbar and drag on the slide to create a rectangle. Double-click the rectangle and specify no line and no fill colors in the Format Object dialog box.

To add a hyperlink to either the text box or the AutoShape, right-click it, choose Hyperlink, and select the file you want to link to. If you plan to use PowerPoint Viewer 2003 to display your presentation, see "Hyperlinks Don't Work in PowerPoint Viewer 2003" for further information.

Hyperlinked Text Changes Color

THE ANNOYANCE: When I click a hyperlink to another slide or program, PowerPoint changes the link to an ugly shade of pea green.

THE FIX: The hyperlink changes color based on the slide color scheme. Create a master slide with a different color scheme and apply it to the slide. The only color you really need to change is the swatch labeled "Accent and followed hyperlink." Otherwise, the new master and color scheme can be identical to the existing master and color scheme.

Slides Don't Animate on Return

THE ANNOYANCE: How do I make the animation reanimate when I link *back* to a slide in my presentation?

THE FIX: When you return to a slide, PowerPoint returns you to the end state of the slide. If you want the slide to reanimate when you return to it, you must return to the beginning of the slide.

First, create a "dummy" slide and place it before the real slide. Give the dummy slide a 00-second automatic transition (see "Slide Transitions Don't Work Right"). Hyperlink to the dummy slide, instead of the real slide. The automatic transition will move you automatically to the beginning of the real slide, forcing it to reanimate.

> **NOTE**
>
> *The dummy slide can be a blank slide, or you may want to experiment with using an un-animated copy of the "real" slide as your dummy slide.*

Slides Don't Appear When Linking

THE ANNOYANCE: I'm trying to create a custom show, but some of my slides don't appear in the custom show dialog. The same thing happens when I try to create a hyperlink to those slides. What's the problem?

THE FIX: You've used a comma in the title placeholder on the slide. PowerPoint uses a comma in its code when it references a slide. If the title has a comma too, PowerPoint gets confused and won't show those slides in the custom show and hyperlink selection dialog boxes.

To fix this, remove the comma from the title placeholder. If that's not an option, create a copy of the placeholder, leave the copy on the slide, and drag the original placeholder off the edge of the slide. Delete the comma from the original placeholder.

> **NOTE**
>
> *The reason you don't want to just delete the original title placeholder is because you will want that text to still show up for navigation (custom shows, web pages, etc.), minus the comma, of course.*

Hyperlinks Stop Working

THE ANNOYANCE: When I save my presentation, all my hyperlinks stop working! Some of them just do nothing, and others link to the wrong things! What have I done?

THE FIX: You've probably hit the upper limit of link information that can be stored in a PowerPoint file. PowerPoint only has 64 KB available to store links, whether they're to other files or to slides within the presentation, and half of this is allocated to presentation properties and other such information. So realistically, you have maybe 32 KB of link storage. The longer the links, the more quickly you hit the limit. And the longer your slide titles, the more quickly you hit the limit.

One workaround is to break the presentation into smaller files and link those together. Each file will have its own link limit then. Make a copy of your presentation and delete part of the slides from the copy. Next, delete the slides now included in the copy from your original presentation. You can establish links between the smaller PowerPoint files in a number of different ways: right-click an object and choose Hyperlink, right-click an object and choose Action Setting, or follow Microsoft PowerPoint MVP Taj Simmons's linking tutorial for a more seamless method (*http://www. awesomebackgrounds.com/powerpointlinking.htm*).

Each link to a slide includes all the text in the title placeholder. By shortening the title, you free up more link storage space. So another workaround, especially if you have many links to slides within your presentation, is to make copies of your slide titles, leave the copies on the slides, enter very short text into the actual title placeholders, and drag the placeholders off the edge of the slides so they won't show during the presentation.

Absolute Versus Relative Links

THE ANNOYANCE: I want to use an action button to hyperlink to another PowerPoint presentation. How can I create a hyperlink without all the *C:\mycomputer\Documents* path rubbish, so that the files will work on any computer or from a CD in any drive?

THE FIX: Place all files in the same folder *before* creating the links to the files. This makes relative links—i.e., links with no path information. If PowerPoint comes across a relative link, it will look for the linked files in the same folder where the presentation is and all will be good with your world.

If you create a link to a file in a different folder, you've created an absolute link, and PowerPoint will look for this *exact* link every time it tries to open the linked file. So if you linked to a file that lives in your *My Documents* folder, the path to it may look something like this: *C:\Documents and Settings\Echo\My Documents\file.xls*. PowerPoint will look for *C:\Documents and Settings\Echo\My Documents\file.xls* on every computer, and if the user profile "Echo" doesn't exist, the link will fail.

If you've already inserted a bunch of files with absolute links, grab RnR PPTools' FixLinks Pro add-in (*http://www.rdpslides.com/pptools/fixlinks/index.html*). The add-in costs $70, but the fully functioning demo version can be used to fix links to images and convert linked images to embedded images. The full version of FixLinks Pro also fixes links to OLE objects (such as Excel spreadsheets), movies, sounds, and other types of linked files.

Hyperlinks Don't Work in PowerPoint Viewer 97

THE ANNOYANCE: I created a presentation, and it works great in PowerPoint 2000. But the hyperlinks don't work in PowerPoint Viewer 97. I've got to get this working before tomorrow morning!

THE FIX: The PowerPoint 97 Viewer doesn't support hyperlinks applied to grouped objects. You'll need to ungroup the objects. If that isn't possible (maybe because of animations), you can put a no-fill/no-line AutoShape on top of the group and apply the link to that instead of to objects in the group. See "Remove Underline from Hyperlinked Text" for specifics.

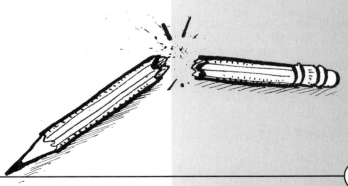

Hyperlinks Don't Work in PowerPoint Viewer 2003

THE ANNOYANCE: I created a presentation, and it works great in PowerPoint 2002. But the hyperlinks don't work in PowerPoint Viewer 2003.

THE FIX: You've probably applied a link to an object that is either 100% transparent or has no fill and no line color. While invisible objects are a great workaround for many issues, PowerPoint Viewer 2003 doesn't like links applied to them.

To fix the issue, add color to the object (Fill Color→More Colors→White) and adjust the transparency to 99%. The object will still look invisible, yet it will have enough color to fool PowerPoint Viewer 2003 (see Figure 7-35).

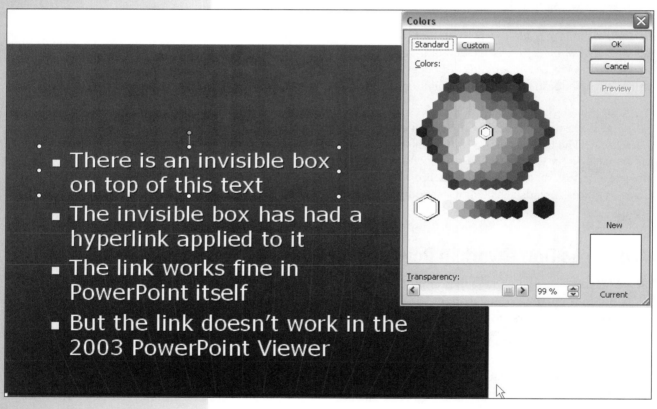

Figure 7-35. PowerPoint Viewer 2003 does not support links applied to objects that are 100% transparent or that have neither a fill nor line color. To fool PowerPoint Viewer 2003, add a color to the object and set transparency to 99%.

Action Settings and Hyperlinks

Force Navigation Via Buttons

THE ANNOYANCE: I made a game for my students, but all they have to do is click the mouse to move to the answer slide. Is there a way to keep them from using the mouse to go to the next slide?

THE FIX: Select Slide Show→Set Up Show→Browsed at a Kiosk (see Figure 7-36). This disables the keyboard, except for the Esc button, and advancing on mouse click. It forces the user to navigate through the presentation by clicking buttons. Don't forget to provide navigation buttons on the presentation if you turn on Kiosk mode.

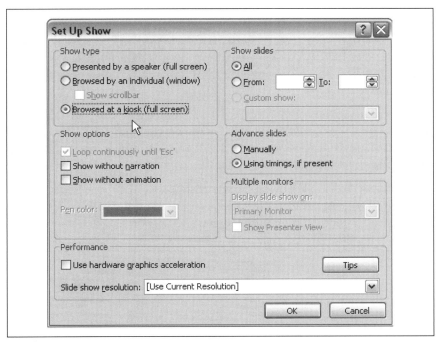

Figure 7-36. Turn on Kiosk mode to force users to move through a presentation using navigation buttons instead of the keyboard or "general" mouse clicks.

A quick and easy way to provide navigation buttons is to add them to the slide masters. Select View→Master→Slide Master, and on the Drawing toolbar, select AutoShapes→Action Buttons→Action Button: Forward or Next. Click on the slide to add the action button and display the Action Settings dialog with "Hyperlink to Next Slide" already in place. Repeat this sequence to add "Action Button: Back or Previous." When you're finished, paste the action buttons on the title master.

If you must also disable the Esc button, use Microsoft PowerPoint MVP Shyam Pillai's free No Escape add-in (*http://skp.mvps.org/noesc.htm*). This add-in works in PowerPoint 2000, 2002, and 2003, and it completely disables the Esc key on the keyboard. If you use this add-in, there won't be any way to close the PowerPoint file, so make sure you've created some way to end the presentation when you're ready. An invisible shape with an Action Setting to End Show is a good option, but if you plan to use PowerPoint Viewer 2003 to display this presentation, see "Hyperlinks Don't Work in PowerPoint Viewer 2003" for further information.

Kiosk Mode Doesn't Reset

THE ANNOYANCE: I set up a kiosk presentation, but I can't make it reset after a short period of inactivity. I thought kiosks were supposed to reset after five minutes. What I'd really like to do is have it reset after two minutes. Is there some way to reset it?

THE FIX: The five-minute reset in Kiosk mode is broken in PowerPoint 2002—kiosk presentations in that version simply do not reset after any period of inactivity. And in no version of PowerPoint is there a way to specify the reset timeframe.

Microsoft PowerPoint MVP Chirag Dalal created a free add-in, Kiosk Assistant (*http://officeone.mvps.org/kioskassist/kioskassist.html*), to fix the lack of kiosk reset in PowerPoint 2002 and provide a way to specify the reset time in PowerPoint 2000, 2002, and 2003.

To use Kiosk Assistant, download and install it, and choose Slide Show→ Configure Kiosk Assistant. Select the reset time and the slide to reset to in the Kiosk Assistant dialog box (see Figure 7-37).

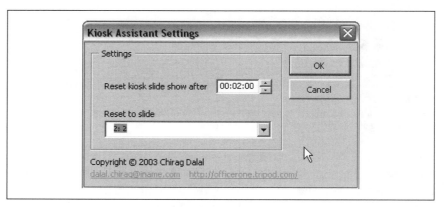

Figure 7-37. This dialog shows the Kiosk Assistant options to reset the presentation to the second slide after two minutes of inactivity.

Sound and Video

8

People use PowerPoint to pull together all kinds of presentation materials, including sound, video, and other types of multimedia. PowerPoint can be pretty picky about the types of media files it gets along with, which can cause all kinds of frustrating scenarios.

In this chapter, we'll walk you through a gazillion ways to deal with sound in your presentations. You'll learn how to rip and play CD audio tracks in your presentation, add background music, embed *.wav* files, and tackle other knotty issues. The chapter also covers annoyances you may face when inserting video and Flash into your presentation.

S O U N D

Hide the Sound Icon

THE ANNOYANCE: I hate that stupid sound icon on my slide. How do I get rid of it? I tried shrinking it and recoloring it, but I can't make it completely disappear.

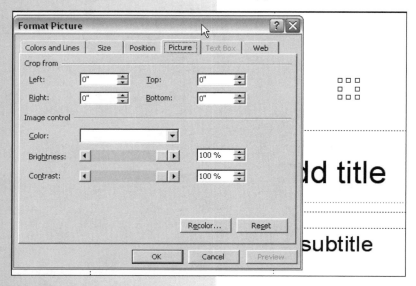

THE FIX: Just drag the icon off the edge of the slide. The sound will still play, but the speaker icon won't show during the presentation.

If your slide background is white, you can right-click the sound icon, choose Format Picture, and change the Brightness and Contrast settings to 100% on the Picture tab (see Figure 8-1). If your background is black, change the Brightness and Contrast to 0%.

In PowerPoint 2002 and 2003, you can also right-click the sound icon, select Edit Sound Object, and check the "Hide sound icon during slide show" box.

Figure 8-1. If your background is white or black, you can change the Brightness and Contrast settings to hide the sound icon. Of course, you can also just drag the icon off the edge of the slide.

CD Track Doesn't Play

THE ANNOYANCE: I put a CD in the drive, selected Insert→Movies and Sounds→ Play CD Audio Track, and clicked the button to play automatically when prompted. I know my CD drive works fine, but the track refuses to play.

THE FIX: You probably have a second CD drive or DVD drive. If you have more than one drive, PowerPoint inserts tracks from the lowest CD drive letter, even if it's really a DVD drive. (For example, if you have two CD/DVD drives named D and E, PowerPoint will look for the audio CD in the D drive.) Put the CD in the other CD/DVD drive and reinsert the track into the presentation.

CD Track No Longer Plays

THE ANNOYANCE: Yesterday I inserted a song from a CD track and it played fine in my presentation. Today, however, the song refuses to play. What happened?

THE FIX: CD audio tracks are linked to your presentation. You need to put the audio CD back in the CD drive so PowerPoint can find it. PowerPoint also links to the track number on the CD. If you inserted Track 2 of an audio CD and then replace it with another CD, PowerPoint will still play Track 2.

If you want to avoid these issues altogether, rip the CD track to your hard drive using an audio ripping application (see the sidebar, "Ripping CD Tracks"), and then insert the resulting .*wav* or .*mp3* file into your presentation using Insert→Movies and Sounds→Sound from File. But be aware that only .*wav* files can be embedded into a presentation (see "WAV File Not Embedded" for more specifics).

Sound Disappears When I Email My Presentation

THE ANNOYANCE: I added .*mp3* files to my presentation and emailed it to a friend, but the sound is missing.

THE FIX: You also must send the .*mp3* file in the email because .*mp3* files are always linked to PowerPoint files. They aren't embedded. The only sound file that can be embedded into PowerPoint is a .*wav* file.

To ensure that your .*mp3* file will play in the presentation on the other end, use this process to insert it:

1. Create a folder on your C drive.

2. Save your PowerPoint file in that folder.

3. Copy the .*mp3* file to that folder.

4. Open the PowerPoint file and select Insert→Movies and Sounds→ Sound from File.

5. Navigate to the .*mp3* file in the folder and click OK.

6. In your email program, be sure to attach both the PowerPoint file and the .*mp3* file. Tell the recipient to save the PowerPoint file and the .*mp3* file into a folder on his hard drive and open the PowerPoint file from that location.

You should always put the .*mp3* file in the same folder with the presentation *before* you insert it into the presentation; otherwise, the sound may not play on the recipient's computer.

This system is a hassle for whoever receives your email. You can use a utility like WinZip to zip the .*mp3* and PowerPoint files together, but it's still a hassle. A better solution is to convert the .*mp3* file to a .*wav* file and embed it into the PowerPoint file (see "WAV File Not Embedded").

WAV File Not Embedded

THE ANNOYANCE: I converted my .mp3 file to a .wav file so I could embed it into my presentation. I inserted the .wav file, but it's not embedded—the file size stayed the same, and when I emailed the file, there was no music.

THE FIX: Before you insert the .wav file into the presentation, select Tools→ Options, click the General tab, and type 50000 into the "Link sounds with file size greater than XXX kb" box (see Figure 8-2). *Then* insert the .wav file using Insert→Movies and Sounds→Sound from File.

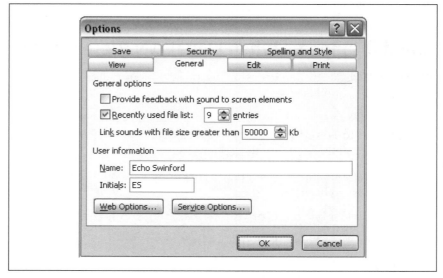

Figure 8-2. The "Link sounds with file size greater than XXX Kb" setting really means "Embed .wav files smaller than XXX Kb." Change this setting before inserting .wav files if you want them to be embedded in your presentation.

The name of this setting hurts my brain. It should read "Embed .wav files smaller than XXX Kb" because it really tells PowerPoint to embed .wav files smaller than the amount you type in the box. The largest number you can input is 50,000 KB, which is just a hair smaller than 50 MB. But you have to set the amount *before* you insert the .wav file into your presentation if you want to make sure it's embedded.

Shrink Your WAV File

THE ANNOYANCE: Okay, okay. I converted my .mp3 file to a .wav file and entered 50000 in the "Link sounds with file size greater than XXX kb" box on the General tab of the Options dialog. Now that it's embedded in my PowerPoint file, the presentation's too big to email! Now what?

THE FIX: Make the .wav file smaller. Using an audio editing program, you can convert from stereo to mono, and the file size will be cut in half.

Resampling can also help—48,000 Hz is DVD-quality sound, 44,100 Hz is CD quality, 22,050 Hz is radio quality, and 11,025 Hz is telephone quality. PowerPoint files generally don't need CD-quality sound. You can often drop the bit-depth from 16-bit to 8-bit when you save the sound as well, which will further cut the file size. Some files sound very bad when dropped to 8-bit; others still sound okay. You'll just have to experiment.

A very slick alternative is to trick PowerPoint. You can make an *.mp3* file look like a *.wav* file by adding a RIFF-WAV header to it. This combines the small size of the MP3 with the WAV header information PowerPoint needs to embed the sound.

To do this, download and install the open source utility CDex (*http://sourceforge. net/projects/cdexos*), choose Convert→ Add RIFF-WAV(s) header to MP2 or MP3 file(s), navigate to the file you want to convert, and click the Convert button (see Figure 8-3). Another utility for this type of conversion is RIFFMP3 (*http:// www.studiodust.com/riffmp3.html*). You can use the program for 30 days without charge, but then you will be asked to make a $10–$25 donation.

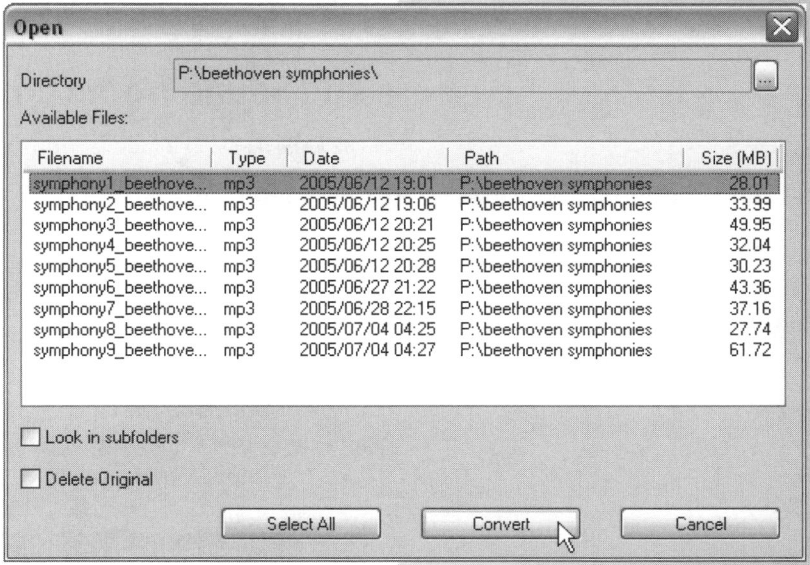

The resulting *.wav* file will be the same size as the original *.mp3* file. Make sure you've changed your settings appropriately in the "Link sounds with file size greater than XXX kb" box in PowerPoint (select Tools→Options, and click the General tab). Finally, select Insert→ Movies and Sounds→Sound from File.

Figure 8-3. In CDex, click the button at the top right to navigate to the folder holding your .mp3 files. Click the Convert button to make your file look like a .wav file.

Reports in the newsgroup *microsoft.public.powerpoint* indicate that these converted *.mp3* files may not play in PowerPoint on Windows 98 systems. This may cause you problems if your presentation will be played on computers running that operating system.

Add Sound from iTunes

THE ANNOYANCE: I want to add music from iTunes to a presentation. When I try, I get an error saying "PowerPoint cannot insert a sound from the selected file. Verify that the path and file format are correct, and then try again." So what's the deal with this file format?

THE FIX: Music from Apple iTunes downloads as an *.m4p* file encoded with proprietary AAC codecs. Not surprisingly, iTunes offers no "Convert to MP3" option. To convert an iTunes *.m4p* file into something PowerPoint can recognize, you must download the file, burn it as an audio CD, rip the file from the CD as an *.mp3*, and save it to your hard drive. Once it's an *.mp3* on your hard drive, you can select Insert→Movies and Sounds→Sound from File to insert it into your presentation.

The iTunes Help files have good information on creating audio CDs. Also, read the "Ripping CD Tracks" sidebar for a list of programs you can use to rip the file from the CD to your hard drive. It's a long way around, but it works.

Add Sound from Clip Organizer

THE ANNOYANCE: If I add sound from the Clip Gallery or Clip Organizer, it doesn't play when I move my presentation to a different computer.

THE FIX: Basically, this boils down to a broken link. PowerPoint's looking for the sound file buried somewhere in your clip art folders. The problem is, *your* clip art folders aren't on the other computer.

If the sound file is a small *.wav* file, it will probably be embedded in your PowerPoint file. But many of the sound files in the Clip Gallery (PowerPoint 97 and 2000) and the Clip Organizer (PowerPoint 2002 and 2003) are *.midi* and *.mp3* files. They are not embedded in your presentation, they're linked (see "Absolute Versus Relative Links" in Chapter 7).

Ripping CD Tracks

You can use a wide variety of software to "rip" CD audio tracks to create sound files, such as *.mp3* or *.wav* files. The following list offers a few of the most popular programs:

- Audiograbber (*http://www.audiograbber.com-us.net/*) is a free program that will convert your CD audio tracks to *.wav* or *.mp3* files.
- Express Rip (*http://www.nch.com.au/rip/*), another free utility, will convert your CD tracks to *.wav* and *.mp3* files, as well as a variety of additional formats.
- dBpowerAMP Music Converter (*http://www.dbpoweramp.com/dmc.htm*) is a good, free ripper and is useful as a sound file format converter.
- Nero (*http://ww2.nero.com/enu/index.html*) costs $80 and includes an audio grabber.

You can find additional audio grabbers by typing "Rip CD" into any search engine.

Overall, it's best not to insert sound and video files from the Clip Gallery or Organizer, as tempting as it might be. Instead, right-click the clip preview in the Gallery or Organizer, choose Preview/Properties, and look at the path to the sound file (see Figure 8-4). Write down or copy the path, navigate to the file on your hard drive, copy it to the folder with your PowerPoint presentation, and then select Insert→Movies and Sounds→Sound From File to insert the copy.

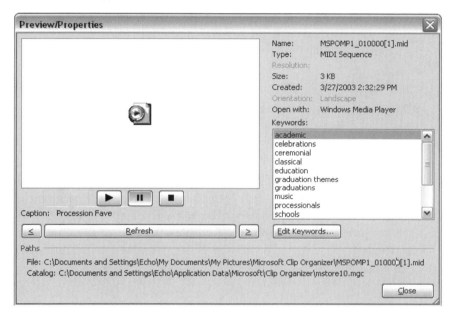

Figure 8-4. If you insert a sound from the Clip Gallery or Organizer, it usually results in a long, convoluted link from the PowerPoint file to the sound, as shown in the Paths area of the Preview/Properties dialog box.

> **NOTE**
>
> *Did you know that you can drag a movie, sound, or image clip from the Clip Gallery or Clip Organizer to the folder with your presentation? First, open the folder with your presentation, and then click the clip in the Gallery or Organizer. When you do this, the folder will minimize to the Windows task bar. Drag the clip from the Gallery or Organizer on top of the folder on the Windows task bar until the folder opens on your screen. Move your mouse to the open folder and let go to copy the clip to the folder.*

Add Background Music

THE ANNOYANCE: When I add background music to my presentation, the slides don't advance. I know the music is the problem because when I remove it, the slides advance just fine. This shouldn't be so freaking hard!

Mother, May I?

Make sure you have appropriate copyrights and permissions before ripping CD tracks to audio files, or even before using any multimedia (and other) files in general. Even if you think you're covered under Fair Use (*http://www.utsystem.edu/ ogc/intellectualproperty/ccmcguid. htm*), it pays to be certain.

Here are some additional licensing resources:

Music

- *http://www.harryfox.com/ index.jsp*
- *http://www.mpa.org/copyright/ copyresc.html*
- *http://www.ascap.com/ index.html*
- *http://www.bmi.com/*
- *http://www.sesac.com/ licensing/obtain_a_license.html*
- *http://www.copyright.gov/*
- *http://www.woodpecker.com/ writing/essays/royalty-politics. html*

Photography

- *http://www.stockindustry.org/ resources/commandments.html*

  When purchasing stock or royalty-free photography, make sure you read the usage guidelines and contract

Written works

- *http://www.copyright.com/*

Additional information

- *http://www.indezine.com/ ideas/copyright.html*
- *http://www.rdpslides.com/ pptfaq/FAQ00435.htm*

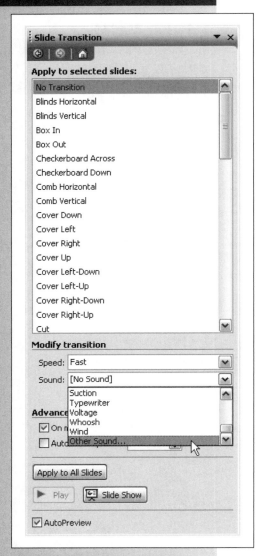

Figure 8-5. Embedding .wav sounds into a slide transition is an easy way to add background music to your presentation.

THE FIX: If you're using a .*wav* file for your background track and it's smaller than 50 MB, you can embed it in your slide transition. Select Slide Show→Slide Transition, and choose Other Sound from the Sound drop-down menu (see Figure 8-5). Navigate to your .*wav* file and select it.

In PowerPoint 97 and 2000, click the Apply button to apply the transition with the sound to the slide. In PowerPoint 2002 and 2003, just select the .*wav* file, and it will be applied to that slide transition automatically. In all versions, if you click the Apply to All Slides button, the .*wav* file will start over every time your slides transition.

Transition .*wav* files are always embedded into PowerPoint, regardless of the size you specify in the "Link sound files greater than XXX kb" area on the General tab (select Tools→Options). The upper size limit for a transition .*wav* file is 50,000 KB, which is a hair shy of 50 MB. If your .*wav* file is larger than 50,000 KB, you can't use it as a transition sound. And yes, you can use a RIFF-WAV in your slide transitions (see "Shrink Your WAV File").

If you are not using a .*wav* file or don't want to embed the background files in the transitions for some other reason, you need to specify how many slides you want the sound to play through in the animation settings.

In PowerPoint 97 and 2000:

1. Go to the slide you want the sound to begin playing on.

2. Select Insert→Movies and Sounds→Sound From File, navigate to the file, and click OK to insert it on the first slide.

3. Click Yes when prompted with "Do you want your sound to play automatically?"

4. Right-click the sound icon and choose Custom Animation.

5. On the Multimedia Settings tab, choose the "Continue slide show" option and enter the appropriate number in the "Stop playing after XXX slides" box (see Figure 8-6).

If you want to add another sound, insert it on the slide where you want it to start playing and specify its Multimedia Settings.

If you have only one sound file to play in the background, type **999** in the "Stop playing after XXX slides" box, which is the largest number you can enter. PowerPoint considers each slide transition a new slide, even if you're going back to previously viewed slides. By using such a large number, you ensure that your sound will keep playing, even throughout long presentations.

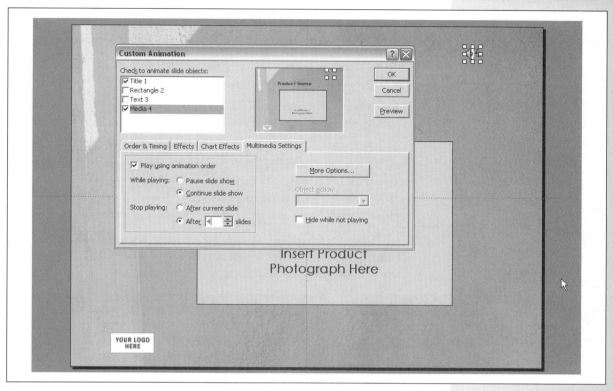

Figure 8-6. If you want to add background music to a PowerPoint 97 or 2000 presentation, make sure you set the appropriate settings in the Custom Animation dialog box.

6. Make sure you set the sound to play automatically and that it's the first object in the animation list (see Figure 8-7). Click OK to exit the dialog box.

In PowerPoint 2002 and 2003:

1. Go to the slide you want the sound to begin playing on.

2. Select Insert→Movies and Sounds→ Sound From File, navigate to the file, and click OK to insert it on the first slide.

3. Click the Yes button when prompted with "Do you want your sound to play automatically?"

4. Right-click the sound icon and choose Custom Animation.

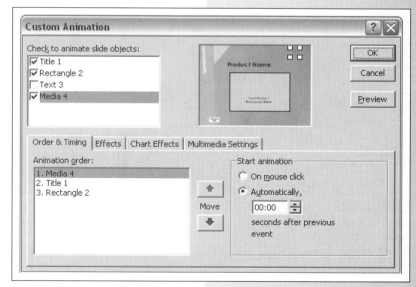

Figure 8-7. Set the order of animated objects in the first tab of the Custom Animation dialog box. Your background music should be the first thing in the list, and it should be set to start automatically.

5. In the Custom Animation task pane, double-click the sound in the list to open the Play Sound dialog box. (You can also right-click the sound in the Custom Animation task pane list and choose Effect Options.)

6. On the Effect tab, enter the appropriate number in the "Stop playing after XXX slides" box (see Figure 8-8).

   If you want to add another sound, insert it on the slide where you want it to start playing and specify its Multimedia Settings.

   If you only have one sound file to play in the background, type **999** in the "Stop playing after XXX slides" box, which is the largest number you can enter. PowerPoint considers each slide transition a new slide, even if you're going back to previously viewed slides. By using such a large number, you ensure that your sound will keep playing, even throughout long presentations.

7. On the Timing tab, select Start After Previous with a 0-second delay. Click OK to close the dialog box (see Figure 8-9).

Figure 8-8. In PowerPoint 2002 and 2003, specify playback settings for background sounds in the Custom Animation Effect Options dialog.

Figure 8-9. Make sure you haven't set your background music to start on mouse click or added an unwanted delay to its start.

8. Make sure your sound file is first in the list of animations on the Custom Animation task pane. If not, use the reorder buttons at the bottom of the task pane to put it at the top of the list.

Use CD Tracks for Background Music

THE ANNOYANCE: I'm using PowerPoint 2002, and I added a couple of CD tracks to my presentation as background music. They're set to play for the correct number of slides, and the timings are all fine. So why doesn't the second one start playing when it's supposed to?

THE FIX: PowerPoint 2002 is really buggy when it comes to handling sound. If you're trying to play more than one CD track in a presentation and it's not working right, try adjusting the settings on the Effect tab.

In the Custom Animation task pane, double-click the sound in the list, or right-click the sound in the list and choose Effect Options, to open the Play Sound dialog box. On the Effect tab, enter **999** in the "Stop playing sound files after XXX slides" box. This should allow your CD track to play and your slides to advance as you expect. For some reason, entering the actual number of slides to play through doesn't always work in PowerPoint 2002, but entering 999 often seems to fix the problem.

The following steps show you how to play multiple CD tracks in PowerPoint 2002:

For example, say your presentation has 100 slides. You want the first CD track to play for slides 1 through 30 and the second CD track to play for slides 31 through 100. Follow these steps:

1. Go to the slide you want the sound to begin playing on. In this case, the first slide.

2. Select Insert→Movies and Sounds→Play CD Audio Track.

3. Choose the Start track and End track. Total playing time shows at the bottom of the dialog box (see Figure 8-10).

4. Click the Yes button when prompted with "Do you want your sound to play automatically?"

5. Right-click the sound icon and choose Custom Animation.

6. In the Custom Animation task pane, double-click the sound in the list (or right-click the sound in the list and choose Effect Options) to open the Play Sound dialog box.

7. On the Effects tab, type **100** in the "Stop playing after XXX slides" box. If you stop playing after 30 slides, the second CD track won't play.

8. Go to slide 31, the slide the second sound should begin playing on, and repeat Steps 2 through 7. You can also enter 999 instead of 100 in the "Stop playing after XXX slides." The point here is you need to put at least the entire number of slides in the presentation in the box, not the actual number of slides you want the sound to stop playing after.

Figure 8-10. In the Insert CD Audio dialog box, you can set the start and end time for each track. Total playing time is shown at the bottom.

Start Sound Partway Through

THE ANNOYANCE: I'm using PowerPoint 2002, and I have a sound file I want to start 30 seconds into the file. When I set the sound start time to 00:30 on the Effect tab, the music doesn't play. If I set the start time to 00:00, it plays fine.

THE FIX: You'll have to edit out that first 30 seconds of the file in a sound editor. PowerPoint 2002 is buggy when it comes to handling sound, and you've just hit one of those bugs.

Or upgrade. You can start a sound at a point other than the beginning in PowerPoint 2003 just fine.

Background Sound Won't Play in PowerPoint Viewer 2003

THE ANNOYANCE: I created a presentation with background sound in PowerPoint 2000. When my friend plays it in PowerPoint Viewer 2003, she doesn't hear any sound.

THE FIX: Often, simply opening the file in PowerPoint 2002 or 2003 and resaving it will resolve this issue.

If not, you'll have to open the file in PowerPoint 2002 or 2003 and disable the new animation effects (select Tools→Options and click the Edit tab). Next, right-click the sound and choose Custom Animation. On the Multimedia Settings tab, choose the "Continue slide show" option. Once you've done this, you can reenable the new animation effects and save the file.

This is a known issue with PowerPoint Viewer 2003. The Viewer doesn't recognize the PowerPoint 97 and 2000 "Continue slide show" setting, because you can't access this setting through the Custom Animation task pane in PowerPoint 2002 and 2003. Unfortunately, you must use PowerPoint 2002 or 2003 to make this fix.

Sound Starts Over When Slides Advance

THE ANNOYANCE: I added some background music to my presentation, but every time the slide changes, the music starts over.

THE FIX: You inserted the music on the master slide, didn't you? Sound files must be inserted on the slide you want them to begin playing on. Remove your sound file from the master slide (View→Master→Slide Master), reinsert it on the appropriate slide in your presentation, and you should be good to go.

It's also possible you inserted the sound as a transition sound and clicked the Apply to All Slides button. If that's the case, remove the sound from the slide transitions by selecting all the slides in Slide Sorter view. Next, select Slide Show→Slide Transition and choose the "No Sound" option. Then reinsert the sound in the appropriate slide's transition, but this time, do not click the Apply to All Slides button.

Change the Sound Volume

THE ANNOYANCE: I changed the volume of my sound in the Sound Settings tab of the Play Sound dialog box, but it didn't do anything. How do you control the volume of the sound in the presentation?

THE FIX: PowerPoint's volume control option ignores sounds that get their volume from the system's volume settings. That means the volume control, even though it's still visible on the Sound Settings tab, does not work for CD tracks, *.wav*, *.mid*, *.midi*, *.mp2*, *.mp3*, *.mpa*, or *.rmi* files. It does work for *.afi*, *.aiff*, *.aifc*, *.au*, *.m3u*, *.snd*, and *.wma* files.

Where is the volume control option? In PowerPoint 2002 and 2003, right-click the sound icon and choose Custom Animation. In the Custom Animation task pane, double-click the sound to open the Play Sound dialog box, and then click the Sound Settings tab (see Figure 8-11). In PowerPoint 97 and 2000, you can't control the volume of sounds in your presentation.

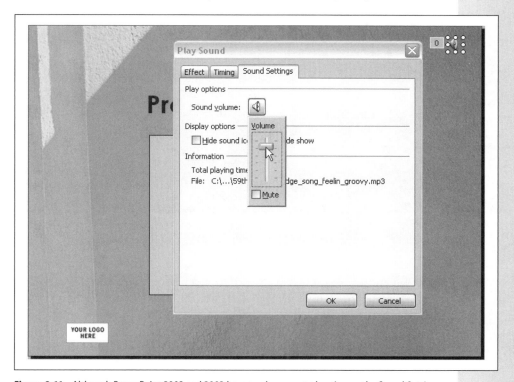

Figure 8-11. Although PowerPoint 2002 and 2003 have a volume control option on the Sound Settings tab, it works only for certain sound file types.

If your computer speaker volume controls prove inadequate, you can change the volume of your sound in other ways. You can edit the volume of the sound file in a sound editor, or convert it to one of the file types supported by PowerPoint's volume settings.

You can also download the $20 Volume Control add-in from Microsoft PowerPoint MVP Chirag Dalal (*http://officeone.mvps.org/volctrl/volctrl.html*). Once installed, select all the slides in your presentation, choose Edit→Volume Control, and click the Set Volume for Slide option. In the Set Volume for Slide dialog box, check the box for the volume you wish to set, and drag the volume slider for the sound (see Figure 8-12). Be sure to choose the Sound ON option as well.

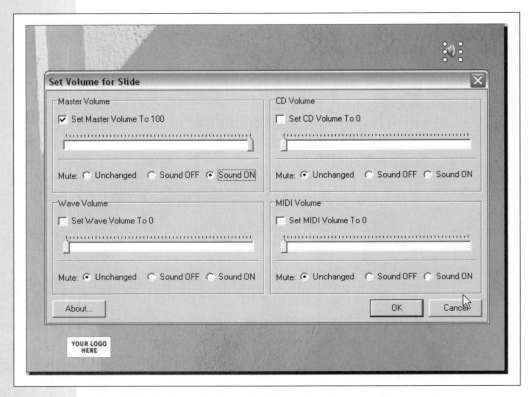

Figure 8-12. The Volume Control add-in lets you adjust the volume of sounds on slides.

After setting the sound for the entire presentation, you can go back and make changes to individual slides. Select the slide, choose Edit→Volume Control, and specify the settings for the slide in the Set Volume for Slide dialog. This is a fantastic way to mute the background sound on one slide in a presentation.

Synchronizing Sound

THE ANNOYANCE: My presentation plays differently every time, which throws my carefully synchronized sounds and photos out of whack. I spent hours making this presentation.

THE FIX: PowerPoint is simply not designed to perfectly synchronize slides and sound.

PowerPoint playback depends on the system itself—the hard drive space available, the RAM installed, the file cache, how defragmented the drive is, the speed of the CD-ROM drive, all kinds of things. That's why PowerPoint files rarely play exactly the same on the same system the second time.

If you really just need some photos set to background music, use the free Windows Movie Maker (*http://www.microsoft.com/windowsxp/downloads/updates/moviemaker2.mspx*) or Photo Story (*http://www.microsoft.com/windowsxp/using/digitalphotography/photostory/default.mspx*) application to create a video file of your photos and sound. It will make your life much easier. If you need more features, consider using Macromedia Flash or Director, although timing can be "off" in files created with these programs as well.

Extract Sound from PowerPoint Files

THE ANNOYANCE: My friend sent me a presentation with some background music of him playing the guitar. He told me I can use it in another presentation, but I can't figure out how to extract the sound file. Help!

THE FIX: Save the PowerPoint file as a web page, and you should get a useable sound file in the resulting HTML and other files.

Follow these step-by-step instructions:

1. Create a new folder somewhere on your hard drive.

2. Open the PowerPoint file, select File→Save as Web Page (Save as HTML in PowerPoint 97), and choose the folder you created in Step 1. In the Save As dialog box, make sure you choose "Web Page (*.htm; *.html)" from the "Save as type" drop-down menu (see Figure 8-13).

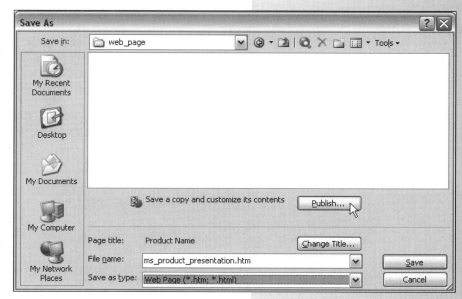

Figure 8-13. To extract sound files, make sure you've selected Web Page (*.htm; *.html) from the "Save as type" drop-down menu.

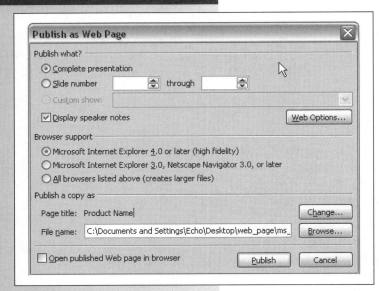

3. Click the Publish button. In the Publish as Web Page dialog box, click the Publish button (see Figure 8-14).

4. Navigate to the folder where you published the presentation. Double-click the folder with the name ending in _files to see all the supporting files (see Figure 8-15). The sound file should be in that folder.

Figure 8-14. In this dialog box, you can change the various web publishing options for your PowerPoint file. If you're just extracting sound, you can ignore them.

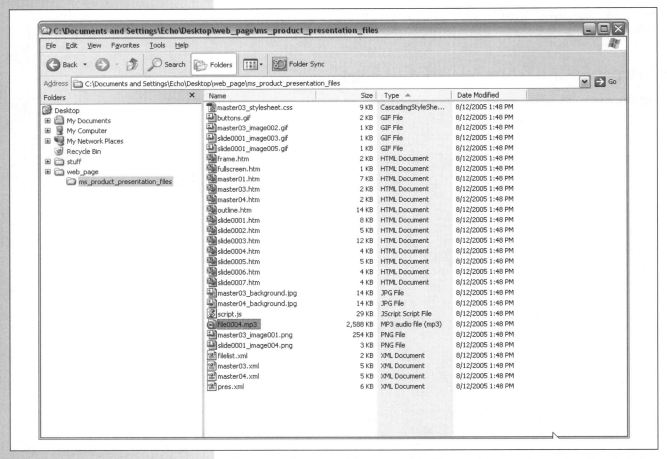

Figure 8-15. After you publish your PowerPoint file as a web page, you'll get an HTM file and a folder full of supporting files. Your extracted sound file will be in the supporting files folder.

WEB PAGES AND FLASH

Sound Doesn't Play on the Web

THE ANNOYANCE: I saved my PowerPoint file as a web page and published it online, but the background sound stops after the first slide. How can I make the sound play during the whole presentation?

THE FIX: You need to create an HTML file that points to the URL for your sound file and then adjust the *frame.htm* file PowerPoint created so it refers to the new HTML file.

For specific instructions on making these adjustments, see Microsoft PowerPoint MVP Kathy Jacobs's web site (*http://www.powerpointanswers. com/article1018.html*).

Show a Web Page on a Slide

THE ANNOYANCE: I need to demo a web page for some colleagues. I'd really like it if the web page could play on my slide instead of having to link to it and wait for my browser to open. Any suggestions?

THE FIX: Download the free Live Web add-in from Microsoft PowerPoint MVP Shyam Pillai (*http://skp.mvps.org/liveweb.htm*). After you install it, select Insert→Web Pages, type the URL of the site you want to display, and complete the wizard (see Figure 8-16). The Live Web add-in creates slides with a web browser control embedded in them.

Because the Live Web add-in uses ActiveX controls, this doesn't work in PowerPoint Viewer 97 or 2003.

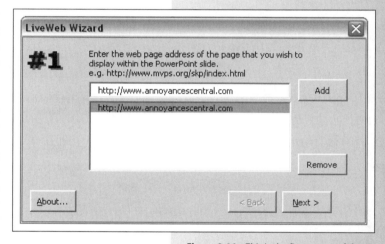

Figure 8-16. This is the first screen of the Live Web wizard. Type the URL of the web site you want to show on your slide.

Play Flash SWF Files in PowerPoint

THE ANNOYANCE: An ad agency sent me a bunch of Flash *.swf* files to use in my PowerPoint file, but I have no idea how to make them work. I tried Insert→ Object→Create From File, but that just inserts the name of the file. How can I play a *.swf* file in PowerPoint?

THE FIX: You'll have to insert a Shockwave Flash Object ActiveX control on your slide. The *.swf* file will play in it.

To insert this control onto your slide, select View→Toolbars→Control Toolbox, click the Hammer tool icon, and choose Shockwave Flash Object from the list (see Figure 8-17). Click and drag with the crosshairs to draw the control on your slide. You'll see a big X on your slide.

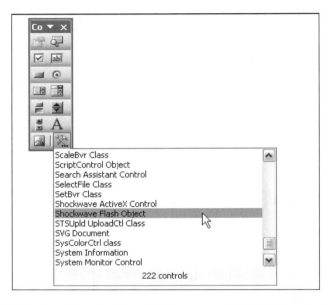

Figure 8-17. The first step to insert a Flash .swf file in your presentation is to choose Shockwave Flash Object from the More Controls button on the Control Toolbox.

With the box selected, click the Properties button on the Control Toolbox toolbar or right-click and choose Properties from the menu. In the Properties options, click the button with the three dots to open the Property Pages dialog box (see Figure 8-18). Type the path to the *.swf* file, click any other options as desired, and click OK to close the dialog. (If you put your *.swf* file on your C drive proper, it makes the path much easier to remember when you have to type it in!) Save and play the presentation in Slide Show view. Sometimes the Flash SWF won't be visible on your slide until you've run the file as a slide show.

To embed the SWF in your presentation, check the "Embed Movie" box in the Property Pages dialog box or set the Embed Movie value to True in the Properties options. It's generally best to leave a little space around the edge of the Shockwave Flash Object ActiveX control on the slide to make it easier to move to the next slide when you're ready. If your control covers the entire slide, clicking the mouse will often restart or click a button on the SWF when you really intended to move to the next slide. Because the *.swf* files use an ActiveX control, they won't play in PowerPoint Viewer 97 or 2003.

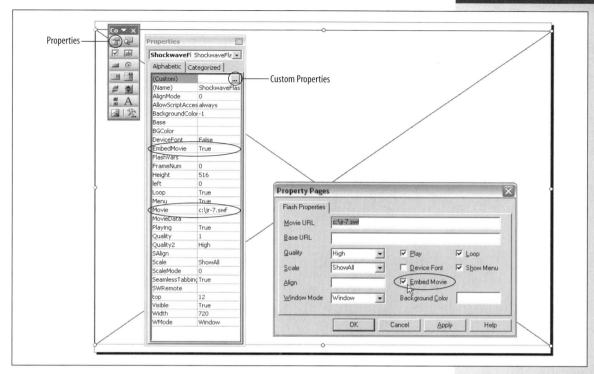

Figure 8-18. Embed your Flash .swf file in the Properties options of the Shockwave Flash Object control.

Make Flash SWF Files Rewind

THE ANNOYANCE: I embedded a *.swf* file in my presentation, but I can't for the life of me get it to rewind. Heck, it won't even rewind if I drop out of Slide Show view and back into Normal (Edit) view. If anybody wants to see it again, I'm sunk.

THE FIX: The free FlashBack add-in (*http://skp.mvps.org/ flashback.htm*) from Microsoft PowerPoint MVP Shyam Pillai will take care of this problem.

Download and extract the *flashback.ppa* file from the Zip file. In PowerPoint, choose Tools→Macros→ Security and make sure your macro security is set to medium. To install it, select Tools→Add-Ins→Add New and navigate to *flashback.ppa*. If prompted, opt to Enable Macros.

To use FlashBack, open the PowerPoint file with the Flash SWF, select Tools→FlashBack→Initialize FlashBack, and choose the options you want (see Figure 8-19). FlashBack will automatically rewind all Flash movies during the slide show.

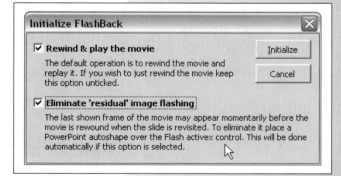

Figure 8-19. Use the FlashBack add-in to rewind Flash SWF movies automatically during your slide shows.

Sounds and Videos Play Only Once

THE ANNOYANCE: How come my sounds and videos don't play again when I go back to a slide?

THE FIX: When you return to a slide, PowerPoint returns you to the end state of the slide. If you want the sound or video to play again when you return, you must return to the *beginning* of the slide.

To force this, create a "dummy" slide and place it before the real slide. Give the dummy slide a 00-second automatic transition. Return to the dummy slide instead of to the real slide. The automatic transition will move you automatically to the beginning of the real slide, forcing the sound or video to play again.

Links to Sound and Video Break When I Move a Presentation

THE ANNOYANCE: I made a presentation with background music and a video on one slide, burned it to a CD, and neither the sound nor the video plays.

THE FIX: All media is linked to a PowerPoint presentation, with the exception of certain *.wav* files and *.swf* files embedded via ActiveX controls. This means you must send the multimedia files along with the presentation and maintain the links when you move the files.

Read "Absolute Versus Relative Links" in Chapter 7 to get a better idea of how to handle your media files.

Now that you've reread it, raise your right hand and repeat after me: I will always put sound and video files in the folder with my presentation *before* I insert them into the presentation. I will include the sound and video files with the PPT file when I move the presentation.

If you've already inserted a bunch of videos and sounds, grab FixLinks Pro (*http://www.rdpslides.com/pptools/fixlinks/index.html*), a $70 add-in from Microsoft PowerPoint MVP Steve Rindsberg. FixLinks Pro will automatically "de-path" the links in your presentation. You'll still have to send the sound and video files along with your presentation, but at least you won't have to go to the trouble of reinserting them.

Path Length Is Too Long

THE ANNOYANCE: I added a bunch of sound and video files to my presentation. Some play, and some don't. I created all the files at the same time, so if one plays, they should all play, right?

THE FIX: The length of the path to your media files is too long. Chances are, the ones with shorter filenames play, but the ones with longer names don't. Because you're right at the edge of the 128-character length limit, you're experiencing the odd situation where some files fall below the limit, while others exceed it.

This happens fairly often when the media files are buried in the *My Documents* folder. The actual path to *My Documents* is not *C:\My Documents*, as many people think; it's more along the lines of *C:\Documents and Settings\Echo Swinford\My Documents*, which accounts for 53 characters.

Move the media files and the presentation to a folder directly on your C drive (*C:\presentation*, for example), and you can avoid this problem.

VIDEO

My Old Video Won't Play on My New Computer

THE ANNOYANCE: I just got a new computer and my existing video files won't play in PowerPoint anymore. What's the problem? Do I have to go back to my old computer?

THE FIX: You're probably missing codecs on your new system. Use a free utility like GSpot (*http://www.headbands.com/gspot/*), MMView (*http://www.nirsoft.net/utils/mmview.html*), or AVICodec (*http://avicodec.duby.info/*) to help determine what codec your videos use and whether they're installed on your system.

Downloading the latest version of Windows Media Player can sometimes rectify this situation by installing missing codecs to your system.

Also, test the media files in the MCI Media Player (see the sidebar "Troubleshooting Video," later in this chapter). If they don't play in that media player, they're not gonna play in PowerPoint.

Put Text on Top of Movies

THE ANNOYANCE: Somebody gave my boss a video to use in a presentation, but he wants to add some caption text to it. I added text boxes to the slide, but I can't get them to stay on top of the video.

THE FIX: You'll have to add the captions in a video editor, as video always plays on top of everything else in PowerPoint.

If you absolutely can't edit the video, Microsoft PowerPoint MVP Chirag Dalal offers instructions on how to do this using two of his add-ins: TransparentShow (free) and PowerShow ($99.95). Visit the OfficeOne web site for more information (*http://officeone.mvps.org/powershow/tips_text_over_video.html*).

Use Video in the Background

THE ANNOYANCE: Well, if video always plays on top, how can I have a moving background?

THE FIX: If you just need something like twinkling stars or moving clouds, you can insert an animated GIF as a background texture, and it will play in the background. Select Format→Background→Fill Effects, click the Texture tab, click the Other Texture button, and navigate to the animated GIF (see Figure 8-20). Click OK to close the dialog box, and then click the Apply to All button to apply it to all the slides. You can also select Format→ Background→Fill Effects, click the Picture tab, and click the Select Picture button. Whether using a Texture fill or a Picture fill is best depends on your animated GIF.

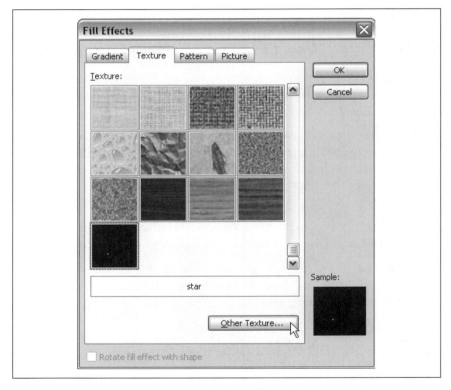

Figure 8-20. Add an animated GIF to your slide background through the Texture options—or even the Picture options—in the Fill Effects dialog box.

If you need more intricate video than an animated GIF can provide, try a third-party add-in such as OfficeFX from Instant Effects (*http://www. instanteffects.com/index.html*). Or consider positioning your video in an area on the screen—along the left edge, in the lower-right corner, etc.— where nothing would have to play on top of it.

Controls for Video Show on Slide

THE ANNOYANCE: I don't want the controls to show when I play a video.

THE FIX: Ah, you used Insert→Object→Create From File to insert your video file on your slide. This calls your default player (often Windows Media Player) to play the video. If you use Insert→Movies and Sounds→Movie From File to insert your video, it forces PowerPoint to play the media with the MCI Media Player, and the controls won't show.

Click to Pause Movie

THE ANNOYANCE: I have .*mpg* movies playing on a series of slides. After the movie finishes playing and I click to the next slide, the MPG starts up again.

THE FIX: Move your mouse so it's not resting on the movie, and then click to transition to the next slide. If your movie covers the entire slide, make it a little smaller so you have a non-movie place to click.

Play Movie Across Multiple Slides

THE ANNOYANCE: I have a little movie of our corporate logo, and I'd like it to play in the lower-right corner of the slides. Any way I can do this without the movie starting over every time I go to a new slide?

Sound Editors

Throughout this chapter, I often recommended using sound-editing software to perform certain tasks like adjusting volume or trimming a few seconds from the beginning of a sound clip. You may be wondering what software to use.

There are a ton of sound editors available. If you have something like Sony Sound Forge (*http://www. sonymediasoftware.com/Products/ShowProduct. asp?PID=961*, formerly Sonic Foundry Sound Forge) or Adobe Audition (*http://www.adobe.com/products/ audition/main.html*, formerly Syntrillium Cool Edit Pro), by all means, use it!

If you don't have high-end sound-editing software, don't worry. You can find several free and inexpensive sound-editing applications to meet your needs. A short list follows:

- Audacity (*http://audacity.sourceforge.net/*) is free.
- WavePad (*http://www.nch.com.au/wavepad/*) is free, but the Master Edition will cost you $49.
- Sound Forge Audio Studio (*http://www. sonymediasoftware.com/Products/ShowProduct. asp?PID=975*) costs $70.
- GoldWave (*http://www.goldwave.com/*) costs $45.
- Internet Audio Mix (*http://www.sonicspot.com/ internetaudiomix/internetaudiomix.html*) costs $30.

If you don't like any of these, go to *http://www.google. com* (or your favorite search engine) and type "sound editor" or "sound editing software" in the search box for a list of possibilities.

THE FIX: Place the video on your slide master, set it to loop, and specify "Continue slide show" or "Stop playing after XXX slides" in the Custom Animation settings.

To do this, first save your presentation and copy the movie file to the same folder where your PowerPoint file is located. Choose View→Master→Slide Master and then select Insert→Movies and Sounds→Movie from File. Navigate to the movie and insert it. Opt to play the movie automatically when prompted.

In PowerPoint 97 and 2000, right-click the movie and choose Custom Animation. In the Multimedia Settings tab, select "Continue slide show" and "Stop playing after **999** slides." Click the More Options button and check the "Loop until stopped" box (see Figure 8-21).

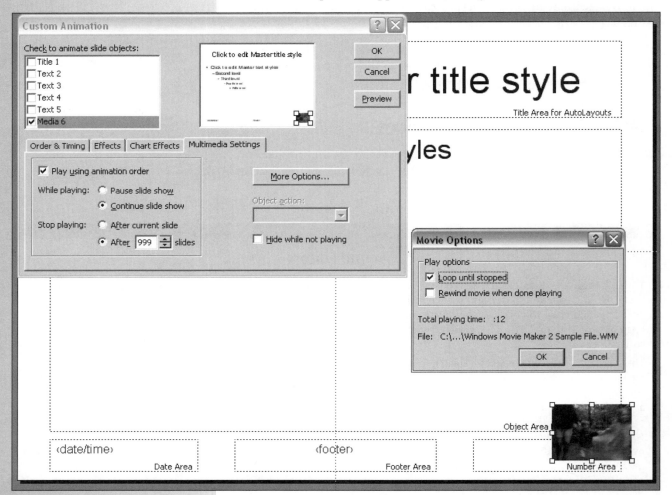

Figure 8-21. Use the Multimedia Settings tab to set a video to play across slides in PowerPoint 97 and 2000.

In PowerPoint 2002 and 2003, right-click the movie and choose Edit Movie Object, and then check the "Loop until stopped" box (see Figure 8-22). Right-click the movie again and choose Custom Animation, and double-click the animation in the task pane to display the Effect tab of the Play Movie dialog. Enter **999** in the "Stop playing after XXX slides" box. Next, click the Timing tab and type **9999** (that's *four* 9s) in the Repeat box (see Figure 8-23). Hit your Tab key and then close the dialog.

Figure 8-22. In PowerPoint 2002 and 2003, right-click the movie and select Edit Movie Object, and check the "Loop until stopped" box.

Figure 8-23. Type 9999 in the Repeat box on the Timing tab.

Mouse Dies When Playing MPEGs

THE ANNOYANCE: Why does my mouse crap out whenever I play an MPEG on my slide? I can't move to the next slide after the MPEG plays.

THE FIX: Updating DirectX should resolve this. You can download and install the latest version from Microsoft (*http://www.microsoft.com/directx/*).

> **NOTE**
>
> *According to Microsoft, "DirectX is a group of technologies designed to make Windows-based computers an ideal platform for running and displaying applications rich in multimedia elements such as full-color graphics, video, 3D animation, and rich audio." Keeping DirectX updated is generally a good idea.*

Play MPEG-2 Files in PowerPoint

THE ANNOYANCE: I inserted some MPEG-2 videos in my presentation, but they don't play. What can I do?

THE FIX: To play MPEG-2 on your system, you must have a DVD decoder installed on the machine. All DVDs use the MPEG-2 format, and it does not ship with Windows. If you can't play MPEG-2 videos on your system, download and install the free Elecard MPEG-2 Video Decoder (*http://www.elecard.com/download/*). Installing this codec may make it possible for the video to play in your presentation.

If not, download and install PFCMedia (*http://www.pfcmedia.com*) and let it convert the MPEG-2 video to a format PowerPoint can play.

Insert Video from a Digital Camera

THE ANNOYANCE: When I insert a video from my digital camera into PowerPoint, I get an error that says "cannot find vids:mjpeg decompressor" or "MMSYSTEM006 There is no driver installed on your system."

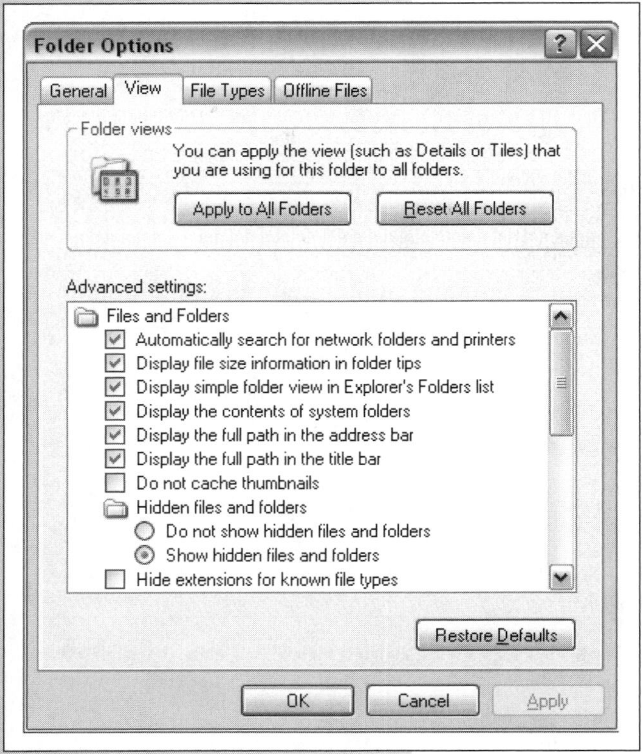

THE FIX: Renaming the file extension from *.avi* to *.mpg* should solve this problem.

Now, usually you can't go around renaming file extensions and still have the files actually work. But many digital cameras seem to use the *mjpg* (motion jpg) codec to create their *.avi* videos, and renaming the *.avi* extension to *.mpg* seems to allow them to play in PowerPoint.

To rename a file extension, first make sure you can actually *see* file extensions in Windows. Open *My Documents*, choose Tools→Folder Options, click the View tab, and uncheck the "Hide extensions for known file types" box (see Figure 8-24). Navigate to the file, right-click it, and select Rename. Type a new name, followed by the new *.mpg* extension. You should be prompted with a warning, "If you change a file name extension, the file may become unusable. Are you sure you want to change it?" Click Yes.

Figure 8-24. Talk about a dumb default. Windows' default setting is to hide file extensions for known file types.

White Box Shows Instead of Video

THE ANNOYANCE: My video shows up as a white box on the slide. What in the world is happening?

THE FIX: The path to the video file is too long (see "Path Length Is Too Long" earlier in this chapter).

Play QuickTime Files

THE ANNOYANCE: I have a bunch of *.mov* files, but I can't play them in PowerPoint. QuickTime is installed on the computer and I can insert the *.mov* files into the presentation, but when I try to play the slide show, PowerPoint crashes.

THE FIX: PowerPoint can't play QuickTime movies, even if the QuickTime Player is installed on the system. You'll have to convert the *.mov* file to something PowerPoint can play—MPG, MPEG, AVI, WMV, etc. QuickTime Pro (*http://www.apple.com/quicktime/buy/*) is the best tool for this type of conversion, but it will cost you $30.

You can find more information on converting *.mov* files at *http://www.indezine.com/products/powerpoint/ppquicktime.html*.

VIDEO AND PROJECTORS

Video Jumps to Full Screen When Projected

THE ANNOYANCE: The video in my presentation plays fine (yay!), but when I hook up the projector, the video clips play full screen instead of on just part of the slide.

THE FIX: Toggle the video so it plays only on the projector, and not on the laptop. You might also try changing your hardware acceleration. (See Chapter 1 for more about toggling the view and for specifics on how to change your hardware acceleration.)

You can set some video cards to display an overlay at a full screen, which might also help. To turn this off on ATI and Nvidia cards, right-click the desktop and choose Properties, click the Settings tab, and then click the Advanced button. Look for an Overlay or Overlay Controls tab (see Figure 8-25). Change the Overlay Display Mode option to "Same on all" (ATI cards) or adjust the video overlay zoom control settings (Nvidia cards). These controls may not be in the same place or even available in all drivers, and you may need to have your projector or other external video hooked up in order to set them.

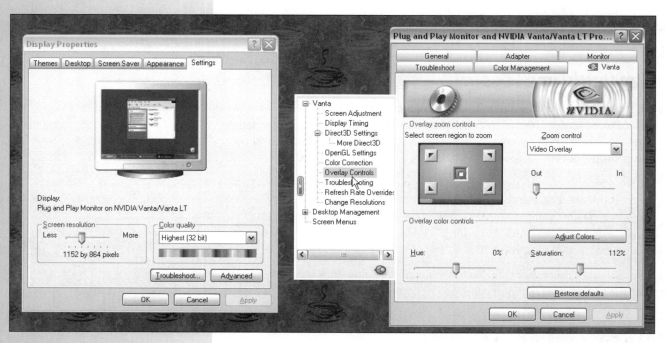

Figure 8-25. Adjusting your video card's Overlay Controls may help if your video jumps to full screen when projected.

Video Doesn't Play When Projected

THE ANNOYANCE: No matter what I do, I can't get my video to show on the projector. The audio plays, but all I see on the projector is a black box.

THE FIX: Toggle the video so it plays only on the projector, and not on the laptop (see "Video Doesn't Show on Projector" in Chapter 1 for more about toggling the view).

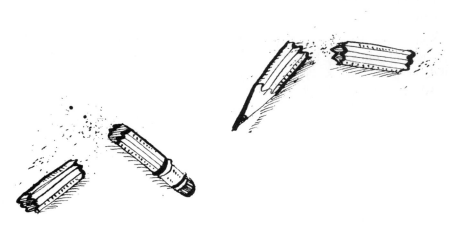

OTHER VIDEO STUFF

Play a DVD in PowerPoint

THE ANNOYANCE: I can't figure out how to play a DVD clip in PowerPoint. The DVD has VOB files and stuff. Can I just insert it like a regular movie?

THE FIX: Select Insert→Object→Create From File and navigate to your DVD software (see Figure 8-26).

Alternatively, use a Windows Media Player ActiveX control. To insert this control, choose View→Toolbars→ Control Toolbox, click the More Controls hammer icon, and choose Windows Media Player from the list (see Figure 8-27). Click and drag the crosshairs to create the Media Player

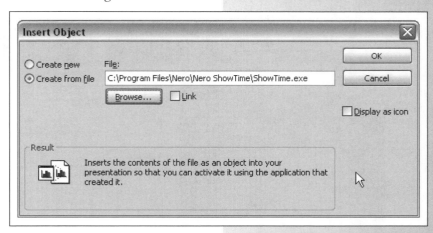

Figure 8-26. One way to play a DVD in your PowerPoint file is to use Insert→ Object→"Create from file" and navigate to your DVD player.

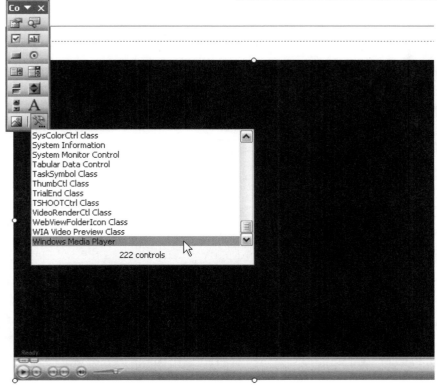

Figure 8-27. A Windows Media Player ActiveX control is another way to play a DVD on your slide. Remember, the PowerPoint Viewers do not support ActiveX controls.

control on the slide. Select the Properties icon on the Control Toolbox and click the button in the Custom property. Click the Browse button and navigate to an appropriate file (see Figure 8-28).

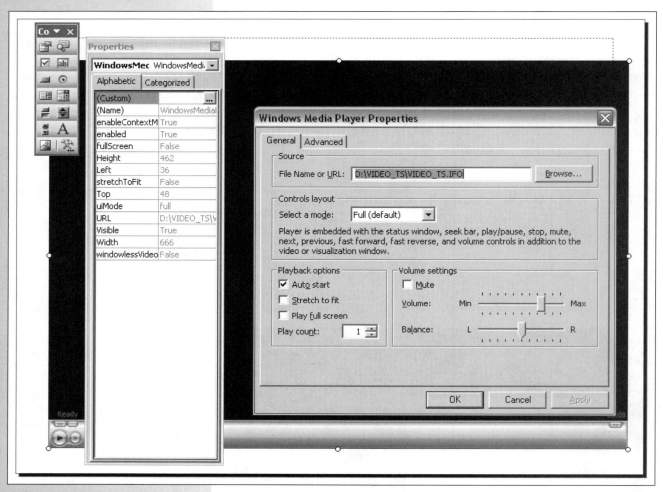

Figure 8-28. Choose Properties on the Control Toolbox and click the box in the Custom property to specify what file to play.

You might also want to try a third-party product, such as the $79 Onstage DVD (*http://www.visiblelight.com/onstage/products/powerpoint/*) or $50 PFCMedia (*http://www.pfcmedia.com/*).

Turn PowerPoint into Video

THE ANNOYANCE: I want to save my PowerPoint file as a video to give to potential clients. That way, they can play the file in any media player.

THE FIX: If your file has animation, you'll have to use screen recording software to capture the presentation as it plays, because there's no magic "save me as video" button in PowerPoint. Be aware that you'll need a pretty hefty system—PowerPoint eats up quite a few resources, and so do screen recorders. Running them both is bound to tax even the speediest computers.

Here are some screen recorders to check out:

Mr. Captor (http://www.fox-magic.com/)
It saves recorded content as standard *.avi* files and will only set you back $29.

My Screen Recorder (http://www.deskshare.com/msr.aspx)
This $30 program saves recorded content as standard *.avi* files.

QuickScreen Recorder (http://www.etrusoft.com/screen-recorder/)
Another $30 program that saves recorded content as standard *.avi* files.

HyperCam by Hyperonics (http://www.hyperionics.com/)
Lets you save recorded content as standard *.avi* files, but costs $40.

Camtasia Studio (http://www.techsmith.com/products/studio/default.asp)
It saves in a variety of video formats, offers a save for CD or Internet (SWF) option, and has Picture-in-Picture recording. It costs $299.

Macromedia Captivate (http://www.macromedia.com/software/robodemo/)
It costs $499 and can export screen recordings as *.swf* files.

ScreenWatch Producer (http://www.screenwatch.com/screenwatch.html)
You can publish your recorded content directly to Blackboard, standard video formats, or RealMedia output. The software costs a hefty $695.

I'm Desperate! Save Me!

You did everything—you tested your presentation with its video files on your computer, and you even showed up early and tested them on the presentation computer. They worked fine. Now here it is, 10 minutes before your presentation begins, and of course, the video files don't work for some crazy reason. What do you do?

Download and install Windows Movie Maker. Import your video, select all the video frames, drag them to the timeline, and choose File→Save Movie File. Save the *.wmv* file to the same folder with your presentation. Delete the original movie and insert the *.wmv* file into your presentation using Insert→Movies and Sounds→Movie From File.

An even better tool is the $50 PFCMedia (*http://www.pfcmedia.com/*), which you can try for free for 14 days. After you install PFCMedia, it will prompt you to download any necessary auxiliary programs, such as Windows Media Encoder or DirectX.

Click the PFCMedia button on your menu bar and choose Insert MultiMedia→Media From File. Click the Windows button, navigate to your media file, and choose the appropriate timing playback option. Click Start Test if you want to see the video play back. When you're satisfied, click Process/Insert to begin the process to ensure your video *"Plays For Certain."*

If your file is really just a series of photographs set to music, use Windows Movie Maker (*http://www.microsoft.com/windowsxp/downloads/updates/moviemaker2.mspx*) or Photo Story (*http://www.microsoft.com/windowsxp/using/digitalphotography/photostory/default.mspx*) to create *.wmv* files (see Figure 8-29). You can download both programs for free from Microsoft.

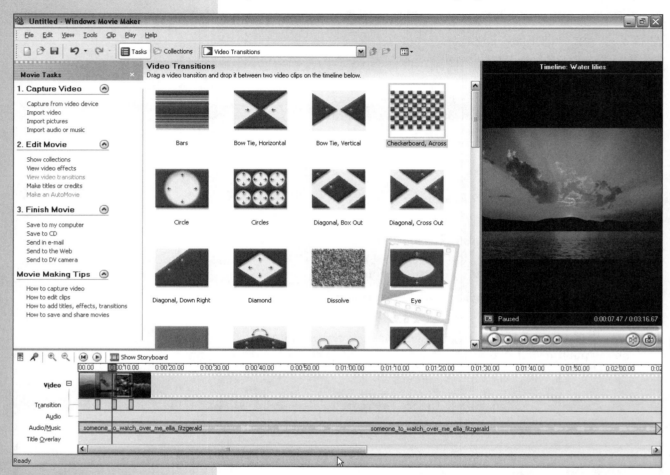

Figure 8-29. Use a program like Windows Movie Maker to create videos of photos set to music. Click Import pictures and Import audio or music, and then drag the pictures and music to the timeline. Click and drag video effects and transitions onto the timeline as well.

Turn PowerPoint into Flash

THE ANNOYANCE: How can I create a Flash file from my PowerPoint file?

THE FIX: You'll need a third-party application to create *.swf* files from PowerPoint. Here's a list of apps:

Articulate Presenter (http://www.articulateglobal.com/)
    The Standard version costs $499; the Pro version will run you $699.

Macromedia Breeze (http://www.macromedia.com/software/breeze/)
    Call for a cost estimate.

PowerConverter (http://www.crystalgraphics.com/powerpoint/ powerconverter.main.asp)
This program will cost you $299.

Impatica (http://www.impatica.com/)
This creates Java files from PowerPoint. Call for a cost estimate.

If you really, really want to do it by hand, Rick Turoczy has a tutorial on converting PowerPoint files to Flash (*http://www.flashgeek.com/ tutorials/09_ppttofla_01.htm*). If you follow this technique, you will need to manually recreate your animations in Flash.

Troubleshooting Video

In case you can't tell from this chapter, troubleshooting video in PowerPoint can be very tricky. Generally speaking, PowerPoint hands off sound and video files to the antiquated MCI Media Player. (PowerPoint 2003 does try to give the file to Windows Media Player if the MCI Media Player can't handle it for some reason. Sometimes it works, sometimes it doesn't.)

If you have difficulty with a video not playing in PowerPoint, see if it will play in the MCI Media Player.

If you're using Windows 2000, NT, or XP, select Start→ Run, type **mplay32.exe**, and click OK (see Figure 8-30). If you're using Windows 98, type **mplayer.exe**. The MCI Media Player will open. Choose File→Open, navigate to your multimedia file, click Open in the dialog box, and

then click the Play button in the MCI Media Player controls (see Figure 8-31).

Figure 8-31. To test your media file in the MCI Media Player, simply choose File→Open and use the media controls on the player.

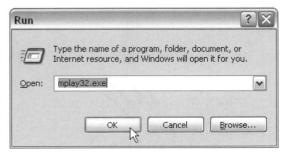

Figure 8-30. Click Start→Run and type "mplay32.exe" to test your video files in the MCI Media Player. PowerPoint doesn't actually play multimedia files—it hands them off to this player.

—continued—

Troubleshooting Video (*continued*)

If the video does not play in the MCI Media Player, it's not gonna play in PowerPoint. Chances are you're missing a codec or a third-party media player (QuickTime, RealPlayer, etc.) has hijacked the MCI settings in your registry. You can read about different ways to troubleshoot these issues at *http://www.soniacoleman.com/Tutorials/PowerPoint/multimedia.htm*. To quickly resolve these issues, download and install the 14-day trial version of PFCMedia (*http://www.pfcmedia.com*), run your video through it, and be on your merry way. If you use video often in your presentations, pay the $50 and add it to your PowerPoint and multimedia arsenal.

If the video file plays in the MCI Media Player, but still won't play in PowerPoint, try the following:

1. Turn down your hardware acceleration. For instructions, see "Presentation Keeps Locking Up" in Chapter 1.

2. Shorten your path length. The MCI Media Player has a path-length limit of 128 characters. If your media files are buried so deep that the path is longer than this, your media won't play (see "Path Length Is Too Long" earlier in this chapter).

3. Update DirectX from Microsoft (*http://www.microsoft.com/windows/directx/default.aspx*).

4. Update Windows Media Player from Microsoft (*http://www.microsoft.com/windows/windowsmedia/default.mspx*). Even though PowerPoint relies on the MCI Media Player, sometimes updating Windows Media Player can affect the MCI Media Player and available codecs.

5. Check for hardware conflicts. For example, some video cards have settings more applicable when editing video than when simply trying to play video from within PowerPoint. If your video card has WYSIWYG DirectShow or other special video-handling options, try disabling them.

6. Check for software conflicts, especially with video/DVD editing and authoring applications. Many multimedia programs overwrite codecs and other files necessary for PowerPoint to be able to play video and sound files. You may have to uninstall the problem software in order for your videos to work properly in PowerPoint.

Printing and Distribution

Even though PowerPoint is truly presentation software—or, perhaps, because it is presentation software—people use it for a wide variety of projects. For example, you often need to print handouts from your presentation or use your presentation as the basis for a video.

In this chapter, we discuss the various output options for your PowerPoint file. It tackles the most common printing pitfalls—everything from printing slides, to printing note pages, to printing posters. It also shows you how to extract images from your presentation slides, save your presentation as HTML, and add video to your slides on the Web. Finally, the chapter shows you how to create Autorun CDs and distribute your presentations without all the hassles.

PRINTING

Print Button Grayed Out in PowerPoint 2002 and 2003

THE ANNOYANCE: The Print button is grayed out when I go to File→Print in PowerPoint 2003. For that matter, Save is also grayed out. I can't do anything with this presentation I just created.

THE FIX: Office XP, 2003, and some versions of Office 2000 require you to activate them. Go to Help→Activate Product to initiate the process (see Figure 9-1).

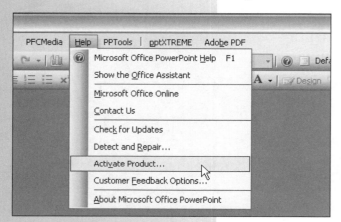

Figure 9-1. If Print and Save are not available in PowerPoint—or any other Office application—you may need to activate it.

Office grants you 50 uses before going into "reduced functionality" mode. In reduced functionality mode, you can open and view your documents, but you can't print or save them. You must activate Office or PowerPoint to return to full functionality.

If your software has already been activated, you'll see a message saying "This product has already been activated." Otherwise, follow the instructions for activating the software over the Web, by phone, etc. Choose whichever is appropriate and follow the wizard.

Print Password-Protected Files

THE ANNOYANCE: I'm using PowerPoint 2002. My boss gave me a presentation to print, but when I hit the print icon, nothing happens. The file has a modify password on it, but I should still be able to print it.

THE FIX: This is a bug. Install Office XP Service Pack 3 (SP3) to fix it. Go to *http://office.microsoft.com/en-us/officeupdate/default.aspx* and click the "Check for Updates" link to begin the SP3 installation process. Alternatively, open your presentation in PowerPoint 2003 and print it.

Pictures Print Twice

THE ANNOYANCE: When I print my slides, all the pictures print twice. PowerPoint's gone wild!

THE FIX: Often, updating your printer driver will resolve this issue. This is generally a Windows 2000 issue. If you're still stuck, Microsoft addresses it more thoroughly with a hotfix (*http://support.microsoft.com/default. aspx?scid=KB;EN-US;843284*).

You can also change the PostScript language level or disable advanced printing features for PCL drivers.

To change the PostScript language level:

1. Click Start, point to Settings, and then click Printers.

2. Right-click the PostScript printer and choose Properties.

3. Click the Advanced tab, click Printing Defaults, and then click Advanced.

4. Expand PostScript Options.

5. Click the PostScript Language Level box, and then type **1** to set the PostScript language level (see Figure 9-2).

6. Close the printer properties dialog box.

To disable advanced printing features for PCL drivers:

1. Click Start, point to Settings, and then click Printers.

2. Right-click the PostScript printer and choose Properties.

3. Click the Advanced tab, click Printing Defaults, and then click Advanced.

4. In the Advanced Printing Features list, click Disabled.

5. Close the printer properties dialog box.

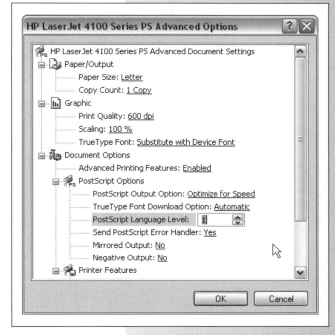

Figure 9-2. The Advanced printer settings dialog has a number of options you can use to control your printer. Disabling some of the advanced features can help troubleshoot some printing issues. Changing PostScript language to level 1 can correct some specific issues with images printing twice.

Landscape File Prints Portrait

THE ANNOYANCE: My presentation is set up to print landscape, but it prints portrait. I went to File→Print, hit the Properties button, and changed the paper layout to landscape. So why does my presentation insist upon printing in portrait orientation?

THE FIX: Updating your printer driver will often resolve this issue. If not, set the default printer settings in Windows instead of using File→Print→Properties in PowerPoint.

Click Start→Settings→Printers or Start→Printers and Faxes, right-click your printer, and choose Properties. Use these options to set the printer's default orientation to landscape. Now start PowerPoint again and try printing.

Margin Prints Around Slides

THE ANNOYANCE: When I print from PowerPoint, a white margin appears around my slides. How do I get rid of it?

THE FIX: You'll have to print to a larger sized paper and trim the whitespace. Or print to special perforated paper so you can tear off the edges.

Most printers can't print clear to the edge of the paper. This is known as edge-to-edge printing, and, while more and more less expensive printers have this attribute, it's still not an everyday feature. You don't usually notice the margin with other types of documents, because you're usually either printing onto white paper, or you're printing onto letterhead that's already been professionally printed. But with PowerPoint and its backgrounds, you tend to notice the margin more often.

Print Slides in the Center of the Page

THE ANNOYANCE: My slides are all cockeyed on the page. What kind of hoops do I have to jump through to get them to print in the center of the page?

THE FIX: Most inkjets have uneven, unprintable areas. A very slick workaround to this limitation is to size the slide thumbnail on your notes page so that it mimics the slide printout correctly, and print notes pages instead of slides.

Modify the notes master using the following steps:

1. Choose File→Page Setup and set notes pages to print in the same orientation as your slide pages (see Figure 9-3).

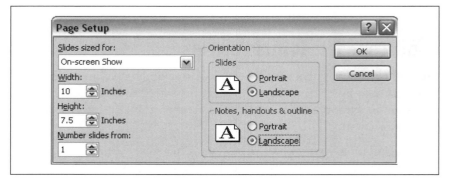

Figure 9-3. For this workaround, make sure your notes orientation is the same as your slide orientation in the Page Setup menu.

2. Choose View→Master→Notes Master (see Figure 9-4).

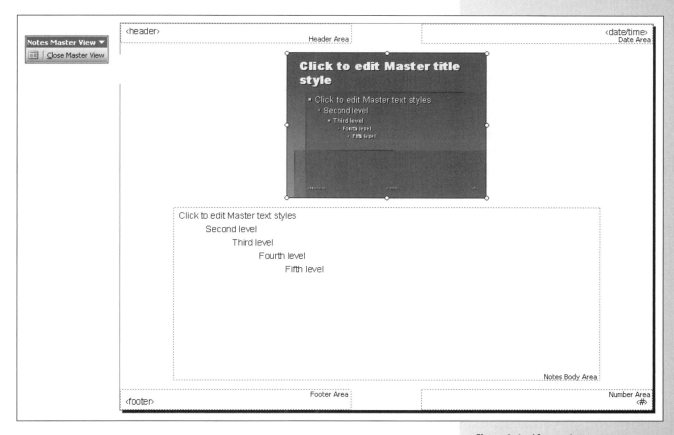

3. Select and delete any placeholders you don't want to appear on your printouts.

4. Select and scale the slide image on the notes master to a larger size, but still somewhat smaller than full page. You need to find out what the margin on your printer is—make the margins on both sides of the slide image at least that large.

5. Print a trial notes page from one of your slides by selecting File→Print and choosing Notes Pages from the "Print what" drop-down menu (see Figure 9-5). The page will probably be off center.

6. Go back to the notes master and move the slide image accordingly. It may take several trial printouts to get it right.

Figure 9-4. After setting your notes page orientation to landscape, this is what the notes master looks like. Scale the slide image larger by holding the Shift key while dragging a corner handle.

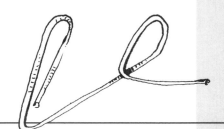

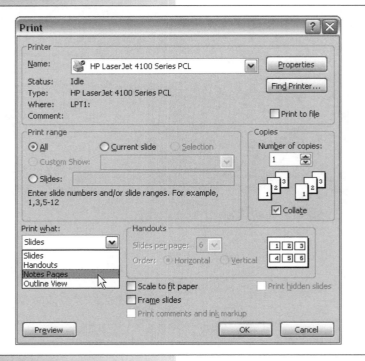

Figure 9-5. The Print dialog is chock full of options for printing your presentation. In the "Print what" box at the bottom of the dialog you can choose to print slides, handouts, notes pages, or outlines.

Print Slides on Notes Pages

THE ANNOYANCE: I printed notes pages using File→Print→Notes Pages, but there's no slide on them.

THE FIX: Apply an outline to the slide placeholder on your notes master.

Choose View→Master→Notes Master, select the slide image placeholder, and add a line to it by clicking the line icon on the Drawing toolbar. Or choose Format→Placeholder and add a line through the dialog box (see Figure 9-6).

Figure 9-6. Choose Format→Placeholder to add an outline to the slide image placeholder on the notes master.

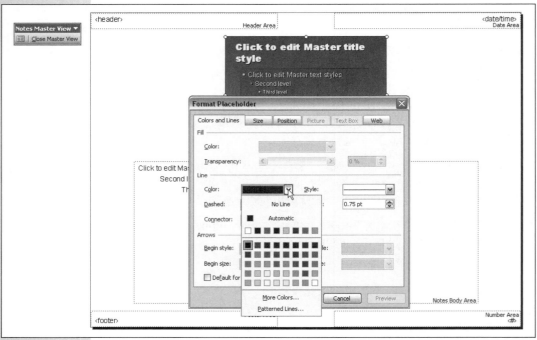

Stubborn Slide Refuses to Print

THE ANNOYANCE: I've got one slide in this file that just doesn't want to print. What can I do?

THE FIX: If the slide has an image on it, make sure it's not hanging off the edge of the slide, as this can sometimes prevent the slide from printing. Use the Crop tool on the Picture toolbar (View→Toolbars→Picture) to crop its edges, if necessary.

Gradient Transparency Won't Print

THE ANNOYANCE: I have some AutoShapes on a slide. I used the gradient transparency for the fill colors in PowerPoint 2002, and while the shapes look great on the screen, they just print as solid colors.

THE FIX: Paste special the gradient shapes as PNG images, which will usually print just fine.

First, make a duplicate of your slide by copying and pasting the slide in Slide Sorter view (View→Slide Sorter) or the Slide Thumbnail pane (View→ Normal (restore panes)), or by selecting the slide in the Slide Thumbnail pane and choosing Edit→Duplicate Slide. On the duplicate slide, select the transparent gradient-filled shape and any other overlapping shapes above or below it. Select Edit→Copy, then Edit→Paste Special and choose Picture (PNG). Delete the original shapes.

This also usually resolves issues with transparent gradient fills not printing at all, so objects below them on the slide show through on printouts.

Print Spool Becomes Huge

THE ANNOYANCE: When I print this presentation, the print spool jumps to like a bazillion MB! What's going on?

THE FIX: You're probably printing slides with transparent objects, and PowerPoint and transparency printing often don't play well together. You need to replace the transparent objects by selecting them, copying them, and choosing Edit→Paste Special→Picture (see "Gradient Transparency Won't Print").

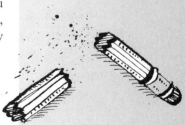

Turn Off Background Printing

THE ANNOYANCE: I want to print my slides without the background. The Help file says to go to Tools→Options, click the Print tab, and uncheck the Background Printing box. I did that, but the slide background still prints. What gives?

THE FIX: To put it bluntly, the Help file is wrong.

When printing a file in black and white, people generally want to drop out the background so the slide prints plain white and the text prints black. Choose File→Print and select either Grayscale or Pure Black and White from the Color/grayscale drop-down menu (Figure 9-7). Click the Preview button (PowerPoint 2002 and 2003) to see what the printed slide should look like. If the option you've selected doesn't omit the background, try the other option.

> **NOTE**
>
> *To change the black and white print settings for objects in PowerPoint 97 and 2000, select View→Black and White. In PowerPoint 2002 and 2003, you have two options. If you choose Grayscale in the Print dialog box (File→Print), select View→Color/Grayscale→ Grayscale and change the settings for your objects. If, on the other hand, you choose Pure Black and White in the Print dialog box, select View→ Color/Grayscale→Pure Black and White. I usually play it safe and make the changes in both places.*

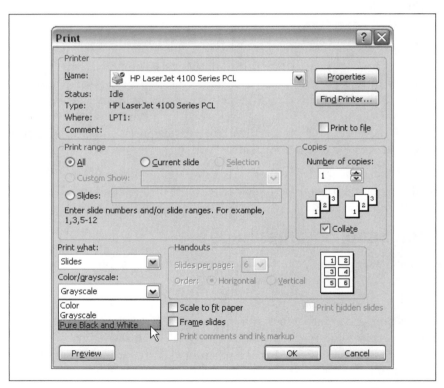

Figure 9-7. Don't miss the Color, Grayscale, and Pure Black and White options at the bottom of the Print dialog box. Also notice the Preview button, which is available in PowerPoint 2002 and 2003.

You can also specify the black and white or grayscale print settings of objects on slides. If you inserted an image on your slide master using Insert→ Picture→From File, use this technique to mask the object for black and white or grayscale printing, as it doesn't change the objects' color settings. Select

View→Master→Slide Master, and then select View→Color/Grayscale→Grayscale (View→Black and White in PowerPoint 97 and 2000). Next, right-click the background picture, select the Grayscale setting (Black and White in PowerPoint 97 and 2000), and choose either White or Don't Show from the list (see Figure 9-8). The large grayscale background image will turn white (or will revert to Don't Show), but the color thumbnail on the left will remain the same. This serves as a reminder that changes to the grayscale and black and white settings do not affect the color slide at all.

Figure 9-8. When you're in black and white or grayscale view, you can right-click objects and specify their print settings. This does not affect the color slide at all.

Figure 9-9. This setting is handy for dropping out elements that interfere when printing, or even just on busy slides in general.

When you're satisfied with the grayscale setting, repeat the process for Black and White in PowerPoint 2002 and 2003. Select View→Color/Grayscale→ Pure Black and White. Right-click the picture, select the Black and White Setting, and choose either White or Don't Show.

If you're using a template with design elements, you can change the black and white or grayscale settings, or you can simply use Format→Background and check the "Omit background graphics from master" box (see Figure 9-9). Turn the background elements back on after you've printed the file.

Print from PowerPoint Viewer

THE ANNOYANCE: I use PowerPoint Viewer to see my professor's presentations. But when I print, I can only print one slide per page. Is there a way I can print more slides on each page?

THE FIX: Both the 2003 and 97 PowerPoint Viewers print only one slide per page. They do not print handouts, notes pages, or outlines.

Some PostScript printer drivers let you specify "N-up" pages per printed page. If your printer driver has this option, you can try specifying N-up—e.g., 4-up—in its preferences to print more than one slide per page (see Figure 9-10).

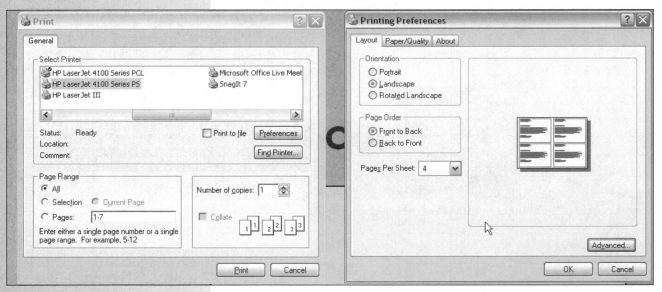

Figure 9-10. To get to the Print dialog in PowerPoint Viewer, press Ctrl+P. Click the Preferences button to set N-up or N-pages-per-sheet printouts. In this example, the printer is set to output four pages per printed sheet.

Print Posters from PowerPoint

THE ANNOYANCE: I have a big conference coming up, and I'm supposed to make a "poster presentation." How can I print a poster of my slides?

THE FIX: PowerPoint's largest slide size is 56×56 inches. Posters are often sized 60×48 inches and larger. In this case, choose File→Page Setup, set your slide size to 30×24 inches, and print the slide at 200%. Be sure to discuss this with the technician who will print your poster so they're aware of how you set up the file.

PowerPoint doesn't have any options to "tile" printing, but your printer driver might. Additionally, recent versions of Adobe Acrobat have tiled printing options, so you could consider creating a PDF of your poster and print it from Acrobat.

You can also print each slide individually and mount them on foam core (or similar mounting board) using spray adhesive.

Specify Global Print Settings

THE ANNOYANCE: How can I specify the print settings for all PowerPoint files? I'm so tired of wasting paper printing out one slide per page, when I really meant to print six-per-page handouts.

THE FIX: You can specify print settings per file. Select Tools→Options, click the Print tab, and select the appropriate options in the "Default print settings for this document" area (see Figure 9-11).

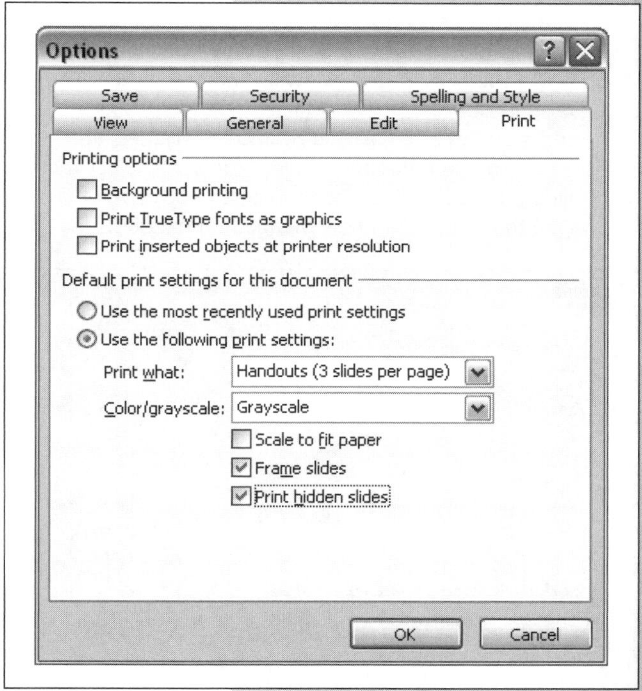

You can also specify these same settings on a template, and they will apply to all presentations based on that template. Be careful, though: applying the template to a presentation will not apply these print settings. You must select File→New to begin the presentation. And in PowerPoint 2002 and 2003, you must also select "Template From My Computer" in the New Presentation task pane.

As an alternative solution, Microsoft PowerPoint MVP Shyam Pillai has developed a free add-in called Save the Trees (*http://skp.mvps.org/savetree.htm*). Download and install this add-in on any system that may print PowerPoint files. The Ctrl+P shortcut will be disabled, and File→Print will open a custom print dialog box.

Pattern Fills Don't Print

THE ANNOYANCE: I made a chart and added some pattern fills. However, they don't print in black and white—I just get solid black bars. How can I make the pattern print?

Figure 9-11. Specify the default print settings for each file in the Print tab.

File→Print→Print What?

When you select File→Print in PowerPoint, you can choose Slides, Handouts, Notes Pages, and Outline View from the "Print what" drop-down menu near the bottom of the dialog box (see Figure 9-5). But what do these terms mean? The following list explains:

Slides

Choosing Slides simply prints one slide per page. Generally speaking, what you see on the slide is what will print on the page.

Handouts

Choose Handouts if you want to print more than one slide per page. Specify the number of slides per page and other options in the Handouts area (see Figure 9-12); the page thumbnail will change to reflect your selections. Select View→Master→Handout Master to add graphics or adjust the position of headers and footers on your handout pages. You can't select the slide thumbnails because the size and position of the slide thumbnails can't be changed on handouts.

Notes Pages

Select Notes Pages to print one slide plus notes. Notes can be added in the notes placeholder when you select View→Master→Notes Master, or they can be added in Normal view by typing in the pane where it says, "Click to add notes" (see Figure 9-13). The slide thumbnail and the notes placeholder can be resized on the notes master, but you're limited to printing one slide plus notes per page.

Outline View

Choosing Outline View prints the text included in the title and text placeholders on each slide ("Click to add title" and "Click to add text"). Text added to "manual" text boxes will not print in Outline view. The easiest way to see what Outline view prints is to select File→Print Preview and choose Outline View from the "Print What" drop down box (see Figure 9-14).

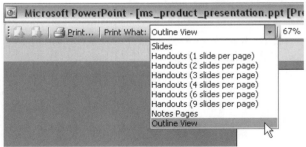

Figure 9-13. You can add slide notes in the notes pane in Normal view.

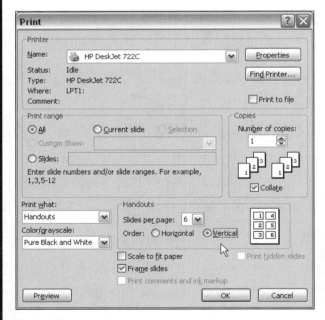

Figure 9-12. Choose Handouts and you can select options to determine the number of slides to print per page, as well as the order of the slide thumbnails on the page.

Figure 9-14. File→Print Preview is available in PowerPoint 2002 and 2003. Choose different print options from the "Print What" drop-down menu to determine what your printout will look like.

THE FIX: Try reversing the colors in the foreground and background of the pattern. Double-click to activate the chart, select Format→Selected Data Series, click the Fill Effects button, click the Pattern tab, and swap the Foreground and Background colors. This will often allow the black and white patterns to print properly.

If not, set the Foreground pattern fill to black and the Background to white. Of course, make sure you set the appropriate grayscale settings for the chart. Select View→Color/Grayscale→Grayscale in PowerPoint 2002 and 2003 or View→Black and White in PowerPoint 97 and 2000. Next, right-click the chart and choose Grayscale Setting (PowerPoint 2002 and 2003) or Black and White (PowerPoint 97 and 2000), and select Automatic.

If *that* doesn't work, then you probably need to update your printer driver.

Print Slides Plus Notes

THE ANNOYANCE: I need to print three slides per page, plus speaker notes. Can I replace the blank lines on a PowerPoint handout with my speaker notes?

THE FIX: Select File→Send to→Microsoft Office Word, choose the "Notes next to slides" option, and click OK (see Figure 9-15). This creates a table in Word with three columns: slide numbers, slide image thumbnails, and notes (see Figure 9-16). You can delete any of the columns, resize them, add headers and footers to the Word document, etc.

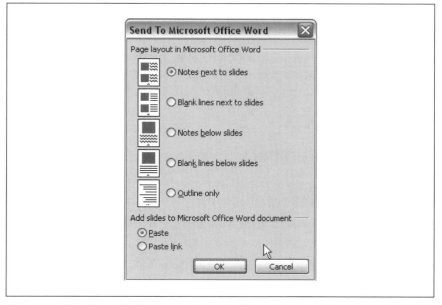

Figure 9-15. Even though the first two sample thumbnails here show two slides per page, the default Word document actually has three slides per page, plus lines or notes.

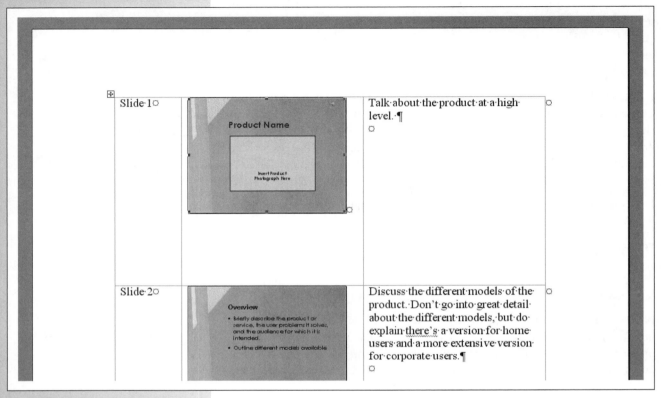

Figure 9-16. The resulting Word document has three columns: slide numbers, slide thumbnails, and either notes or blank lines. You can format this Word document as you would any other Word document.

If you wish to resize the slide thumbnails in the Word document, select one, choose Format→Object, click the Size tab, and increase the percentage. (Immediately select the next slide and hit your F4 key or press Ctrl+Y to repeat this action.)

Update Page Numbers

THE ANNOYANCE: I printed all my handouts two days ago. Today, I had to change one slide and reprint that page, but now it has the wrong page number.

THE FIX: Select View→Master→Handout Master, and type the appropriate page number in the Number Area. Reprint the page.

PowerPoint's printing capability is very rudimentary when it comes to things like page numbering, and it starts over at page one each time. If you need to force a page number, you can type it onto the handout or notes master, you can use File→Send To→Word, or you can use a third-party handout utility (see the sidebar "Extend PowerPoint's Handout Printing Features," later in this chapter).

Best Practices for Send To Word

When you select File→Send To→Microsoft Office Word, it tends to create huge Word files because PowerPoint sends an OLE slide object to Word for each slide in the presentation.

To see this in action, open a presentation, choose File→Send To→Microsoft Office Word, choose the "Notes next to slides" option, choose the Paste option in the "Add slides…" area, and click OK (see Figure 9-15). In the resulting Word document, double-click one of the slide thumbnails. It will become editable because it's an embedded OLE object.

That's all well and good, but the resulting Word file might be 20 times the size of the original PowerPoint file! For example, the PowerPoint file you see in Figure 9-16 is 295 KB; the Word document it created via File→Send To→Word jumped to 7.7 MB!

One workaround is to force a linked OLE object when you use the Send To command by choosing the Paste Link option in the "Add slides…" area. In the resulting Word

document, select all the slides, choose Edit→Links, and click the Break Link button (see Figure 9-17). Continuing with the previous example of a 295 KB PowerPoint file, the Word document is about 2.5 MB after the links have been broken.

So why not maintain the OLE links and update the Word document as you update the PowerPoint presentation? In a perfect world, this would be a great tactic to create handouts easily. But as you know, the world isn't perfect, and neither is PowerPoint.

In a nutshell, the OLE link between the presentation and the Word document is not very robust. Additions, deletions, and reordering of slides in either the PowerPoint file or the Word document are all ignored. Changes made in PowerPoint to individual slides already included in the Word document will show up in the Word document if you update links, but changes to notes will not. Changes to the notes in the Word document will not be reflected in the PowerPoint file, either.

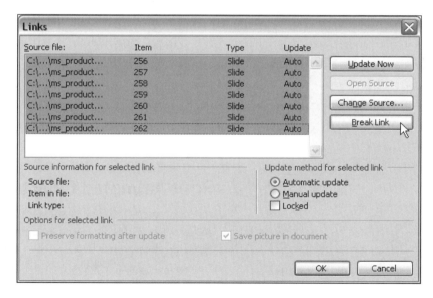

Figure 9-17. Choosing the Paste Link option when sending to Word forces the slide thumbnails to be linked OLE objects. That means you can select Edit→Links and click the Break Links button to make the file size smaller.

Number Slides on Printouts

THE ANNOYANCE: I want to print handouts, but I need to number the slides. I also want the numbers to be on the page *next* to the slides, not on the slide itself.

THE FIX: Use File→Send To→Microsoft Office Word and choose the option closest to the layout you want (three slides per page or one slide per page). The resulting file automatically includes the slide numbers. PowerPoint handouts and notes pages printouts don't offer an option to number the slides themselves.

Omit Objects from Slides When Printing

THE ANNOYANCE: I have some text on the slide that shouldn't be printed in the handouts. Do I have to delete the text boxes?

THE FIX: If you're printing in black and white or grayscale, select View→ Color/Grayscale→Pure Black and White or Grayscale in PowerPoint 2002 and 2003 or View→Black and White in PowerPoint 97 and 2000. Right-click the text box, select Black and White or Grayscale Setting, and choose Don't Show from the list (see Figure 9-8). This lets you keep the text box perfectly intact on the color slide, but specify that it not printed in black and white or grayscale.

If you're printing in color, you'll have to delete the text box before printing. Perhaps you could create a copy of your presentation before deleting the text boxes. Open the file, choose File→Save As, and change the name of the file in the Save As dialog box. Delete the text boxes, print, and close this file. You can save the changes or not, as this is only a copy of your original file.

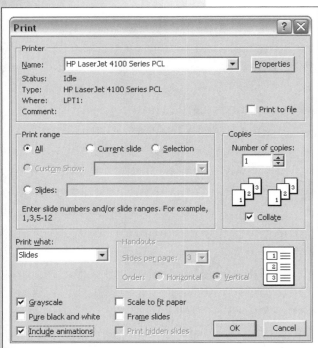

Figure 9-18. In PowerPoint 97 and 2000, you can opt to print animations in the Print dialog. This option is not available in PowerPoint 2002 and 2003.

Print Animated Objects

THE ANNOYANCE: I have a presentation that has several slides with multiple animated objects. It works fine in the slide show, but when I print it, the animation doesn't show up. Is there a way to print a series of animations?

THE FIX: If you're using PowerPoint 97 or 2000, select File→Print and check the "Include animations" box at the bottom of the dialog box (see Figure 9-18). This option is available only if you choose Slides from the "Print what" drop-down menu; if you've chosen Handouts, Notes Pages, or Outline View, the option to print animations will be grayed out.

PowerPoint 2002 and 2003 introduced nonlinear animations so the "Include animations" option was removed from the Print dialog.

If you need to print a series of animations in those versions of PowerPoint, you can use the free Capture Show add-in from Microsoft PowerPoint MVP Shyam Pillai (*http://skp.mvps.org/cshow.htm*). Download and install the add-in, select Tools→Capture Show, choose the appropriate capture mode and output type from the dialog box, and click the "Begin" button (see Figure 9-19). (If your presentation uses trigger animations, you may prefer to choose Semi-automatic as the Capture mode.) Capture Show will play the presentation, create images of each animation step, and place the images in a new PowerPoint file. When this process is complete, you can print the resulting PowerPoint file.

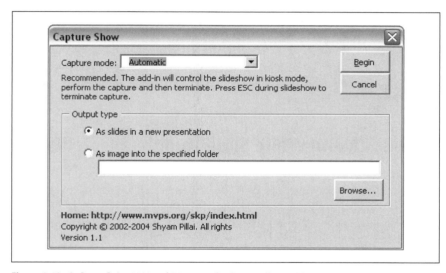

Figure 9-19. In PowerPoint 2002 and 2003, use the Capture Show add-in to automatically grab images of each animation step and place them on slides in a new presentation. You can then print the resulting file.

Line Prints on Filled Text Box

THE ANNOYANCE: I created some text boxes with background-colored fills to hide some text underneath. Everything looks like it should until I print black and white slides or handouts—those text boxes print with a line around them. The line doesn't show up in Print Preview or Pure Black and White view or Grayscale view, and I've triple-checked to make sure no line

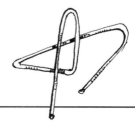

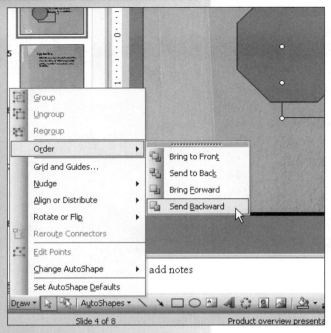

Figure 9-20. Select Draw→Order→Send Backward to place a filled AutoShape behind a text box. Alternatively, choose the text box and choose Draw→Order→Bring to Front.

is applied to the text box. How can I get rid of this stupid line on the printouts?

THE FIX: You'll have to work around this by creating an AutoShape with a background-colored fill, placing it behind the text box, and removing the fill from the text box itself. Then change the black and white or grayscale setting of the AutoShape to White or another appropriate option.

Basically, the fill on the text box is what causes the line to print when you print black and white or grayscale. To prevent the line, you have to remove the fill from the text box. If you filled the text box so it would cover something on the slide, create an AutoShape and apply the fill to it. (See "Turn Off Background Printing" for specifics on how to change the AutoShape's black and white or grayscale print setting.) Finally, select Draw→Order→ Send Backward to place the AutoShape behind the text box (see Figure 9-20).

Send Black and White Slide Thumbnails to Word

THE ANNOYANCE: In PowerPoint 2000, I could select View→Black and White and then File→Send To→Microsoft Word to create better handouts using black and white slide thumbnails. When I try this in PowerPoint 2002 or 2003, however, I always get colored slide thumbnails. Is there a workaround?

THE FIX: The best solution to this problem is to keep a copy of PowerPoint 97 or 2000 around, as Send To Word in black and white is broken in PowerPoint 2002 and 2003.

When you need to send black and white thumbnails to Word in PowerPoint 97 or 2000, make sure all of the following are true:

- You're in Normal view (View→Normal), not in Slide Sorter or Notes Page view.

- You're in Black and White view (View→Black and White).

- You select Paste Link in the File→Send To→Microsoft Word dialog box.

Otherwise, PowerPoint will send color slide thumbnails to Word.

If you're using PowerPoint 2002 or 2003, it will always send color slide thumbnails to Word. You can, however, apply a new black and white color scheme to a copy of your slides and send it to Word. (Depending how closely you followed the slide color scheme when developing the presentation, this could be a real pain.) Also, if you have a picture background on your slide, you'll have to manually change the image to black and white.

You may want to experiment with two add-ins that increase PowerPoint's handouts capabilities: Handout Wizard and SlideIntoWord. Depending on your file, these may help you overcome some of PowerPoint's printing limitations (see the sidebar "Extend PowerPoint's Handout Printing Features").

Create PDFs from PowerPoint

THE ANNOYANCE: I need to send a PowerPoint file to a copy shop to print, but they don't have PowerPoint. Any suggestions?

THE FIX: Create a PDF from your file. Any copy shop worth its salt will be able to print a PDF.

To create a PDF from PowerPoint, download and install a PDF printer driver. Choose File→Print and choose the PDF printer driver from the Printer Name area at the top of the dialog box. Specify what to print elsewhere in the dialog box, just as you would if you were printing to a physical printer. Click the Properties button near the printer name to make adjustments to the PDF output itself.

There are a number of PDF drivers available. Here's a list:

PrimoPDF (http://www.primopdf.com/)
> This free converter works as a PDF printer driver.

PStill (http://www.pstill.com/)
> The Personal version of the program will cost you $23; the Commercial version $43. Both work as a PDF printer driver.

PDFcamp (http://www.verypdf.com/pdfcamp/pdfcamp.htm)
> The company offers a $29 Standard and $38 Pro version of its PDF conversion software.

Win2PDF (http://www.daneprairie.com/)
> The $35 Standard and $69 Pro version let you create PDF files from any Windows application.

FlashPaper (http://www.macromedia.com/software/flashpaper/)
> This $79 program can convert files to PDF or Flash. It includes a toolbar with one-click conversion for Microsoft Office applications.

Jaws PDF Creator (http://www.jawspdf.com/pdf_creator/)
> For $84 you get a toolbar plug-in for Word and PowerPoint with one-click PDF creation.

Adobe Acrobat (http://www.adobe.com/products/acrobat/main.html)
> Arguably the most well known of the PDF creators, the Standard and Professional versions cost $299 and $449, respectively. Acrobat also has a plug-in for Microsoft Office applications that creates PDFs with one click.

Extend PowerPoint's Handout Printing Features

If you do a lot of printing from PowerPoint, you owe it to yourself to try two commercial add-ins: Handout Wizard and SlideIntoWord.

Handout Wizard (*http://skp.mvps. org/how/*) costs $40 and provides a wizard-like interface, which walks you through various options you can include in your handout. The handout can be further edited and formatted before printing. Several layout options are available, and you can also *create* your own.

SlideIntoWord (*http://billdilworth. mvps.org/SlideIntoWord.htm*) is a kinder, gentler version of the Send To Word command, and only costs $20. It creates Word documents preformatted to include a heading, page numbering, and the main table with slides, slide numbers, and lines or notes. SlideIntoWord also lets you specify the size of slide images and include an indication of how many manual animation advances are on each slide.

IMAGES

Extract Images from a PowerPoint File

THE ANNOYANCE: I created a PowerPoint file with a bunch of pictures I took on vacation. I just realized I accidentally deleted my vacation pictures from my computer. Can I extract them from the PowerPoint file?

THE FIX: You can get your photos out of the presentation file in quite a few ways.

If you're using PowerPoint 2002 or 2003, right-click the image, select Save As Picture, and choose Save Original Picture by clicking the little arrow next to the Save button (see Figure 9-21).

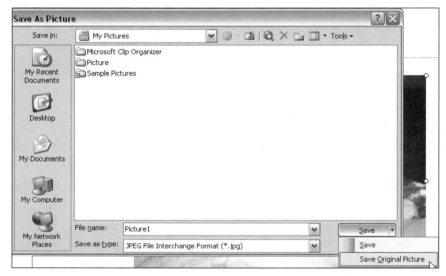

Figure 9-21. When you right-click a picture in PowerPoint 2002 and 2003, you have the option to save the original picture.

In any version of PowerPoint, you can select File→Save as Web Page. The resulting folder full of files will include your images as either JPGs or PNGs.

You can also select the picture on the slide, copy it, and paste it into any image-editing application.

Increase the Resolution of Exported Slide Images

THE ANNOYANCE: I want to save my PowerPoint slides as images, but the text on them is really ragged when I do screenshots. How can I increase the resolution so the slide images look better?

THE FIX: Select File→Save As and choose an image type from the "Save as type" drop-down menu. You'll see a box asking if you want to save all the slides or just the current slide. Click the appropriate button, and the save process will complete (see Figure 9-22).

Figure 9-22. When you choose to save a PowerPoint file as an image, PowerPoint 2002 and 2003 ask if you want to save every slide or the current slide. PowerPoint 97 and 2000 ask "Do you want to export every slide in the presentation".

When you save a file as an image, PowerPoint uses the slide size specified in the Page Setup dialog to determine the size of the saved image. If you need more pixels than you're getting with your regular slide size, choose File→ Page Setup and increase the size of your slide proportionately (see Figure 9-23). Be sure to check the file after changing the Page Setup size, as doing so can cause strange formatting issues on some slides.

> **NOTE**
>
> *Text slides generally look cleaner when saved as .png files than they do when saved as .jpg files.*

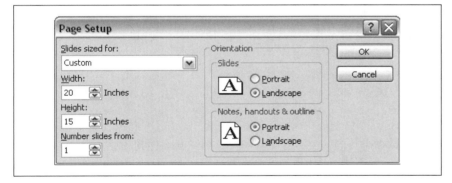

Figure 9-23. Choose File→Page Setup to increase the size of your slide, which increases the image resolution when you save the file as an image.

In PowerPoint 2003, you can change the slide image export size in the Windows registry. Visit Microsoft to learn how to do this (*http://support. microsoft.com/default.aspx?scid=kb;en-us;827745&Product=ppt2003*).

In all versions of PowerPoint, you can also use the $30 RnR Image Exporter add-in (*http://www.rdpslides.com/pptools/FAQ00005.htm*). The Image Exporter lets you specify export size, choose image type, append the filenames, and specify a range of slides to export, all in one dialog box (see Figure 9-24).

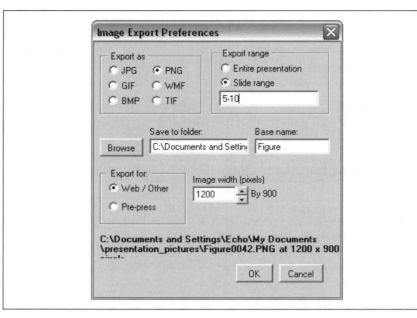

Figure 9-24. The RnR Image Exporter add-in offers a number of options to create images of your slides.

Create Black and White Slide Images

THE ANNOYANCE: I'm making a syllabus in InDesign, and I need to create black and white *.png* files of my PowerPoint slides. Is this even possible?

THE FIX: Sure, but you'll need PowerPoint 97 or 2000 to do it. Select View→ Normal, View→Black and White, and finally, File→Save As. In the "Save as type" drop-down menu, choose either Tag Image File Format (*.tif; *.tiff) or Windows Metafile (*.wmf), which are the only black and white image formats PowerPoint will export. Use an image-editing application to resave the *.tif* or *.wmf* files as *.png* files.

If you only have PowerPoint 2002 and 2003, you can select File→Save As and choose PNG Portable Network Graphics Format (*.png) from the "Save as type" drop-down menu. You'll have to open the *.png* files in an image editor and convert them to grayscale.

If your slide background is dark or is a picture, and if you want the exported images to use a white background with black text, you should remove the background picture or color and apply a new black and white color scheme to a copy of your file. Because PowerPoint 2002 and 2003 can only export color images of the slides, removing the slide background and applying a black and white color scheme might even make it possible for you to save "black and white" colored images directly from PowerPoint 2002 and 2003 without having to convert the images in an image-editing application.

Create EPS Images

THE ANNOYANCE: I'm publishing an article in a scientific journal, and they've requested *.eps* files. Is it even possible to create *.eps* files from my PowerPoint slides?

THE FIX: Select File→Save As and choose Windows Metafile (*.wmf) from the "Save as type" drop-down menu. This is a good place to start because both *.wmf* and *.eps* files are vector-based. Open the *.wmf* file in a vector image editor such as Illustrator or Corel Draw, create outlines from the type, and select File→Export or File→Save As to create the *.eps* file (see Figure 9-25).

Or you can follow these steps:

1. Print a single slide to a single-page PDF from within PowerPoint (see "Create PDFs from PowerPoint" earlier in this chapter).

2. Open the PDF in Adobe Illustrator, and then export to an EPS format.

Since PDF and EPS are based on the same technologies, you'll get much better quality than using WMF as an intermediate format.

This trick works with any application that cannot export to an EPS file.

Figure 9-25. Save your slide as a .wmf file and then open it in a vector-based image editor, such as Adobe Illustrator. Select Type→Create Outlines to create outlines from the text, and select File→Save As to save the file as an .eps file.

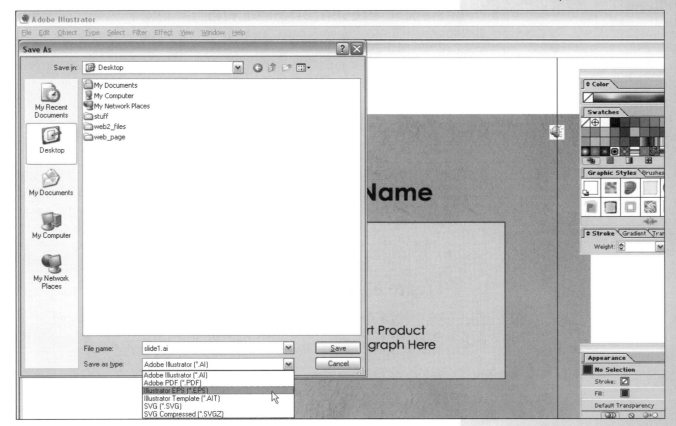

Convert PowerPoint File to Video File

THE ANNOYANCE: How can I create a video of my PowerPoint file? On the Mac, there's an option to "Save as QuickTime Movie." How come PowerPoint doesn't have that on the PC?

THE FIX: If your slides have animation, you'll need to use screen-capturing software. If your slides are pictures with background music, you're better off using something like Windows Movie Maker (*http://www. microsoft.com/windowsxp/downloads/updates/moviemaker2.mspx*) or Photo Story (*http://www.microsoft.com/windowsxp/using/digitalphotography/ photostory/default.mspx*) to create the video file. You can download both programs from Microsoft for free. (See "Turn PowerPoint into Video" in Chapter 8 for more information.)

Microsoft and Apple, the creator of QuickTime, are competitors, so the chances of PowerPoint on the PC incorporating a "Save as QuickTime Movie" option are slim to none.

Record Presentation to VHS

THE ANNOYANCE: How can I record my presentation to VHS?

THE FIX: Look for an S-Video Out or an F-Connector on the back of your computer where your video card is located. This outputs your computer's display to other devices. Connect the computer's "video out" connection (the S-Video Out or F-Connector) to your VCR's "video in" connection using a cable with the proper plugs on either end. (You can usually get these at Radio Shack or similar stores.) Press the Record button on your VCR and play the presentation on your computer.

If you need professional quality video, contact a production house and let a professional do this conversion. If you really want to do it yourself, read the tutorial found on the following web site: *http://www.soniacoleman.com/ Tutorials/PowerPoint/recordvhs.htm*.

Create a DVD

THE ANNOYANCE: I want to put my presentation on a DVD my friends can watch on a regular DVD player hooked up to their TV. What's the best way to do this?

THE FIX: Creating a video DVD from a PowerPoint file is *not* a trivial thing to do. You must create an MPEG video of your PowerPoint file (see "Convert PowerPoint File to Video File") and use DVD-authoring software to create the DVD interface. Some higher-end DVD-authoring software imports PowerPoint files, but beware—the software simply imports the slides as a series of images.

A couple of third-party tools create DVDs from your PowerPoint presentations. Each has a fully functioning trial version you can use to test with your presentation before purchasing. Because of the difficulty in translating PowerPoint files to DVD, you would be well advised to try before you buy:

Product	Price
PPT2DVD *http://www.ppt-to-dvd.com/*	$100 Personal
PowerPoint DVD Maker *http://www.prodvd.net/product/productinfo.asp?pid1=PDM*	$149

If you're looking to create a DVD from a PowerPoint presentation, read Betsy Weber's how-to article (*http://www.indezine.com/articles/powerpointtodvd.html*). Also, Microsoft PowerPoint MVP TAJ Simmons has a very nice tutorial on creating DVDs from your presentations (*http://www.awesomebackgrounds.com/powerpoint-to-dvd.htm*). If you decide to capture video and use DVD-authoring software to create the interface, try one of the following authoring programs:

Product	Price
Movie Studio+DVD *http://www.sonymediasoftware.com/*	$90
Nero Vision Express *http://ww2.nero.com/nero7/enu/Nero_Express_7.html*Vegas	$100
MyDVD Studio *http://www.roxio.com/en/products/mydvd/index.jhtml*	$150
Ulead DVD Workshop Express *http://www.ulead.com/dws/runme.htm*	$199
Sonic DVDit *http://www.sonic.com/products/professional/dvdit/*	$300
Adobe Encore DVD *http://www.adobe.com/products/encore/main.html*	$349
Ulead DVD Workshop *http://www.ulead.com/dws/runme.htm*	$395
Vegas+DVD Production Suite *http://www.sonymediasoftware.com/*	$675

If your presentation is mostly pictures and background music, you might look into tools created specifically for putting photos on DVD and bypass PowerPoint altogether:

Product	Price
MyDVD SlideShow *http://estore.sonic.com/enu/mydvd/slideshow.asp*	$30
Ulead CD & DVD PictureShow *http://www.ulead.com/dps/runme.htm*	$50
Photo2DVD Studio *http://www.photo-to-dvd.com/*	$50
DVD Photo Slideshow *http://www.dvd-photo-slideshow.com/*	$50

NOTE

If you want to create a Flash file from your PowerPoint file, you'll need a third-party application to create .swf files from PowerPoint. See "Turn PowerPoint into Flash" in Chapter 8 for a list of converter applications.

WEB PAGES

Save as HTML

THE ANNOYANCE: I want people to be able to see my presentation on my web site. How do I convert my presentation to HTML?

THE FIX: In PowerPoint 2000, 2002, and 2003, select File→Save as Web Page. In PowerPoint 97, select File→Save as HTML. Next, choose your options and click the Save button. You'll get an HTML file with a folder full of supporting files. Upload these to your web site and create a link to the HTML file from your main web page.

It's generally best to create a folder on your hard drive, publish your web page to it, and use FTP software to upload the files to your web page when you're finished. Select File→Save as Web Page, navigate to the folder on your hard drive in the "Save in" area, change the page title if you wish, and click the Publish button to see more options (see Figure 9-26).

NOTE

PowerPoint is not a good tool with which to create your web site. Instead, use software designed for developing web sites—such as Macromedia Dreamweaver or Microsoft FrontPage—to create the bulk of the site.

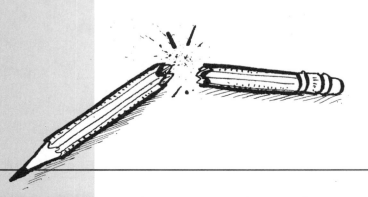

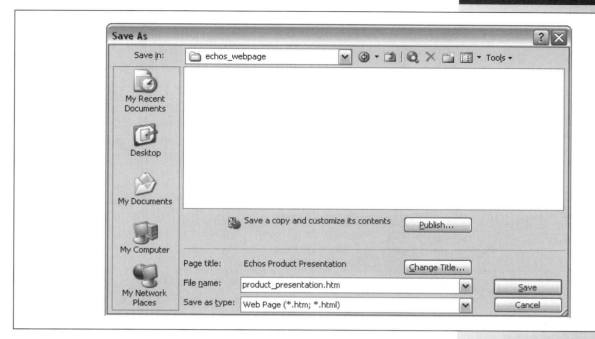

Figure 9-26. **Figure 9-26.** If you want to use PowerPoint's default web publishing settings, just click the Save button. To see more options, click the Publish button.

The Publish as Web Page dialog box lets you select basic options for your web page (see Figure 9-27). Click the Web Options button to see even more options, although the default settings in the Web Options dialog are usually sufficient. If you uncheck "Add slide navigation controls," make sure you've included automatic transitions or navigation buttons on the slides themselves so viewers have a way to advance the presentation.

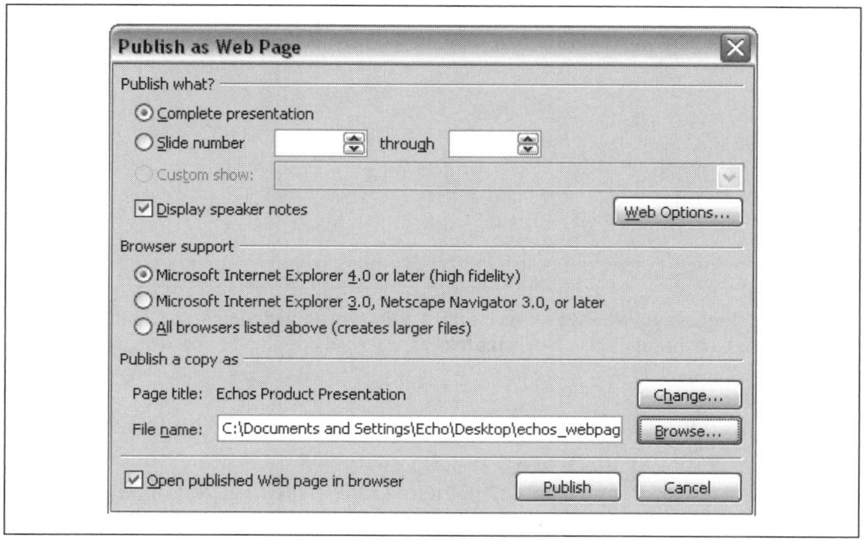

Figure 9-27. Opt to publish the entire presentation or a range of slides, and choose whether to include speaker notes. Click Web Options to see even more publishing options, or click the Publish button if you're ready to save your file as a web page.

Don't be fooled by all the different names for the "I'm finished, get on with it" button. When you've made all your selections and are ready to save your PowerPoint file as a web page, click the button at the *bottom* of the dialog box you happen to be on no matter if it says Publish or Save. Clicking the Publish or Web Options buttons near the *top* of the dialog boxes will take you to another screen of options.

If you check the "Open published web page in browser" box in the Publish as Web Page dialog (see Figure 9-27), your web page will open after you click the Publish or Save button. If not, navigate to the main *.htm* file and double-click it.

Open your web site and create a link to the main *.htm* file you created. In this case, the link might be something like *http://www.mywebpage.com/product_presentation.htm*. Finally, upload the main *.htm* file and the folder of supporting files to your web site (see Figure 9-28).

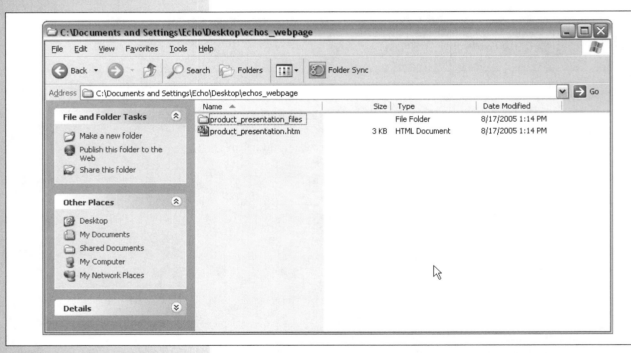

Figure 9-28. The Save as Web Page option creates a main .htm file and a folder full of supporting files. Make sure you keep the supporting files in the folder and upload the .htm file and the folder to your web page.

If you created your web page in PowerPoint 2002 or 2003 and used the new animations available in those versions, you may want to put a link to the free Office Animation Run-Time (*http://www.microsoft.com/downloads/details. aspx?FamilyID=4033A84A-24C7-40B2-8783-D80ADA33CFF8&displayla ng=en*) program on your main page for users to download and install before they open your presentation. The Run-Time program makes the new animations work in Internet Explorer 5.0 and later, and is necessary only for users who don't have PowerPoint 2002 or 2003 installed on their computers.

Get Rid of Slide List

THE ANNOYANCE: How do I get rid of the list of slide titles down the left side of the screen when I save my PowerPoint file as a web page?

THE FIX: Select File→Save as Web Page, click the Publish button, click the Web Options button, and uncheck the "Add slide navigation controls" box on the General tab. Make sure you've included automatic transitions or navigation buttons on the slides themselves so users have a way to advance the presentation.

Get Rid of Frames

THE ANNOYANCE: PowerPoint's HTML has frames. How can I prevent frames?

THE FIX: To hide the frames, select File→Save as Web Page, click the Publish button, click the Web Options button, and uncheck the "Add slide navigation controls" box on the General tab. However, this doesn't actually disable frames. To do that, you'll need a third-party tool. The $70 PPT2HTML from RnR PPTools (*http://www.rdpslides.com/pptools/ppt2html/index.html*) lets you convert PowerPoint files into "standard" HTML, rather than the HTML created when you choose Save as Web Page in PowerPoint. PPT2HTML also includes an Accessibility Assistant, useful for making the pages Section 508-compliant.

Put Your PowerPoint File on the Web

THE ANNOYANCE: I don't want to go through all that HTML hassle. Can I just put my PowerPoint file on the Web for people to download?

THE FIX: Absolutely! Simply upload your PowerPoint file to your web site and create a link to it from one of the pages on your site. One caveat, though—the PowerPoint file might open in some users' web browsers, not in PowerPoint itself. See the next annoyance, "Make PowerPoint Open in PowerPoint."

If the file has sound or video attached, you may want to zip the presentation together with the media files and upload the zipped file instead. Your users will have to download and unzip the file.

Make PowerPoint Open in PowerPoint

THE ANNOYANCE: When users on my web site click a link to a PowerPoint file, I want it to open in PowerPoint, not in their web browser. Is this possible?

THE FIX: No. This is a local user preference that you can't control from your site.

If it's really important that your users open the file in PowerPoint rather than in their web browser, you might consider zipping the PowerPoint file and linking to that instead. Your users should be prompted to save a zipped file.

If you want to configure Internet Explorer on your own system to open PowerPoint files on the Web in PowerPoint itself, use the following steps:

1. Open *My Documents*.

2. Select Tools→Folder Options and click the File Types tab.

3. In the Registered file types list, choose Microsoft PowerPoint Presentation (PPT) and click the Advanced button.

4. Uncheck the "Browse in same window" box and click OK (see Figure 9-29).

5. Repeat for Microsoft PowerPoint Slide Show (PPS) files.

Additionally, you can modify your registry as described at *http://support. microsoft.com/?scid=kb;en-us;162059*.

Figure 9-29. Uncheck the "Browse in same window" box if you want PowerPoint files on the Web to open in PowerPoint and not in a web browser.

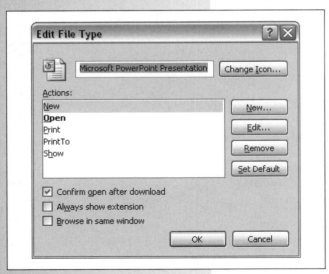

Slide Titles Missing in Navigation Pane

THE ANNOYANCE: I saved my presentation as a web page, but some of the titles on the left don't have the correct slide titles. And a couple just say "Slide 6" or something similar. What have I done?

THE FIX: PowerPoint's HTML picks up the slide titles used in the navigation pane from the title placeholders on the slides. If your slide has no text in the title placeholder, the navigation pane will use text from the text placeholder and enclose it in quotation marks. If there's no text in either the title or the text placeholder, PowerPoint will simply use the word "Slide" plus the slide number.

If you're planning to save your file as a web page, make sure all slides have slide title placeholders with text in them. If you don't want title text to appear on a particular slide, simply drag the title placeholder off the edge of the slide where it won't show.

Charts Look Awful When Saved as Web Page

THE ANNOYANCE: When I save my presentation as a web page, the slides with charts look terrible! What can I do to make them look better?

THE FIX: You have to fake this one by saving the slide as an image and inserting that image onto an empty slide to replace the real slide. Then use File→Save as Web Page. The downside of this is it usually creates larger file sizes.

Add Video to Slides on the Web

THE ANNOYANCE: We videotaped a colleague doing a training session. Now we're trying to figure out if we can combine the tape with slides and put it on the Web. Any suggestions?

THE FIX: This is a perfect use for Producer (*http://www.microsoft.com/ downloads/details.aspx?FamilyId=1B3C76D5-FC75-4F99-94BC-78491946 8E73&displaylang=en*), a free download for PowerPoint 2002 and 2003.

Download and install Producer, and then open it via Start→Programs. You'll be presented with options to use the new presentation wizard, start a new blank project, or open an existing project (see Figure 9-30). Choose the new presentation wizard and click OK.

Figure 9-30. This dialog box opens when you start Producer, giving you the option to start a new blank presentation, choose an existing presentation, or walk through the new presentation wizard.

The new presentation wizard walks you through choosing a template, importing files, capturing new audio or video, and synchronizing elements.

If you click the option to synchronize elements, the new presentation wizard will open the Synchronize Slides dialog box (see Figure 9-31). Click the Play button to begin reviewing or synchronizing the slides with the other media. Click the Next Slide button to move to the next slide at the appropriate time.

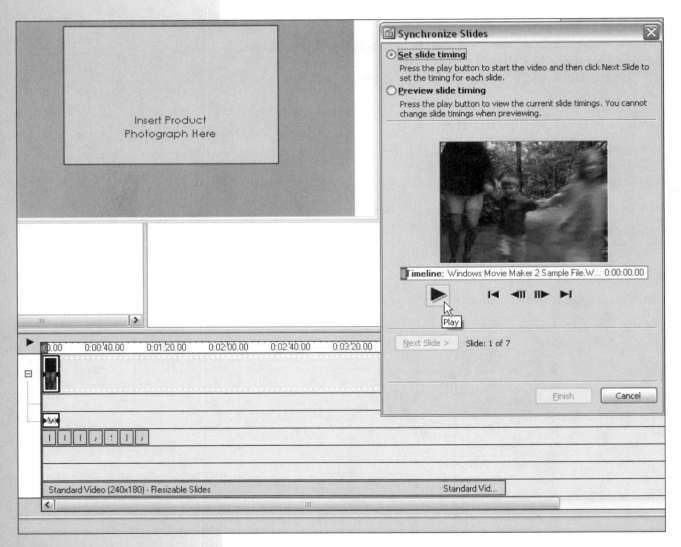

Figure 9-31. Click the Play button to begin previewing or synchronizing slides with other media files.

You can also drag and drop PowerPoint files, images, audio, and video to the Producer timeline. Click and drag on the timeline to adjust an object's timing (see Figure 9-32). Click the Publish button when you're ready to create the web page; you'll have the option to create the file on your computer, on a network shared drive, or on a web server. It's usually best to create the file on your computer and then move it to the final location afterward.

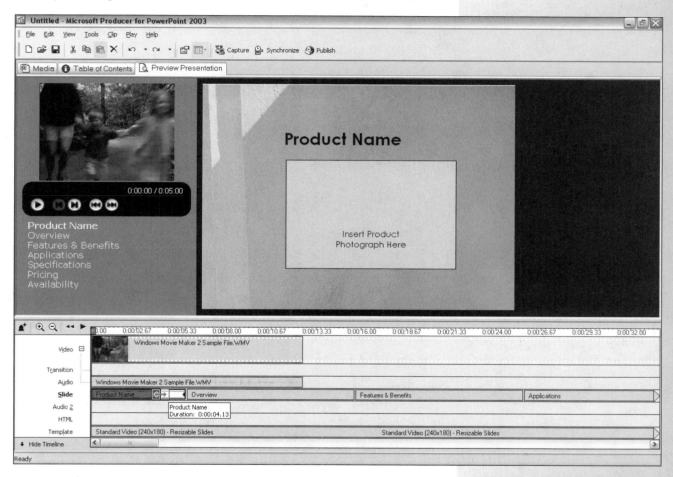

Like the Save as Web Page option in PowerPoint, Producer creates a main HTM file and a folder full of supporting files. Upload them and the additional files Producer creates to your web site (see Figure 9-33). Create a link from your web page to the main HTM file.

Figure 9-32. Drag and drop objects such as audio and video to the Producer timeline. Click and drag in the timeline to adjust the timing of individual objects.

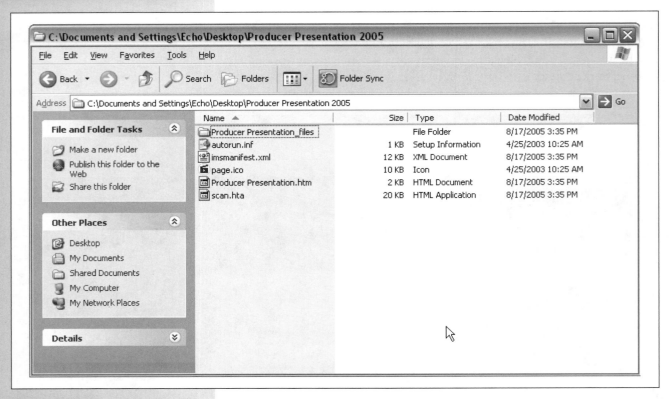

Figure 9-33. **Figure 9-33.** Producer creates a main HTM file, a folder full of supporting files, and some additional "loose" supporting files. Upload the folder and all the loose files to your web site, and create a link from your site to the main HTM file (in this case, Producer Presentation.htm).

PACK AND GO

Open PPZ Files

THE ANNOYANCE: Someone emailed me a *.ppz* file. When I try to open it in PowerPoint, I get an error message that says "PowerPoint can't open the type of file represented by *pres0.ppz*." What is this file, and how do I open it?

THE FIX: A *.ppz* file is one of the files created when you select File→Pack and Go in PowerPoint 97, 2000, or 2002. Pack and Go was the precursor to Package for CD; it packages your presentation, any linked media files, and, if you want, PowerPoint Viewer 97. The Pack and Go process creates two files, *pres0.ppz* and *pngsetup.exe*, both of which are necessary to unpack and view the presentation. If you create a Pack and Go file, you'll want to send both *pres0.ppz* and *pngsetup.exe* to the recipient.

If you have a *.ppz* file with no associated *pngsetup.exe* file, you can create your own. Open a new, blank PowerPoint file, choose File→Pack and Go, and walk through the Wizard. Choose to Pack and Go to your desktop or *My Documents* folder, and choose the "Don't include the Viewer" option when prompted (see Figure 9-34).

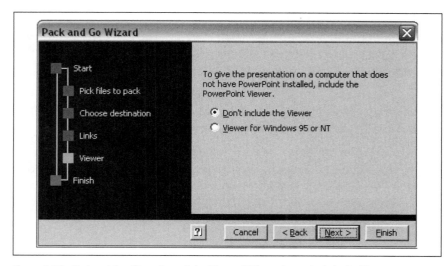

Figure 9-34. Pack and Go will use PowerPoint Viewer 97 if you elect to include the Viewer.

Replace the *pres0.ppz* file your Pack and Go process just created with the existing *.ppz* file. Double-click *pngsetup.exe* to unpack the Pack and Go file and view the presentation.

Occasionally the Pack and Go process will create a third file, *pres0.pp1*. This file doesn't affect the packed presentation and can be deleted.

CDS

Package for CD Uses Incorrect Drive

THE ANNOYANCE: I can't get PowerPoint 2003 to recognize my second CD drive when I select File→Package for CD. It keeps trying to write to my DVD drive. Is there any way to change this?

THE FIX: You would have to re-cable your CD and DVD drives, because PowerPoint automatically uses the drive cabled as the "master" drive when you use File→Package for CD. If you don't want to re-cable your CD drives so they have different drive letters, you can always just put the CD in the DVD drive and let it burn the CD. Better yet, choose File→Package to Folder and burn the files in the folder to the CD using your CD-burning software.

> **NOTE**
>
> *In PowerPoint 2003, the Package for CD option relies on Windows XP's CD burning functionality to create CDs. If you're not using Windows XP, or can't get Package for CD to work, choose File→Package for CD→Copy to Folder instead. You can then burn the files in the folder to CD using your usual CD burning software. Do not burn the folder itself—you want to burn the contents of the packaged folder.*

Make an Autorun CD

THE ANNOYANCE: I want to put my presentation on CD and give it to my friends, but most of them don't have PowerPoint. How do I make a presentation that runs from the CD?

THE FIX: To create an Autorun CD, you need to include the following files on the CD: your presentation file, any linked files such as audio or video, the PowerPoint Viewer files, and an *autorun.inf* file.

If you have PowerPoint 2003, you're in luck—just choose File→Package for CD, walk through the wizard, and be done with it. If you have any other version of PowerPoint, you'll have to do it the long, involved, manual way.

Choose your instructions based on the PowerPoint version and the type of animations and transitions you used to create your file (see Table 9-1).

Table 9-1. Use this table to help you determine which technique and Viewer to use when creating files for an Autorun CD.

Version	Viewer	Notes
PowerPoint 2003	PowerPoint Viewer 2003	Select File→Package for CD.
PowerPoint 2002	PowerPoint Viewer 2003	Use PowerPoint Viewer 2003 if the file includes "new" animations and transitions not available in PowerPoint 97 and 2000. You must, however, set it up manually. Alternatively, select File→Pack and Go and choose to include the Viewer (PowerPoint Viewer 97 by default). Test the file in the Viewer before you start the Pack and Go process.
PowerPoint 2000	PowerPoint Viewer 97	Select File→Pack and Go and choose to include the Viewer (PowerPoint Viewer 97 by default). You can also use PowerPoint Viewer 2003, but you must set it up manually. Test the file in the Viewer before you burn it to CD.
PowerPoint 97	PowerPoint Viewer 97	Select File→Pack and Go and choose to include the Viewer (PowerPoint Viewer 97 by default). You can also use PowerPoint Viewer 2003, but you must set it up manually. Test the file in the Viewer before you start the Pack and Go process.

The following sections show you how to create an Autorun CD with different versions of PowerPoint and PowerPoint Viewer.

PowerPoint 2003

To create a CD that runs your presentation in PowerPoint Viewer 2003 without installing anything on the recipient's computer, follow these steps:

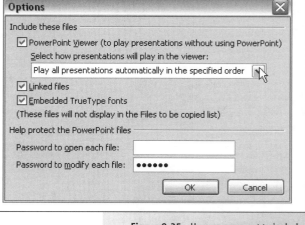

1. Save your PowerPoint file and select File→Package for CD.

2. Type in a name for the CD and click the Options button.

3. In the Options dialog box, check the boxes to include the PowerPoint Viewer and any linked files (see Figure 9-35). Generally, you want to leave the Play option set to "Play all presentations in the specified order." If you want, embed TrueType fonts and add passwords. A Modify password helps keep people from making changes to your files. An Open password prevents users without the password from viewing the file. Click OK to close the dialog.

Figure 9-35. Here you can opt to include PowerPoint Viewer 2003 and any files linked to your presentation.

4. Click the Copy to Folder button and click OK (see Figure 9-36).

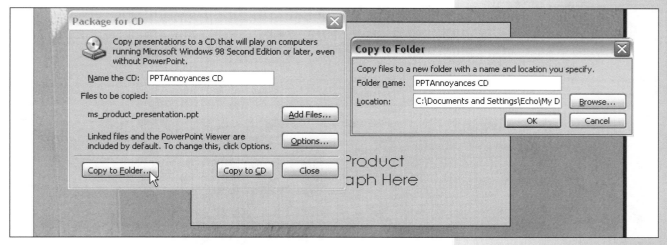

5. Click the Close button when the packaging process is complete. Your files will be saved to a folder with the name you specified in Step 4. If you chose to include PowerPoint Viewer 2003, you'll see *pptview.exe*, *pvreadme.htm*, and a number of *.dll* files. You should also see your presentation file and any linked media, along with files the CD uses when it autoruns (*play.bat*, *playlist.txt*, and *autorun.inf*).

6. Burn all of these files to CD. Don't burn the folder itself, just burn the *contents* of the folder and leave the files "loose" on the CD.

Figure 9-36. Click the Copy to Folder button to open another dialog box where you can specify the folder to save the Package for CD files to. Click OK here when you've made all your selections to begin processing the files.

PowerPoint 97 and 2000 with PowerPoint Viewer 97

To create a CD that runs your presentation in PowerPoint Viewer 97 without installing anything on the recipient's computer, follow these steps:

1. Download and install PowerPoint Viewer 97 from Microsoft (*http://www.microsoft.com/downloads/details.aspx?FamilyID=7c404e8e-5513-46c4-aa4f-058a84a37df1&DisplayLang=en*).

2. Save your PowerPoint file and select File→Pack and Go.

Figure 9-37. The Pack and Go wizard will prompt you to save the packed files to your hard drive or to the A:\ drive. Don't try to package to the A:\ drive.

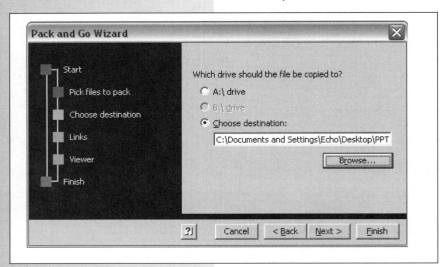

3. When asked to which drive the file should be copied, browse your hard drive and create a folder for the packed files (see Figure 9-37). Do not try to Pack and Go to the A:\ drive.

4. Make sure you check the "Include linked files" box and choose the "Viewer for Windows 95 or NT" option (see Figure 9-38).

5. Click Finish to complete the wizard and begin Pack and Go processing.

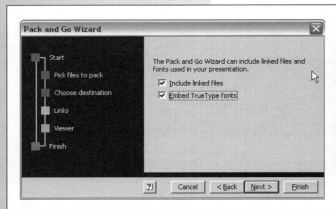
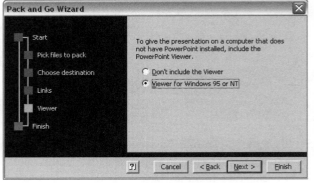

Figure 9-38. As you walk through the Pack and Go wizard, click to include linked files (left) and PowerPoint Viewer 97, which is referred to as "Viewer for Windows 95 or NT" (right).

6. Double-click the *PNGSetup.exe* file created by the Pack and Go process. It should be located in the folder you created in step 3.

7. Type a name for the folder where you want to unpack the files (see Figure 9-39). A folder will be created automatically if it doesn't already exist. If you look at the unpacked files, you will see *ppview32.exe*, 15 *.dll* files, an *.olb* file, your presentation file, any linked files such as audio or video, and a *playlist.lst* file.

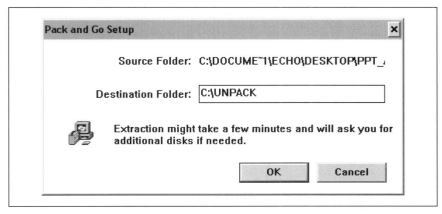

Figure 9-39. Double-click PNGSetup.exe to unpack your presentation and resolve links to any files. Type the name of the folder where you want to unpack the files.

8. Create an *autorun.inf* file and save it in the same folder with the unpacked files.

    a) Open Notepad. In Windows XP, select Start→All Programs→ Accessories→Notepad.

    b) Type the following:

    ```
    [autorun]
    open=ppview32.exe present\playlist.lst
    ```

    c) Select File→Save As, type **autorun.inf** in the "File name" box, navigate to the same folder with the unpacked files, and click the Save button.

9. Inside the folder with the unpacked files, create a folder called *present* and another called *setup* (select File→New→Folder).

10. Drag your presentation file, any linked files, and the *playlist.lst* file to the *present* folder.

11. Search your hard drive and copy all the other files the PowerPoint Viewer needs to run from the CD to the unpacked folder (see the list below). The Pack and Go process did not include these files because

Pack and Go was never intended to run directly from CD. You will need to set your search options to search hidden and system files.

• *base.srg*	• *msorfs.dll*	• *rappt.dll*
• *docobj.dll*	• *msppt8vr.olb*	• *selfreg.dll*
• *hlink.dll*	• *msv7enu.dll*	• *servrdep.srg*
• *hlinkprx.dll*	• *pp4x322.dll*	• *servrind.srg*
• *msimrt.dll*	• *pp7x32.dll*	• *sshow.srg*
• *msimrt16.dll*	• *ppintlv.dll*	• *t2embed.dll*
• *msimrt32.dll*	• *ppview.dll*	• *urlmon.dll*
• *msimusic.dll*	• *ppview32.exe*	• *wininet.dll*
• *mso97v.dll*		

12. Drag the *ppview.dll* file to the *setup* folder.

13. Burn the *setup* folder (and the file inside it), the *present* folder (and the files inside it), and all the files inside the unpacked folder to your CD (see Figure 9-40). Do not burn the unpacked folder itself to the CD.

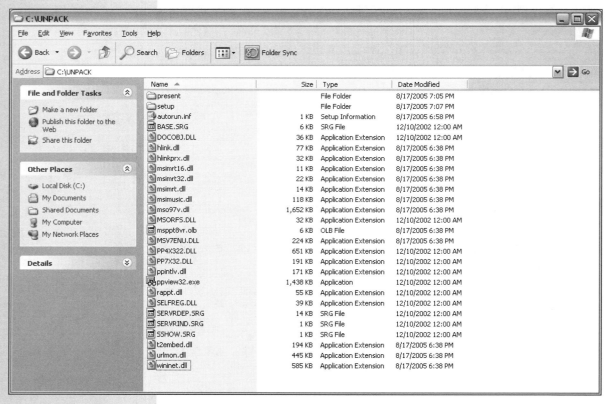

Figure 9-40. Burn the setup folder, the present folder, and all of the remaining "loose" files inside the unpacked folder to the CD to create your Autorun CD using PowerPoint Viewer 97.

PowerPoint 2002 with PowerPoint Viewer 2003

To create a CD that runs your presentation in PowerPoint Viewer 2003 without installing anything on the recipient's computer, follow these steps:

1. Download and install PowerPoint Viewer 2003 from Microsoft (*http://www.microsoft.com/downloads/details.aspx?FamilyId=428D5727-43AB-4F24-90B7-A94784AF71A4&displaylang=en*).

2. Save your PowerPoint file and select File→Pack and Go.

3. When asked to which drive the file should be copied, browse your hard drive and create a folder for the packed files (see Figure 9-37). Do not try to Pack and Go to the *A:* drive.

4. Make sure you check the "Include linked files" box (see Figure 9-38).

5. Choose the "Do not include the Viewer" option when prompted. Pack and Go only recognizes PowerPoint Viewer 97. Since you want to include PowerPoint Viewer 2003 to run your PowerPoint 2002 animations correctly, you will have to manually add its files later.

6. Click Finish to complete the wizard and begin Pack and Go processing.

7. Double-click the *PNGSetup.exe* file created by the Pack and Go process. It should be located in the folder you created in step 3.

8. Type a name for the folder where you want to unpack the files (see Figure 9-39). A folder will be created automatically if it doesn't already exist. If you look at the unpacked files, you will only see your presentation file, any linked files such as audio or video, and a *playlist.lst* file.

9. Locate the PowerPoint Viewer 2003 files on your hard drive and copy them to the unpacked folder (see the list below):

   - *gdiplus.dll*
   - *intidate.dll*
   - *pptview.exe*
   - *ppvwintl.dll*
   - *pvreadme.htm*
   - *saext.dll*
   - *unicows.dll*

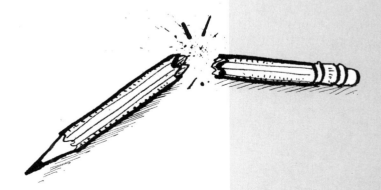

10. Create a *playlist.txt* file and save it in the folder with the unpacked files:

    a) Open Notepad. In Windows XP, select Start→All Programs→ Accessories→Notepad.

    b) Type the name of your presentation. If you used a long filename, the Pack and Go process may have shortened it, so make sure you check before typing. If you have more than one presentation, type all the filenames, pressing Enter after each one to create a list. Make sure you remember the *.ppt* or *.pps* extension.

    c) Select File→Save As, type **playlist.txt** in the "File name" box, navigate to the folder with the unpacked files, and click the Save button.

11. Delete the *playlist.lst* file from your unpacked folder. PowerPoint Viewer 2003 uses a *playlist.txt* file instead of a *.lst* file.

12. Create an *autorun.inf* file and save it in the folder with the unpacked files.

    a) Open Notepad again.

    b) Type the following:

    ```
    [autorun]
    open=pptview.exe /L "playlist.txt"
    ```

    The /L tells PowerPoint Viewer 2003 to read the playlist, which is contained in the file *playlist.txt*.

    c) Select File→Save As, type **autorun.inf** in the "File name" box, navigate to the folder with the unpacked files, and click the Save button.

13. Create a *play.bat* file save it in the folder with the unpacked files.

    a) Open Notepad again.

    b) Type the following:

    ```
    @pptview.exe /L "playlist.txt"
    ```

    c) Select File→Save As, type **play.bat** in the "File name" box, navigate to the folder with the unpacked files, and click the Save button. You don't absolutely have to have a *.bat* file on your Autorun CD. The *.bat* file will actually run your CD automatically, even if autorun has been turned off on the recipient's CD drive—which may irritate the recipient. You can double-click the *play.bat* file to test your files before you burn them to CD.

14. Burn all of the files in the unpacked folder to CD. Don't burn the folder itself, just burn the *contents* of this folder and leave them "loose" on the CD (see Figure 9-41).

You can use this technique with PowerPoint 97 and 2000, if you want to show those files with PowerPoint Viewer 2003. Make sure you test them with the Viewer before you create the Autorun CD files.

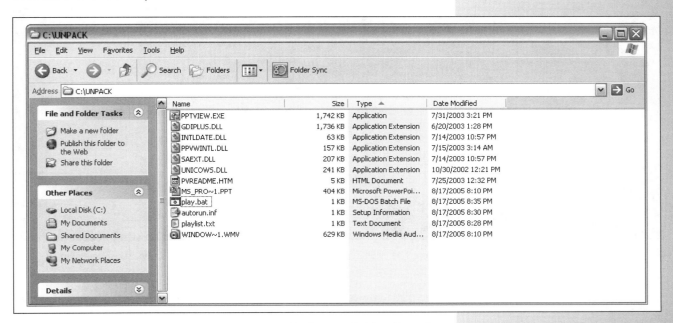

Figure 9-41. When you're done, your folder should look something like this. Burn all of these files to CD.

NOTE

Not into do-it-yourself Autorun PowerPoint CD creation? PowerLink Plus ($50; http://www.soniacoleman.com/Tutorials/PowerPoint/acdpc.htm) resolves all your linked files, copies all the files to a folder, adds the necessary PowerPoint Viewer files, and generates the autorun.inf file. All you have to do is burn the files to CD.

Make an EXE File

THE ANNOYANCE: Can I just create an *.exe* file from my PowerPoint file?

THE FIX: Follow the steps to create an Autorun CD using PowerPoint Viewer 2003 (see "Make an Autorun CD"), but don't burn the files to CD. Click Start→Run and type *iexpress* in the box, click OK, and follow the IExpress wizard.

When you reach the "Packaged Files" screen, click the Add button, navigate to the folder with your autorun CD files, select all the files, and click the Open button to add them to the IExpress package (see Figure 9-42). In the Install Program to Launch screen, type **PPTVIEW.EXE /L /S playlist.txt** in the Install Program box. The /L tells the Viewer to read the playlist, and the /S eliminates the splash screen.

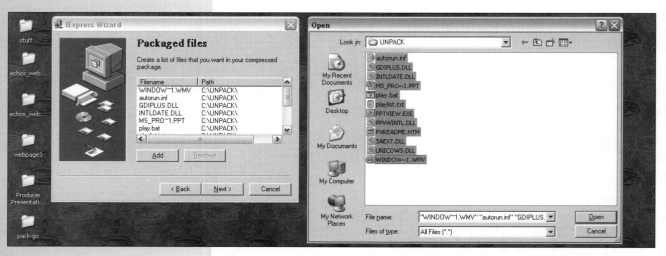

Figure 9-42. Add the files for an Autorun CD when you reach this screen of the IExpress wizard.

Microsoft PowerPoint MVP Geetesh Bajaj developed this technique. You can find more specific instructions on his web site (*http://www.indezine.com/products/powerpoint/pp2003/ppt2exe.html*).

Index

Symbols

3D objects, 147–150

A

absolute hyperlinks, 217
acetates, white background, 6
advancing slides, 3
alignment tools
  grayed out, 76, 133
  object distribution, 134–135
animated GIFs, 109–110
animation
  After Previous setting, 209
  bullet points
    first point, 187
    individual, 187
  charts
    categories, 195
    series, 195
  credits, 196
  effects, options, 188
  exit objects, 196
  Grow/Shrink, 209–211
  motion paths
    animating twice, 192
    editing, 193
    end, 194
    object jumping, 194
  objects
    multiple, 190–191
    multiple, simultaneous, 196
    printing, 270–271
    selecting for, 200–201
  restoring, 25

return to slide, 215
sequence, repeating, 205
slide remains on screen after, 206
spin angles, 201
  fulcrum, 202
text
  levels, 189–190
  one word in text box, 203–204
timeline, 207–220
transitions and, 205–206
versions of PowerPoint, 186
from Web, 108
With Previous setting, 209
arrows, hide on screen, 10
arrow keys, move objects too far, 77
audio, no sound, 2
AutoFit, placeholders and, 20–45
automatic contrast, 62
autorun CDs, creating, 290–298
AutoShapes
  connectors, 126–127
  fills, slide background, 148–150
  settings, default, 73
  word wrap, 140
axes, charts
  break, creating, 166
  labels
    alignment, 154
    length, 152
    missing, 152–153
  secondary, 163
  X-axis, dates in, 161
  Y-axis
    percent markers, 170
    title text, 152

fonts, 72
   charts, 160–161
graphs, 66
masters, new, 62
organization charts, 66
pasting action, 108
slide layout, 34
templates, 32, 62
diagrams
   objects, grouping/ungrouping, 123
   text boxes, moving, 124
digital cameras, video from, 246–253
distribution of objects, alignment
   tools and, 134
drag-and-drop, graphics, 86–112
drawing
   edit points and, 131–132
   half-circles (semi-circles), 129–130
   lines,invisible, 74
   Pen tool, straight lines, 11
   rectangles, invisible, 74
   saving drawings, 148–150
DVDs
   creating, 278–280
   playing, 249–250

E

editing
   motion paths, 193
   organization charts, 114–115
edit points
   drawing and, 131–132
   grayed out, 133
email, sound in, 223–253
embedding WAV files, 224–253
end of show screen, 10
EPS images, 277–298
equipment setup
   crooked slides, 2
   slides skinny on bottom, 2
Excel
   charts
      chartsheets, 101
      embedded, extracting data from, 99–100
      fonts, 102
      pasting, file size and, 182–183
      pasting workbook with, 100
   data, font size, 101–112
   footers, 103

gridlines, deleting, 99–112
headers, 103
importing charts, 182–184
pasting data to presentation, data cut off, 97–112
EXE files, creating, 297–298
exit objects, animation, 196

F

fade through black transition, 4
Fast Saves, file size and, 29
File→New command, 37
filenames, 67
files
   hyperlinked, warning message, 12
   size, 29–32
      Fast Saves and, 29
      Save as Type option, 29–30
   sound extraction, 235–237
   SWF, 237–238
      rewinding, 239
file access from presentation, 11
fills
   AutoShapes, slide background, 148–150
   pattern, printing, 265–298
   text boxes, printing and line appears, 271
Flash SWF files (see SWF files)
fonts
   changing, 122
   charts
      default, 160–161
      distorted, 154
      size, 156–157
   charts (Excel), 102–112
      pasted, 160
   datasheets (charts), 160
   default, 72
   Excel data, 101
   jagged appearance, 159–160
   lockups and, 75
   memory and, 115–116
   moving text and, 21–23
   outlined, 139–140
   size
      charts, 156–157
      increments, setting, 83
      Title Master, 56
footers, Excel, 103–112

formatting
   changing, 122
   grouped objects, 137
formulas, 204–205
frames, HTML, 283
Freeform tool, edit points and, 131
full menus, 23
fuzzy clip art, 107

G

Gantt charts, 110–112
GIFs, animated, 109–112
gradient transparency, printing, 261
graphics
   drag-and-drop, 86–97
   pasting, 86–97
   rotating, 92, 95–97
   transparency, 88–90
      black sections, 91
   (see also images; pictures)
graphs, defaults, 66
grayed out items
   alignment tools, 77, 133
   align tools, 76
   commands, restoring, 24–45
   edit points, 133
   Print button, 256
gridlines (Excel), deleting, 99–112
grids
   settings, 76
   visibility, 76
grouping charts after pasting, 31–45
groups
   diagrams, 123
   objects, 75
      formatting one, 137
Grow/Shrink animation, 209–211

H

half-circles, drawing, 129–130
hanging indents in bulleted text, 79
hardware acceleration, transitions and, 5
headers, Excel, 103–112
Help files online, 40
hidden slides, navigating to, 8
hotspots, triggering, 212–220
HTML
   frames, hiding/showing, 283–298

Office, reactivating, 39
on-the-fly object rotation, 136
organization charts
 boxes, adding, 118–150
 default, 66
 editing, 114–115
 size limits, 122
 space in boxes, 116
outlined fonts, 139–140
outlines (Word), importing, 110–112
Outline View icon, 27–29
out of memory error message,
 115–116
overlapping objects, transparency,
 149–150

P

page numbers, printing, 268
password protection
 files, printing, 256
 presentations, 42
pasting
 buttons, from Web, 109–112
 charts
 color changing when pasted,
 175–177
 Excel, file size and, 182–183
 grouping and, 31–32
 including workbook, 100
 charts (Excel), fonts, 160–184
 default action, 108
 Excel data to presentations, data
 was cut off, 97–112
 graphics, 86–97
 text, placeholders and, 77
paths
 sound, length, 240–253
 video, length, 240–253
pattern fills, printing, 265–298
pausing movies, 243
PDFs
 creating, 273–274
 importing, 111–112
Pen tool, drawing straight lines and,
 11
percent markers, Y axis, 170, 171
photo albums, adding pictures to,
 95–112

pictures
 data points, charts, 172
 inserting
 layout and, 20–21
 size, 87–88
 photo albums, adding to, 95–112
 printing, print twice, 256
 soft edges, 144
 transparency, 88–90
 black sections, 91
 (see also graphics; images)
pie charts
 jagged appearance, 157–159
 less than 100%, 180
placeholders
 AutoFit and, 20
 masters, 56
 pasting text and, 77
 slide layouts, 36
portrait printing, 257
posters, printing, 264
PowerPoint
 files, sound extraction, 235
 open minimized, 6
 reactivating, 39
 Word and, importing, 78
PowerPoint Viewer 2003, hyperlinks
 in, 218–220
PowerPoint Viewer 97, hyperlinks in,
 217–220
PPS files, editing, 40
PPZ files, 288–298
precision in object rotation, 135
presentations
 backups
 during, 9
 convert to video, 278
 corrupt, 43
 file access, 11
 looping continuously, 15
 masters
 multiple, 58
 preserving, 55
 navigation, 8
 password protection, 42
 recording to VHS, 278
 saving
 as Flash, 252
 as HTML, 280–283

 to Web, 283
 self-running, 14
 as video, 250
presenter's skills, 3
Presenter View, notes size, 13
printing
 background, turning on/off, 262
 black and white, 177–178
 centering, 258–259
 fills, pattern files, 265
 global settings, 265
 landscape, 257
 margins, 258
 objects, animated, 270
 page numbers, updating, 268
 password protected files, 256
 pictures, print twice, 256
 portrait, 257
 posters, 264–265
 slides
 notes and, 267–268
 numbering, 270
 omitting objects, 270
 on notes page, 260
 spool size, 261–298
 text boxes, line appears, 271
 transparency, gradient, 261
 troubleshooting, 261
 from Viewer, 264
Print button, grayed out, 256
projection
 video, troubleshooting, 248–253
 video at full screen, 247–248
projector, images not showing, 3

Q

qualifying product, 25–26
question mark in blue circle, 109
QuickTime, playing files, 247–253

R

range of slides, 15
reactivating PowerPoint, 39
recording to VHS, 278
rectangles, drawing but nothing
 shows, 74
rehearsal, single monitor and, 13

title slide, numbers in, 70
toolbars, moving icons, 23–45
tools
  alignment
    grayed out, 76, 133
    sticky, 128–129
transitions
  animation and, 205–206
  fade through black, 4
  Hardware Accelerator and, 5
  troubleshooting, 206
transparency
  gradient, printing, 261–298
  overlapping objects, 149–150
  pictures, 88–90
    black sections, 91

U

underlined text, hyperlinks, 215–220
username, comments, 26–45

V

VHS, recording to, 278
video
  background, 242
  controls, hiding/showing, 243
  converting presentation to, 278
  from digital camera, 246

DVDs, playing, 249
full screen, projection and, 247
importing, batches and, 93–112
links, breaking when presentation,
  240
path length, 240
play once, 240
projection and, troubleshooting,
  248–253
projector and, 6
saving presentations as, 250
slides on web page, 285–288
text over, 241
troubleshooting, 241
white box instead, 247
(see also movies)
Viewer, printing from, 264
visibility of grid, 76
volume, 233–234

W

watermarks, 145
WAV files
  embedding, 224
  size, 224–225
web pages
  opening in PowerPoint, 284
  on slides, 237

sound, 237
video and, 285
white background, acetates, 6
white box instead of video, 247
Word
  black and white thumbnails,
    272–273
  importing to PowerPoint, 78
  outlines, importing, 110–112
Word Art, spell check, 138
word wrap in AutoShapes, 140

X

X-axis (charts), dates in, 161

Y

Y-axis, charts
  percent markers, 170
  title text, 152

Z

zoom, 212–215

About the Author

Echo Swinford has been using PowerPoint professionally since 1997 and became a Microsoft PowerPoint MVP in 2000. She is currently a freelance presentation specialist and New Media graduate student in the School of Informatics at Indiana University.

Colophon

The cover fonts are Myriad and Myriad Pro. The text and heading fonts are Linotype Birka and Adobe Myriad Condensed; the sidebar font is Adobe Syntax; and the code font is LucasFont's TheSans Mono Condensed.

Better than e-books

Buy *Fixing PowerPoint Annoyances* and access
the digital edition FREE on Safari for 45 days.

Go to www.oreilly.com/go/safarienabled
and type in coupon code 9HM7-51TM-Q2C2-8AM1-7D31

Search
thousands of
top tech books

Download
whole chapters

Cut and Paste
code examples

Find
answers fast

Search Safari! The premier electronic reference
library for programmers and IT professionals.

O'REILLY NETWORK
Safari® Bookshelf.

Addison
Wesley

Adobe Press

Sun
microsystems

O'REILLY®

SAMS

ALPHA

New
Riders

Java
For Everything

Cisco Press

Microsoft
Press

QUE®

Peachpit
Press

macromedia
PRESS

PRENTICE
HALL
PTR

Related Titles from O'Reilly

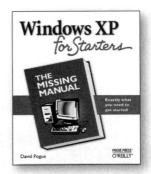

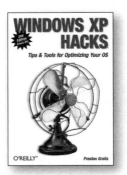

O'REILLY®

Our books are available at most retail and online bookstores.

To order direct: 1-800-998-9938 • *order@oreilly.com* • *www.oreilly.com*

Online editions of most O'Reilly titles are available by subscription at *safari.oreilly.com*

The O'Reilly Advantage

Stay Current and Save Money

Order books online:
www.oreilly.com/order_new

Questions about our products or your order:
order@oreilly.com

Join our email lists: Sign up to get topic specific email announcements or new books, conferences, special offers and technology news
elists@oreilly.com

For book content technical questions:
booktech@oreilly.com

To submit new book proposals to our editors:
proposals@oreilly.com

Contact us:
O'Reilly Media, Inc.
1005 Gravenstein Highway N.
Sebastopol, CA U.S.A. 95472
707-827-7000 or
800-998-9938
www.oreilly.com

Did you know that if you register your O'Reilly books, you'll get automatic notification and upgrade discounts on new editions?

And that's not all! Once you've registered your books you can:

» Win free books, T-shirts and O'Reilly Gear

» Get special offers available only to registered O'Reilly customers

» Get free catalogs announcing all our new titles (US and UK Only)

Registering is easy! Just go to www.oreilly.com/go/register